ASEAN
Centrality

The ISEAS – Yusof Ishak Institute (formerly Institute of Southeast Asian Studies) is an autonomous organization established in 1968. It is a regional centre dedicated to the study of socio-political, security, and economic trends and developments in Southeast Asia and its wider geostrategic and economic environment. The Institute's research programmes are grouped under Regional Economic Studies (RES), Regional Strategic and Political Studies (RSPS), and Regional Social and Cultural Studies (RSCS). The Institute is also home to the ASEAN Studies Centre (ASC), the Singapore APEC Study Centre, and the Temasek History Research Centre (THRC).

ISEAS Publishing, an established academic press, has issued more than 2,000 books and journals. It is the largest scholarly publisher of research about Southeast Asia from within the region. ISEAS Publishing works with many other academic and trade publishers and distributors to disseminate important research and analyses from and about Southeast Asia to the rest of the world.

ASEAN Centrality

An autoethnographic account by a Philippine Diplomat

ELIZABETH P. BUENSUCESO

 YUSOF ISHAK INSTITUTE

First published in Singapore in 2021 by
ISEAS Publishing
30 Heng Mui Keng Terrace
Singapore 119614

E-mail: publish@iseas.edu.sg
Website: <http://bookshop.iseas.edu.sg>

All rights reserved. No part of this publication may be reproduced, stored in a retrieval system, or transmitted in any form or by any means, electronic, mechanical, photocopying, recording or otherwise, without the prior permission of the ISEAS – Yusof Ishak Institute.

© 2021 ISEAS – Yusof Ishak Institute, Singapore

The responsibility for facts and opinions in this publication rests exclusively with the author and her interpretations do not necessarily reflect the views or the policy of the publisher or its supporters.

ISEAS Library Cataloguing-in-Publication Data

Name(s): Buensuceso, Elizabeth P., author.
Title: ASEAN centrality: an autoethnographic account by a Philippine diplomat/by Elizabeth P. Buensuceso.
Description: Singapore : ISEAS - Yusof Ishak Institute, 2021. | Includes bibliographical references.
Identifiers: ISBN 978-981-4951-64-7 (soft cover) | ISBN 978-981-4951-65-4 (pdf)
Subjects: LCSH: ASEAN. | Southeast Asia—Politics and government.
| Regionalism (International organization).
Classification: LCC JZ5333.5 A9B92

Typeset by Stallion Press (S) Pte Ltd
Printed in Singapore by Mainland Press Pte Ltd

CONTENTS

List of Figures ix
Abbreviations xi
Foreword xiv
Acknowledgements xvi

1. Introduction   1

  Why This Book?   1
  The Precursors of ASEAN   5
  A Brief History of ASEAN   8
  ASEAN Community Post-2025 Vision   14
  The Application of Timor-Leste as the 11th Member
    of ASEAN   15
  Is There an ASEAN Community?   16

2. Autoethnography: Memoir, Biography, Auto-What?   18

  Analytical Framework   18
    A Word About Reflexivity   21
    Some Ethical Considerations   23
    Nature and Sources of Data   24

3. ASEAN Diplomacy and ASEAN Centrality   26

Insistence on ASEAN Centrality an Offshoot of
   Post-Colonialism and Cold-War Stigma   26
What They Say About ASEAN Diplomacy   29
What They Say About ASEAN Centrality   32
What I Say About ASEAN Diplomacy and
   ASEAN Centrality   37

4. ASEAN Centrality as an Expression of ASEAN Leadership in the Region: The Philippine Chairmanship of ASEAN in 2017   39

Framework Agreement on the Code of Conduct in the
   South China Sea   45
The Consensus on the Protection and Promotion of the
   Rights of Migrant Workers   46
The Philippine Mission to ASEAN and the Philippine
   Chairmanship   50

5. ASEAN Centrality as a Principle of Diplomacy Among Member States   64

Conceptual Framework of the Jakarta Platform   65
Jakarta, the Hub of Regional Multilateralism   67
ASEAN Centrality in the ASEAN Committee of
   Permanent Representatives (CPR)   69
Strengthening ASEAN Centrality through the CPR
   and the JCM   73
Format of the CPR Meeting   76
Who Participates in the Meetings of the CPR?   77
The Agenda of the CPR   78
ASEAN Centrality In Spite of Conflicting
   Bilateral Disputes   81
ASEAN Centrality through ASEAN Consensus
   or Without   82
ASEAN Consensus on the South China Sea Issue   82

ASEAN Consensus on Illegal Unreported and Unregulated Fishing (IUUF)	87
ASEAN Consensus on Use of the Name of the Chemical Weapon "VX sarin" in the ASEAN Text of the EAS Leaders' Declaration	89
ASEAN Centrality Despite Inability to Amend/Update the ASEAN Charter	89
The Tone and Language of the CPR	93
ASEAN Centrality in the ASEAN Connectivity Coordinating Committee (ACCC)	96
ASEAN Centrality in the ASEAN Institute for Peace and Reconciliation (AIPR)	101

6. ASEAN Centrality as a Principle of Diplomacy with ASEAN's External Partners — **107**

ASEAN Centrality in the CPR Interface with High Level Officials of External Partners	111
CPR Refusal to Meet with Unfriendly Partners	115
ASEAN Centrality in the Relations of the ASEAN Connectivity Coordinating Committee (ACCC) with External Partners	116
ASEAN Centrality in the EAS Ambassadors' Meeting in Jakarta (EAMJ)	119
ASEAN Leadership in Negotiating the Four EAS Statements	122
EAS Leaders' Statement on Chemical Weapons	124
EAS Leaders' Statement on Anti-Money Laundering and Countering the Financing of Terrorism	127
EAS Leaders' Statement on Cooperation in Poverty Alleviation	128
EAS Leaders' Statement on Countering the Ideological Challenge of Terrorism and Terrorist Narratives and Propaganda	129
Negotiations on the Manila Plan of Action on EAS Cooperation with focus on the Regional Security Architecture (RSA)	131

Extended Plan of Action (POA) or a Negotiated New POA and Inclusion of Maritime Cooperation as an EAS Priority Area of Cooperation	131
ASEAN Resolution on the Title of the EAS Plan of Action	132
ASEAN Says No to the Continued Delay in Negotiating the EAS Terms of Reference (TOR)	135
Procedures Employed in Negotiating EAS Documents	138
ASEAN Centrality in the ASEAN+1 Mechanism	140
ASEAN + USA: The CPR and Vice President Michael Pence	144
ASEAN-China JCC	145
ASEAN Says No to Lecturing by External Partners	146
ASEAN Centrality in the ASEAN Plus Three (APT) Meeting	149
Failure to Practise ASEAN Centrality in ASEAN's Dealings with its External Partners in Jakarta	152
7. ASEAN Centrality as an Aspiration to Raise the Level of Awareness About ASEAN	**156**
A Final Word from the Author	165
Bibliography	169
Annexes	173
Annex A List of documents issued by ASEAN in 2017	175
Annex B Terms of Reference for the Joint Consultative Meeting (JCM)	178
Annex C Terms of Reference for the ASEAN Connectivity Coordinating Committee (ACCC)	182
Annex D Terms of Reference for the ASEAN Institute for Peace and Reconciliation (AIPR)	186
Index	193
About the Author	204

LIST OF FIGURES

Figure 1.1	ASEAN Timeline	16
Figure 4.1	Logo of the Philippine Chairmanship of ASEAN	44
Figure 4.2	Routing Slip of the Philippine Mission	52
Figure 4.3	EAMJ Mangrove Planting Event Organized by the Philippine Mission	59
Figure 4.4	Receiving the Best DFA Organization Award from Secretary Alan Peter Cayetano	62
Figure 5.1	Conceptual Framework	66
Figure 5.2	Chairing a CPR Meeting	69
Figure 5.3	CPR and the ASEAN Disability Forum	71
Figure 5.4	Format of the CPR Meeting	77
Figure 5.5	Proposed Amendments to the ASEAN Charter	91
Figure 5.6	8th ASEAN Connectivity Symposium	99
Figure 5.7	Launch of the ASEAN Women for Peace Registry	104
Figure 6.1	CPR Meeting with Foreign Minister Wang Yi	113
Figure 6.2	Physical Format of the EAMJ	120
Figure 6.3	Format of an ASEAN-China JCC Meeting	140

Figure 6.4	Format of the Joint Sectoral Cooperation Committee (JSCC)	142
Figure 6.5	Co-Chairing ASEAN+1 Meeting with Vice President Michael Pence	144
Figure 6.6	Format of the ASEAN Plus Three (APT) Meeting	149
Figure 7.1	Speaking at the Habibie Center	159
Figure 7.2	Co-panelist in the Perspective Show of Channel News Asia	160
Figure 7.3	Speaking at the Maritime Security Conference in Victoria, Canada	162
Figure 7.4	Speaking at the ASEANNALE 2018	164

ABBREVIATIONS

AADCP II	ASEAN-Australia Development Cooperation Program II
ACB	ASEAN Center for Biodiversity
ACC	ASEAN Coordinating Council
ACCC	ASEAN Connectivity Coordinating Committee
ACJCC	ASEAN-China Joint Cooperation Committee
ACTIP	ASEAN Convention Against Trafficking in Persons, Especially Women and Children
ADF	ASEAN Disability Forum
ADMM-Plus	ASEAN Defense Ministers' Meeting Plus
AEC	ASEAN Economic Community
AEMM	ASEAN Economic Ministers' Meeting
AFDM	ASEAN Finance and Central Bank Deputies' Meeting
AFRP	ASEAN Secretariat Financial Rules and Procedures
AIIB	Asian Infrastructure Investment Bank
AMS	ASEAN Member States
APCSS	Asia-Pacific Center for Security Studies
APSC	ASEAN Political-Security Community
APT	ASEAN Plus Three
ARF	ASEAN Regional Forum
ASA	Association of Southeast Asia
ASCC	ASEAN Socio-Cultural Community

ASEAN-IPR	ASEAN Institute for Peace and Reconciliation
ASEAN	Association of Southeast Asian Nations
ASRR	ASEAN Secretariat Staff Rules and Regulations
AWPR	ASEAN Women for Peace Registry
BRI	Belt and Road Initiative
COC	Code of Conduct in the South China Sea
CPR	Committee of Permanent Representatives
DENR	Department of Environment and Natural Resources, the Philippines
DFA	Department of Foreign Affairs, the Philippines
DFAT	Department of Foreign Affairs and Trade, Australia
DOC	Declaration on the Conduct of the Parties in the South China Sea
DPs	Dialogue Partners
DSG	Deputy Secretary General
EAMJ	EAS Ambassadors' Meeting in Jakarta
EAS	East Asia Summit
ECO	Economic Cooperation Organization
ERIA	Economic Research Institute for ASEAN and East Asia
EU	European Union
FOIP	Free and Open Indo-Pacific
GAM	Free Aceh Movement
GCC	Gulf Cooperation Council
GMM	Global Movement of Moderates
GMMF	Global Movement for Moderates Foundation
IAI	Initiative for ASEAN Integration
ICJ	International Court of Justice
ILEA	International Law Enforcement Academy
IPS	Indo-Pacific Strategy
IRRI	International Rice Research Institute
IUUF	Illegal Unregulated and Unreported Fishing
JBIC	Japan Bank for International Cooperation
JCC	Joint Cooperation Committee
JCLEC	Jakarta Centre for Law Enforcement Cooperation
JCM	Joint Consultative Meeting
JOIN	Japan Overseas Infrastructure Investment Corporation

JPM	Joint Preparatory Meeting
JPM	Philippine Mission to ASEAN
JSCC	Joint Sectoral Cooperation Committee
LIB	Lead Implementing Body
MAPHILINDO	Malaysia-Philippines-Indonesia Organization
MFA	Ministry of Foreign Affairs, Norway
MOU	Memorandum of Understanding
MPAC	Master Plan on ASEAN Connectivity
NAM	Non-Aligned Movement
NEXI	Nippon Export and Investment Insurance
ODA	Official Development Assistance
PCA	Permanent Court of Arbitration
PCs	Participating Countries
PPP	Public Private Partnership
PR	Permanent Representative
RCEP	Regional Comprehensive Economic Partnership
RSA	Regional Security Architecture
SDP	Sectoral Dialogue Partner
SEARRCT	Southeast Asia Regional Centre for Counter-Terrorism
SEATO	Southeast Asia Treaty Organization
SEOM	Senior Economic Officials' Meeting
SOM	Senior Officials' Meeting
STOM	Senior Transport Officials' Meeting
TAC	Treaty of Amity and Cooperation
TOR	Terms of Reference
TVET	Technical and Vocational Education and Training
UN	United Nations
UNCLOS	United Nations Convention on the Law of the Sea

FOREWORD

The book, *ASEAN Centrality: An Autoethnographic Account by a Philippine Diplomat*, written by the Department of Foreign Affairs' resident ASEAN specialist, Ambassador Elizabeth P. Buensuceso proves the point that diplomats and scholars should join forces to make this world a more coherent, more compassionate and more affable place to live in.

Ambassador Buensuceso's evocative, direct, uncomplicated but authoritative style is a refreshing departure from the boring reportage of ASEAN reports and treatises on the one hand and on the other, the incomprehensible balderdash of some academics pretending to interpret diplomacy from their distorting lenses of the wrong grade. Never since the renowned former ASEAN Secretary General Rodolfo Severino do we find the rare combination of the academic perspective beautifully blended with the actual experience of a seasoned diplomat as in this author.

ASEAN Centrality is a concept that has, time and again, been put to the test. Once again, the world is experiencing a creeping polarization among the powers and countries of the world. And once again, their chosen theater is the region where the ASEAN Member States are in the midst of two of the most volatile flashpoints in the world—the Korean Peninsula and the South China Sea. The region has gotten a new name: the Indo-Pacific arena, resurrected from its uncertain beginnings in 1994 when it was first broached. The big powers are now testing and approaching ASEAN for alliances and cooperation. How ASEAN will take advantage of the opportunities of this renewed interest and not be swept away in the currents of contending forces will once again bring ASEAN Centrality to the fore and its greatest test. Even political instability among its members, as in the current crisis in Myanmar, is a clarion call for ASEAN Centrality to play its part and acquire substantive meaning beyond mere intention.

Ambassador Buensuceso makes an inventory of various definitions and views on ASEAN Centrality, juxtaposes them with her own take, and concludes that indeed, ASEAN Centrality should be understood from the point of view of one who has experienced and practised it. Her definition is fact-based and practical. It can be operationalized, observed, and put to test easily. It can serve the interest of ASEAN in a practical manner. She is able to define her parameters of what constitutes ASEAN Centrality that makes for an interesting, informative reading.

I am honoured that the book is published during my term as Secretary of Foreign Affairs of the Philippines. I would urge all students and practitioners of ASEAN diplomacy, especially diplomats of the Philippines and ASEAN Member States, to read this book and savour its unique approach and style. It does not merely inform, it educates, uplifts and sometimes, entertains.

TEODORO L. LOCSIN, JR.
Secretary of Foreign Affairs

ACKNOWLEDGEMENTS

I give back all glory and honour to God Almighty who is the Author of all good and perfect things and the source of all wisdom.

I thank Claire for her invaluable technical help and research support.

I am grateful to Dr Jean Saludadez, Program Chair and Vice Chancellor of the UPOU, Dean Joefe Santarita and Dr Grace Alfonso of the UP Asian Center.

I dedicate this book to the officers and staff and their families of the Philippine Mission to ASEAN in Jakarta, circa 2013–2019. I also appreciate Karen and Sab for always being there for me.

1
INTRODUCTION

Why This Book?

On 20 March 2019, I represented the Philippines at a High-Level Dialogue on Indo-Pacific Cooperation hosted in Jakarta by the Minister of Foreign Affairs of Indonesia, Retno Marsudi, and which was attended by Ministers, Senior Officials and Ambassadors of the eighteen countries belonging to the East Asia Summit (EAS). At the ASEAN Summit with the United States held in Manila in November 2017, President Donald Trump had first broached the concept of a Free and Open Indo-Pacific Strategy (FOIPS). Soon after, the so-called Quad (the United States, India, Japan and Australia) also expounded on the strategy, but downplaying any adversarial implications that might be associated with it in view of the impression that it was an isolationist strategy to exclude or contain an emerging China in the regional political and security architecture. From then on, much speculation and discussion have been generated on the so-called Indo-Pacific Strategy (IPS) and Indonesia, projecting herself as a leader in ASEAN and always zealous to surface ASEAN Centrality in the emerging regional security architecture, took pains to host this event.[1] High level delegations from the eighteen EAS members attended the event. At that meeting which was the first ministerial-level forum to explore ideas on this emerging area of cooperation, almost all delegates stressed the importance of and support for ASEAN Centrality in the evolving political/security and economic architecture of the region which straddles the Indian and Pacific oceans, including the Member States of ASEAN. Yet, while prefacing their interventions with support for ASEAN Centrality, non-ASEAN countries expounded on their own particular initiatives on how they understood the Indo-Pacific approach, strategy or concept, including the FOIPS of the United States, the Belt and Road Initiative of China, the Quality Infrastructure Program of Japan, the Indo-Pacific Foreign Policy of Australia, and others, giving the impression that the participants did not have the same views as myself on what ASEAN Centrality meant and how it should be implemented. The implication, of course, is that their respective Indo-Pacific strategy or concept is the norm to be followed to ensure the political stability and economic prosperity of the region. After all the participants had spoken, as the Russian Ambassador and I were the most junior in the group in terms of rank, we were the last in the speaking order, but he spoke first before I did. His intervention was anticlimactic, asking rhetorical questions like why should there be any discussion on the IPS at all and why we were having the meeting even. Responding to what I heard, I set aside my prepared speech and conveyed the Philippines' message to the Conference in a few minutes: first, in reply to the Russian Ambassador, I said that indeed we needed to have a meeting to surface a clear understanding of what ASEAN Centrality is. If discussions on the IPS were to continue, I said, ASEAN Centrality should be the foundational principle upon which it should be moved forward. ASEAN Centrality should mean using ASEAN-led mechanisms, the surrounding principles should be those enshrined in ASEAN seminal documents such as the ASEAN Charter, the tone or atmosphere should be those with which ASEAN has conducted its cooperation, bereft of naming and shaming but conducted in a friendly, non-confrontational "family style" ASEAN Way and that the topics and agenda of IPS should be those already spelled out by ASEAN. Foreign Minister Retno Marsudi and all the ASEAN delegates applauded this intervention.

This and many other experiences impressed on me that although other countries and diplomats continue to expressly manifest their "support" for ASEAN Centrality, there is, in fact, no exact definition of what it is.

The expression "ASEAN Centrality" largely depends, therefore, on who is saying it. The definitions propounded by other writers, as discussed in another section of this book, also do not reflect the same reality that I experienced. This disparity has prompted me to advance a publication exploring what to me is a more authentic meaning of ASEAN Centrality from the point of view and experience of one of its own practitioners—myself, a diplomat from one of ASEAN's five founding members. Hopefully, such a definition would bridge the gap of understanding among the students and practitioners of ASEAN diplomacy and lead to a deeper realistic understanding of ASEAN and thereafter to a more productive relationship among the countries concerned.

On a personal note, I have always wanted to tell the story of my life as a female foreign service officer coming from humble beginnings. My colleagues in the Philippine foreign service will bear witness to the fact that I have had one of the most colourful, most challenging and most dramatic careers serving my country and people abroad and at home—from being falsely accused of betraying an overseas migrant worker, an incident which had upended how we conducted Philippine foreign policy, to being instructed to boycott a Nobel Peace Prize ceremony, instructions I refused to obey at first, to many firsts in the service, including the purchase of chanceries in Belgium and the Mission in Jakarta. Capping this colourful career was my assumption of the Chairmanship of six ASEAN bodies during its 50th Founding Anniversary, a once-in-a lifetime opportunity in any diplomat's life. And yet, I could not write about the truths of these experiences through the usual route of memoirs. I hate writing memoirs, because the lack of scholarly discipline characteristic of memoirs might lead me to hurt the feelings of people whom I have related with over the years. In my life serving our nationals abroad, I have been witness to the fact that it is oftentimes the poor and underprivileged who are at the receiving end of the hurt, the blame and the abuses of people like us who tell stories about them. I did not want to hurt them even more. They must tell their own stories. But I desperately needed to tell others even just a glimpse of my story through another platform. Now, after an earlier state of hesitation, I fell in love with autoethnography and sometimes think that it was invented just for me to tell a small piece of my story.

In one birthday video message which my nephew, Paolo now twenty-five years old, sent to me, I was awakened to an epiphany: I am a storyteller! *"Happy birthday to the family storyteller! I grew up being taught and entertained by your stories, about the books you read, the places you've been to, the stories of your childhood and the stories in the foreign service"*, he said to me. Having majored in Literature for my undergraduate degree, of course, I have always had illusions of being a tribal folklorist, like the Vikings of old had one, keeping stories in my heart and mind and retelling them to family and friends. The Filipino tribal folklorist needed to tell her story about ASEAN.

This book seeks to problematize the concept of ASEAN Centrality, to generate a fresh definition of the term based on the author's experience as a member of the community of diplomats practising this principle in their interaction with each other and with ASEAN's external partners, and how this definition influenced or defined her involvement in the community of ASEAN and other diplomats. Corollarily, the study also wants to demonstrate that such a topic as ASEAN diplomacy can be studied using the atypical method of autoethnography.

Autoethnography is a non-conventional research method of arriving at a truth—a definition of ASEAN Centrality—by capturing the unique perspective of and recounting the lived experiences of a Filipino diplomat (myself) participating in a community engaged in intra-ASEAN and inter-ASEAN relations, an exercise which, I hope, will contribute to new scholarship both in the study of ASEAN diplomacy and the employment of autoethnography as a valid research method.

I tell the story of how I formed this definition of ASEAN Centrality by recounting how it was manifested in the ability of the ASEAN Chair, particularly the Philippines, to take on a leadership role and deliver important accomplishments to benefit the region, a role I imposed upon myself as well, as a Filipino diplomat in the thick of those circumstances.

As a direct participant and Chair of various subgroups in this community, I recount vignettes of my exploitation of the intimate elements such as format, tone and language, agenda, processes and procedures etc. of this singular community of diplomats engaged in ASEAN relations. This community is made up of subsets namely, the Committee of Permanent Representatives (CPR), the ASEAN Connectivity

Coordinating Committee (ACCC), the ASEAN Institute for Peace and Reconciliation, the ASEAN Plus One (JCC and JSCC), the ASEAN Plus Three (APT), and the East Asia Summit (EAS) Ambassadors' Meeting in Jakarta (EAMJ). From this account, I define ASEAN Centrality as a principle of diplomacy with ASEAN playing a dominant role as practised by ASEAN diplomats participating in the various ASEAN-led mechanisms based in Jakarta, discussing and advancing ASEAN's agenda, following ASEAN-approved formats, procedures and processes enunciated in a tone or language, bereft of naming and shaming but conducted in the friendly, non-confrontational "family style" ASEAN Way.

My definition of ASEAN Centrality is also projected as an aspiration to raise the level of awareness about ASEAN, which I illustrated in this study by recounting my engagements in several forums where I spoke about ASEAN and explaining why at the age of sixty-two and having been already a practitioner of ASEAN diplomacy for many years, I had become a student of and a speaker on ASEAN studies, explaining to anyone who cared to listen about the nature, mechanisms, objectives and aspirations, accomplishments, and challenges as well as the weaknesses of ASEAN.

Those expecting to find a sensationalized memoir in the following pages will be disappointed. I also tried not to sound like the tedious reports of the ASEAN Secretariat. What I intend to do is to submit a new definition of ASEAN Centrality by marrying the rigours of an academic discipline and my practical experiences as a practitioner of ASEAN diplomacy. I lament the fact that these two groups of people—academics and practitioners—oftentimes find each other's world apart in the study of ASEAN.

The Precursors of ASEAN

As a student of Asian and ASEAN studies and a diplomat promoting Philippine interests abroad, I have been intrigued by the failure of earlier attempts at regionalism in my part of the world. My analysis of the precursors of ASEAN entails answering two important "why" questions, the answers to which have influenced me in how I view ASEAN today: why did the proponents of the earlier attempts of regional organizations seek to establish them? The second "why" is to explain the reasons behind the failure of these earlier experiments at regional organizations. Failure in this sense denotes their inability to attain their objectives, their inability to attract more members and the fact that they no longer exist today. It is also important to describe the backdrop or the setting of the decade in which they were born, i.e., the raging Cold War that enveloped the region and the concomitant attempts by the major powers, the United States, China and the then USSR, to extend their sphere of influence in Southeast Asia as well as the nascent rise of post-colonial nationalism among the countries in the region. The retreat of the UK as a colonial power and the defeat of the French in Indo-China also influenced the formation and demise of these earlier attempts at regionalism; they left the United States as the lone Western superpower in the region vis-à-vis a perception of the growing influence of China.

Looking back at these earlier attempts at regional cooperation explains for me the motivation and circumstances, as well as the lessons learned, that led to the establishment of ASEAN in 1967.

The precursors of ASEAN are the following:

1. Southeast Asian Treaty Organization (SEATO)—The SEATO was established in 1954 by the United States, France, Great Britain, New Zealand, Australia, the Philippines, and Thailand to prevent communism from spreading in the region. Its only two Southeast Asian members, the Philippines and Thailand, joined for the obvious reason of preventing communism from invading their respective territories and because of their close ties with the United States. Contrary to popular notions about the nature and objective of SEATO, John Franklin (2006) offers a more nuanced explanation of the failure of SEATO, which he believes, was never intended by its chief proponent, the United States, to be a military alliance, but an American design to justify its presence in the region and an instrument to act as a deterrence for the spread of communism. Franklin says that SEATO failed because it never developed into a regional organization that provided economic prosperity for Southeast Asian countries and therefore, has not attracted additional membership from them.

There is also suspicion by nationalist leadership, particularly in Indonesia and Malaysia, that it was an instrument of the United States to wield influence in the region, a notion shunned by policymakers of nations which have only a few decades ago, yanked the yoke of colonialism in their countries. On the part of the two Southeast Asian members, the Philippines and Thailand, the raging war in and eventual fall of Viet Nam, the upsurge of communist insurgents along their borders, and the Lao crisis of 1960–61 in which, the French and British governments refused to intervene, were stark reminders that SEATO was not the defense organization that they hoped it was going to be.

2. The Association of Southeast Asia (ASA)—ASA was formed in 1961 and included the Philippines, Thailand and Malaya. Its ostentatious goals were to develop economic, socio-cultural cooperation among its members, as stated in its main document, the Bangkok Declaration of 1961. In the beginning, there was much enthusiasm in its potential as could be gleaned from a glowing dispatch by Professor Gayl D. Ness to the Institute of Current World Affairs in which he praised the Association's first fruits (a medical mission, a railway, and so forth) and considered it a genuine attempt by the proponents to free themselves from colonial influence. Despite these avowed goals, however, ASA did not attract membership from the other countries in the region and instead earned damning criticism of being a pro-Western, anti-communist group whose motive was to promote the interests of the United States. Vincent K. Pollard (1970) recounts the painstaking efforts and statements of its founders to defend it from such criticism which he says, only exacerbated outsiders' suspicions that it was an instrument by the United States to contain China. The Philippine claim to Sabah in 1962 was also a big hindrance in its development to a full-blown regional organization, since it led to non-recognition of the new federation of Malaysia in 1963 by the Philippines, automatically including this State, which the Philippines claim, is an integral part of its territory.

3. Malaysia-Philippines-Indonesia organization (MAPHILINDO)— Formed in 1963, MAPHILINDO was an initiative of President

Diosdado Macapagal. Each of the proponents had a different motivation in agreeing to its establishment. The Philippines had intended it to diffuse regional hostility while endowing it with a leadership role in the region, and perhaps finding an amicable solution to the Sabah issue. Indonesia, on the other hand, had used it as a vehicle for removing western influence in the region with Sukarno's "Asian solutions to Asian problems by Asian people". Malaysia's Tunku Abdul Rahman spoke of "the revival of the Malay race after a period of division due to Western domination" leading to "efforts to build closer integration among peoples of Malay origin in the whole region". Touted to be a better solution than ASA was because of its more non-aligned composition with Indonesia as a member, it soon deteriorated into becoming a failure because of the now infamous *Konfrontasi* between Indonesia and Malaysia whereby Indonesia, to show its displeasure over Malaysia's expansion to include Borneo (known as Kalimantan in Indonesia), supported and staged belligerent actions against the latter, including supporting guerilla warfare in air and sea attacks in Sarawak and Sabah and harsh language and propaganda against Malaysia. Also aggravated by the Philippine claim of sovereign jurisdiction over Sabah in 1962, the fledgling organization had no chance of surviving, much less of attracting other members to join.

The fall of Sukarno in 1967 led to calmer relations among the three protagonists and various mediation efforts led to the end of the *Konfrontasi* and engendered the establishment of a regional organization that attracted the buy-in of, first of the founding five, and then the ten Member States that now make up ASEAN.

A Brief History of ASEAN

The first artwork that catches one's attention when visiting the ASEAN Gallery of Art at the ASEAN Secretariat Headquarters in South Jakarta is a rendition into canvas of the iconic photograph depicting the Five Founding Fathers of ASEAN signing the Bangkok Declaration on 8 August 1967. As one of my initiatives, the painting was commissioned by the Committee of Permanent Representatives of which I was the Chair at the time and the artist was a young Filipino painter, Peter

Paul Blanco, who depicted on the faces and hands of Adam Malik of Indonesia, Tun Abdul Razak of Malaysia, Thanat Khoman of Thailand, Narciso Ramos of the Philippines, and S. Rajaratnam of Singapore, their grim determination to bind together the destinies of their peoples to form ASEAN. The fledgling organization of five countries which was then established by that act was not given a chance to survive, much less prosper, by political analysts and observers, including the Nobel Laureate Gunnar Myrdal (1968) in view of the dismal political and socio-economic conditions of the Southeast Asian region at the time of its birth. The Viet Nam War was raging, the countries were mired in abject poverty and the people did not even know of the existence of their next-door neighbours. And yet, more than fifty years hence, I am awed that ASEAN, despite its many failings and weaknesses and the many challenges and the dire circumstances under which it was born and nurtured, is now a robust organization of ten Member States and considered to be one of the most important regional organizations in the world. It is a region which, although characterized by territorial disputes, differing colonial and post-colonial backgrounds, wracked by religious and cultural animosities, post-Cold War experiences and more recently by the tug-of-war of big power rivalry, has survived and thrived even. It has a total GDP of US$243 trillion and an FDI of over US$120 billion, making it the 4th largest economy in Asia and the 7th in the world with a young population of about 630 million. It has become the convenor of strategic forums, such as the EAS, ARF, ADMM-Plus etc. Former Foreign Minister Marty Natalegawa, in reply to the question, Does ASEAN Matter?, unequivocally says "absolutely". Without ASEAN, the past five decades could have been witness to an entirely different experience including incessant conflict, distrust, animosity, and poverty. Instead, ASEAN has made a difference; it has mattered, he adds.

I note the following milestones in the history of ASEAN after the 1967 signing of the Bangkok Declaration which should be taken into consideration in trying to understand the ASEAN of today:

1976—The ASEAN Treaty of Amity and Cooperation (TAC) was signed. To date, forty-three countries have acceded to the TAC with a few more waiting in the line to be granted approval to sign it. The most recent signatories were South Africa, Thailand, and Cuba.

1984—Soon after its declaration of independence, Brunei Darussalam joined ASEAN. I do not remember any major issue connected with their joining since it was a natural consequence of their being a sovereign nation.

1992—The ASEAN Free Trade Area which aimed to lower intra-regional tariffs through the Common Effective Preferential Tariff (CEPT) Scheme to a 0–5 per cent tariff range, was launched. There was stiff resistance to this scheme in the beginning. I remember being called to a House of Representatives hearing, assuaging the apprehension of the body that the liberalization being sought in the scheme would harm their constituents' agricultural products.

1995—Viet Nam[2] joined ASEAN.

1976—The Bali Concord 1 was issued.

1997—Myanmar and Lao PDR joined. The ASEAN Vision 2020 was adopted.

1999—Cambodia joined. The Hanoi Action Plan was launched.

The end of the Cold War in 1991 found the communist-leaning Southeast Asian countries—CLMV (Cambodia, Laos, Myanmar, and Viet Nam)—without strong backers. Their membership in ASEAN was, therefore, natural and expected. Particularly in the case of Viet Nam, its joining in 1995 was a two-way solution to the dilemma of the ASEAN-6 on the one hand and Viet Nam on the other. On the one hand, the ASEAN-6 had to keep into their network a country which they once suspected of spreading the communist fever in their region, the so-called "domino effect" paranoia of communism while Viet Nam had to address its urgent need to rise from the ashes of war that ravaged its economy and caused social upheavals in its society. *Strategic Comments* had predicted it accurately when they said in 1996 that Viet Nam needed the umbrella of ASEAN to attain good regional citizen credentials to gain the business confidence of the world. Today, Viet Nam posts one of the fastest growing economies in ASEAN. It has surpassed even Indonesia and the Philippines in some of their United Nations Substainable Development Goals (UNSDG) indexes.

The membership of the CLMV in ASEAN was also a realization of the vision of the Founding Fathers of the inclusion of all Southeast Asian countries in one regional organization to enable them to peacefully discuss issues that have torn them apart in previous decades and chart a common destiny together. Their membership was not without issues, in fact they are the same ones that ASEAN is confronted with regarding the accession of Timor-Leste at the moment. The admission of the CLMV countries into ASEAN brought the challenge of integration of market diversity given that the four countries were transitional economies. This "development gap" is manifested not only in the difference between the average per capita income of the six older ASEAN Member States (AMS) and that of the newer four, but also in terms of human resources, institutional capacity, the state of the infrastructure and their level of competitiveness.

2003—The Bali Concord was signed.
2004—The Vientiane Action Programme (VAP) was issued.
2007—The ASEAN Charter was signed and deposited in the United Nations. The Cebu Declaration was signed.
2009—The Roadmap for an ASEAN Community was launched.
2015—The KL Declaration and the ASEAN Community Vision 2025 and its Blueprints were launched.
2020—The Regional Comprehensive Economic Partnership was signed.

I also advise ASEAN Studies students to take note of the major documents related to realizing the ASEAN Community as listed in Table 1.1.

TABLE 1.1
Major Documents Related to Realizing the ASEAN Community

Declaration of ASEAN Concord, Bali, Indonesia (Bali Concord I) 1976	The Declaration, more commonly known as Bali Concord I, was signed in Bali on 24 February 1976 by the Leaders of Indonesia, Malaysia, the Philippines, Singapore, and Thailand.
	It declared ASEAN's objectives and principles in pursuit of political stability in the region. It also adopted a programme of action as a framework for ASEAN cooperation, which included the following priorities: political, economic, social, cultural and information, security, and improvement of the ASEAN machinery.

TABLE 1.1 (*Continued*)

ASEAN Vision 2020	The ASEAN Vision 2020 was adopted on 15 December 1997. It encapsulates ASEAN's vision for the year 2020 as a concert of Southeast Asian Nations, a partnership in dynamic development identifying various areas of economic cooperation. This document also focuses on fostering a community of caring societies, and an organization of outward-looking countries with intensified cooperation with external partners.
Hanoi Plan of Action (1999–2004)	The Hanoi Plan of Action is the first in a series of action plans building up to the realization of the ASEAN Vision 2020. In recognition of the need to address the economic situation in the region in the late 1990s, ASEAN came up with initiatives to hasten economic recovery and address the social impact of the global economic and financial crisis. These measures reaffirm ASEAN commitments to closer regional integration and are directed at consolidating and strengthening the economic fundamentals of AMS. The Plan of Action focuses on the following areas: (i) strengthening macroeconomic and financial cooperation; (ii) enhancing greater economic integration; (iii) promoting science and technology development and developing information technology infrastructure; (iv) promoting social development and addressing the social impact of the financial and economic crisis; (v) promoting human resource development; (vi) protecting the environment and promoting sustainable development; (vii) strengthening regional peace and security; (viii) enhancing ASEAN's role as an effective force for peace, justice, and moderation in the Asia-Pacific and in the world; (ix) promoting ASEAN awareness and its standing in the international community; and (x) improving ASEAN's structures and mechanisms.
Declaration of ASEAN Concord II (Bali Concord II) 2003	The second Bali Concord or Bali Concord II was signed by the Leaders of Brunei, Cambodia, Indonesia, Lao PDR, Malaysia, Myanmar, the Philippines, Singapore, Thailand, and Viet Nam on 7 October 2003 in Bali. It noted the expansion of ASEAN from five to ten Member States from the adoption of Bali Concord I.

1. Introduction

TABLE 1.1 (*Continued*)

	The Declaration charted ASEAN's goal to establish an ASEAN Community comprising three pillars: political and security cooperation, economic cooperation, and socio-cultural cooperation. It also adopted a framework to achieve this goal. The end goal of economic integration as outlined in the ASEAN Vision 2020 is also reiterated in this Declaration.
Vientiane Action Programme (VAP) 2004–2010	The VAP was adopted by the Leaders at the 10th ASEAN Summit in 2004. It was adopted as a successor action plan to the Hanoi Plan of Action and to implement Bali Concord II. It serves as a guide towards the ASEAN Vision 2020. It enshrines specific goals, strategies, and measures per ASEAN community: ASEAN Security Community, ASEAN Economic Community, and ASEAN Socio-Cultural Community, as well as for narrowing the development gap. In order to attain these goals, implementation mechanisms are also indicated in the document, which focuses on resource mobilization, strengthening existing institutions, and developing a monitoring and evaluation framework.
Cebu Declaration on the Acceleration of the Establishment of an ASEAN Community by 2015	At the 12th ASEAN Summit in January 2007, ASEAN Leaders affirmed their strong commitment to accelerate the establishment of an ASEAN Community by 2015 and signed the Cebu Declaration on the Acceleration of the Establishment of an ASEAN Community by 2015.
Roadmap for an ASEAN Community (2009–2015)	In 2009, ASEAN Leaders agreed that the Roadmap for an ASEAN Community constitute the ASEAN Economic Community Blueprint (adopted at the 13th ASEAN Summit on 20 November 2007 in Singapore), the ASEAN Political-Security Community Blueprint, the ASEAN Socio-Cultural Community Blueprint, and the Second Initiative for ASEAN Integration Work Plan (all adopted at the 14th ASEAN Summit on 1 March 2009 in Thailand), and shall ensure their timely implementation. The Roadmap replaced the Vientiane Action Programme.

TABLE 1.1 (*Continued*)

Kuala Lumpur Declaration on the ASEAN 2025: Forging Ahead Together	The Declaration was adopted at the 27th ASEAN Summit in November 2015 and welcomed the formal establishment of the ASEAN Community 2015 comprising the ASEAN Political-Security Community (APSC), ASEAN Economic Community (AEC), and ASEAN Socio-Cultural Community (ASCC) and adopted the ASEAN Community Vision 2025, the APSC Blueprint 2025, the AEC Blueprint 2025, and the ASCC Blueprint 2025, constituting the "ASEAN 2025: Forging Ahead Together".
ASEAN Community Vision 2025 and its Blueprints	The ASEAN Community Vision 2025, issued in Kuala Lumpur in 2015, consists of the APSC Blueprint 2025, AEC Blueprint 2025, and the ASCC Blueprint 2025, and succeeds the Roadmap for an ASEAN Community (2009–2015). The Blueprints serve as frameworks and include strategic measures that are implemented by the relevant sectors and bodies in ASEAN. It envisions a peaceful, stable and resilient Community with enhanced capacity to respond effectively to challenges, and ASEAN as an outward-looking region within a global community of nations, while maintaining ASEAN Centrality. This Community encompasses all facets of life, as reflected by its political-security, economic, and socio-cultural pillars.

ASEAN Community Post-2025 Vision

Work and discussions towards the development of an ASEAN Community Post-2025 Vision is ongoing. Brunei as 2021 Chair will work together with other Member States and the ASEAN Secretariat to develop a draft roadmap for the Post-2025 Vision and the Terms of Reference (a must in any ASEAN major undertaking) of a High-Level Task Force (HLTF) as the targeted outcomes for 2021. This HLTF will be composed of eminent persons knowledgeable about ASEAN who will chart the future of ASEAN for the next thirty years. They will identify the strengths, shortcomings and challenges of ASEAN and will propose ways forward to make ASEAN sustainable, relevant and successful. The documents will be referred to each ASEAN Member State before being submitted to the Joint Consultative Meeting (JCM) for endorsement, and subsequently to the ASEAN Coordinating Council (ACC) and the 38th ASEAN Summit for approval.

The Application of Timor-Leste as the 11th Member of ASEAN

On 17 November 2011 at the 19th ASEAN Summit in Bali, the Leaders of ASEAN formally welcomed the application of Timor-Leste as the 11th member of ASEAN. As mentioned, this application has presented a number of challenges both for the applicant and the organization. The Leaders tasked the ACC through the establishment of an ASEAN Coordinating Council Working Group (ACCWG), to discuss all relevant aspects related to the application as well as its implications to ASEAN. The ACCWG, comprising the Senior Officials' Meeting (SOM), Senior Economic Officials Meeting (SEOM) and Senior Officials Committee for the ASEAN Socio-Cultural Community Council (SOCA), shall make recommendations to the ACC on the application by Timor-Leste based on whether or not Timor-Leste is able to meet the requirements of Article 6 of the ASEAN Charter.[3]

Since its establishment, the ACCWG on Timor-Leste has convened eight times. All three pillars have submitted their reports to the ACC and such reports indicate efforts by both sides to overcome considerable challenges particularly in the area of human resources capacity and policies and regulations consistent with ASEAN. The Philippines and Indonesia have been ardent champions of Timor-Leste's membership for obvious reasons. While enormous challenges have been identified in this endeavour, I have always believed that these are minor compared with the political-security implications of Timor-Leste's non-membership. I believe that a Timor-Leste outside the framework of ASEAN would pose more security threat to the region than one that is within it. Outside ASEAN, Timor-Leste would be more susceptible to the sway of big power rivals and might become a haven for transnational crime. Philippine support for Timor-Leste's application for ASEAN membership continues up to this day, as it recognizes that Timor-Leste deserves to be part of the organization in order to fulfill the vision of its Founding Fathers to unite the countries in Southeast Asia under ASEAN. I have included in my interventions in ASEAN meetings the Philippines' willingness to provide language and conference diplomacy training to the diplomats of Timor-Leste to help them when they finally become the 11th ASEAN Member State.

The timeline in Figure 1.1 provides an overview of the milestones in ASEAN's history.

FIGURE 1.1
ASEAN Timeline

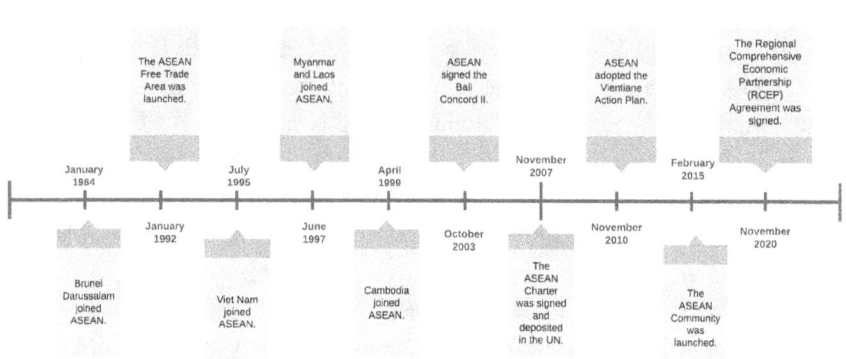

Is There an ASEAN Community?

Many political and economic observers have found ASEAN to be lacking in many aspects. A number of articles and books have been written about its alleged inability to respond to critical issues such as human rights, particularly the political and individual rights of its peoples, and a seemingly lack of consensus on issues like the South China Sea dispute and the adoption of the Regional Comprehensive Economic Partnership (RCEP) before it was signed in November 2020. While I agree to some extent with these observations, having been at the receiving end of ASEAN's lack of unity on many issues, the following facts have been established over the course of these fifty-three years:

1. Regional political stability and security have been attained, without a major single region-wide conflict despite the preponderance of reasons for conflict in the region. I consider this the single biggest achievement of ASEAN, without which socio-economic progress would not have been achieved;
2. The ASEAN Charter has been enshrined as the document that provides ASEAN its legal personality and which embodies the norms, principles and aspirations of ASEAN;
3. The Treaty of Amity and Cooperation has been instituted and any country wishing to establish formal relations with ASEAN

is invited to accede to it. To this date, a total of forty-three countries, including the world's major powers, have done so; and
4. The ASEAN Community, with its three pillars, the ASEAN Political-Security (APSC), the ASEAN Economic Community (AEC) and the ASEAN Socio-Cultural Community (ASCC), has been launched.

Whether or not there has indeed been an ASEAN Community to speak of has been the target of debate. The answer depends on what we mean by "Community". In the general sense that it means complete integration in comparison with other regional institutions which have introduced common currencies, a regional language, supranational institutions with legally enforceable policies, etc., then ASEAN does not fit the term Community. But ASEAN never claimed nor aspired to be like the European Union which fits this description. In the sense that ASEAN Community refers to the achievement of some of the objectives and outcomes outlined in the Vision 2025, including the attainment of peace and stability, the achievement of a considerable degree of economic integration and the level of economic progress it has attained as well as the fostering of a more resilient, inclusive, and people-oriented, caring and sharing Community, then, indeed what we have today is an ASEAN Community.

Notes

1. Later, Indonesia introduced a concept paper on the IPS which the senior officials negotiated. The finished product is called the ASEAN Outlook on the Indo-Pacific (AOIP) which is now being sold as another centrepiece of ASEAN Centrality in response to the other IPSs being touted by ASEAN's Dialogue Partners.
2. The Ambassador of Viet Nam told me this is their preferred spelling.
3. Article 6 outlines the qualifications for admission into ASEAN. While Timor-Leste fulfills all the other criteria listed in Article 6, namely, geographical proximity, recognition by all AMS, and accession to the TAC, there remain huge challenges in fulfilling (d) of the Article, i.e., ability and willingness to carry out the obligations of membership.

2

AUTOETHNOGRAPHY: MEMOIR, BIOGRAPHY, AUTO-WHAT?

Analytical Framework

Before I undertook writing this book, I had never heard of the term "autoethnography". I have, of course, read a number of memoirs and autobiographies of diplomats recounting their experiences. In fact, during a seminar on the same topic where I presented the results of my study, many in the audience, including professors, had mistaken my work as an autobiography. I took pains then, as I do now, to make a differentiation between autoethnography and other genres of reflective writing.

Auto-what? was my initial response when a professor from the University of the Philippines Open University, Dr Jean Saludadez, suggested it to me. As I read up on the research method, I came to realize that this analytical framework was the perfect way to guide me in writing this book. I also came to the conclusion that many people were like me, either ignorant of the existence of such a beautiful research method or knowing about it but dismissing it as a second-rate framework that does not merit being placed side-by-side more formal, more "academic-sounding" approaches.

Autoethnography is a valid research method. I take inspiration from Ellis, Adams, and Bochner (2011) who define autoethnography as a type of research that seeks to describe and systematically analyse the researcher's personal experiences in order to understand cultural phenomena. They rationalize that autoethnography goes beyond data, but attempts to combine personal experiences with methodological tools. They popularized autoethnography as an approach to research and writing that seeks to describe and systematically analyse personal experience as a valid method of research. There should be no shame nor guilt in using personal narratives and perspectives in the quest for truth and knowledge, they say, and instead, regard the result of such a method as one that best approximates the truth, being based on personal experiences.

The *Handbook of Autoethnography* by Jones, Adams and Ellis (2016) distinguishes autoethnography from ordinary emotive writing by citing four of its characteristics, namely: (i) purposefully commenting on/ critiquing culture and cultural practices; (ii) making contributions to existing research; (iii) embracing vulnerability and purpose; and (iv) creating a reciprocal relation with the audience.

Careful not to be dismissed as another boring memoir of a retired diplomat, I take pains to incorporate the above-mentioned characteristics and goals into my book. I mention here memoirs, oral histories and vignettes, especially by retired diplomats and their families, only to illustrate the fact that the emotive, subjective, and informal recollection of diplomatic experience has been the subject of literally thousands of published works and recorded oral histories by diplomats, particularly in the United States where diplomats, their wives and family members are encouraged to talk reflectively about their experiences in the foreign service. However, this similarity between memoirs with autoethnography ends there since memoirs, although oftentimes offering rare insights into the stories behind the headlines, do not necessarily follow the rigours of scholarship required in autoethnographies.

The Handbook also details the purposes or goals of autoethnography as follows:

(i) disrupting norms of research practice and representation;
(ii) working from insider knowledge;
(iii) maneuvering through pain, confusion, anger and uncertainty and making life better;

(iv) "breaking silence and (re)claiming voice and writing to write" quoting Bolen (2012); and
(v) making work accessible.

As the Handbook preaches, autoethnography should be able to challenge conventional methods of analysing diplomacy, all preferring the objective, content-analysis approach. One of the objectives of this publication is to disrupt norms of research practice and representation, especially in the area of diplomacy which even the noted champions of autoethnography have not included in their lists. With my insider knowledge and experience, being not just a participant observer who penetrates a cultural setting and then leaves to tell my story, but a day-to-day member (and in 2017, leader) of the very same cultural community I am studying, I am able to represent events, causes and effects, motivations, realpolitik in the give-and-take, scratch-my-back-I'll-scratch-yours practices which we, diplomats euphemistically call QPQs, used when negotiating difficult documents or wanted to push our own agenda and interests. This is what I suspect is lacking in statistics-based or content analysis studies of ASEAN and its mechanisms, thus resulting in inaccurate and judgmental assessment of this regional organization. By running the risk of exposing confidential information such as negotiating techniques and strategies, revealing otherwise hidden bottom lines to achieve national interests of my country and those represented by the other members of my community, the book is one way of breaking silence on the study of diplomacy.

In *The Aesthetic Turn in International Political Theory*, Bleiker (2001) suggests that in studies on International Relations (IR), an aesthetic approach, including autoethnography, is needed as it "assumes that there is always a gap between a form of representation and what is represented therewith". He describes current IR theory as reliant on objectivity with a detachment between the observer and the subject, thus paying less attention to the relationship between the represented and its representation. The aesthetic approach, he says, welcomes this relationship and sees it not as a threat to knowledge production but rather an inevitable development. With the legitimization of aesthetic approaches, such as images and narratives, scholarship is made less rigid and moves away from exclusive sources of data, he posits. Bleiker justifies the aesthetic approach in studies concerning IR as it aids in "supplementing its social scientific conventions with approaches that problematise representation". This refreshing take on IR scholarship shows me that support for different methods of study exists in the academic community, thus reaffirming my choice to discuss ASEAN Centrality through an autoethnography. An aesthetic approach does not take away from a subject's validity, but can even strengthen it.

In place of field notes, I used Facebook posts, notes to myself, draft speeches and interventions, Google calendars, Department of Foreign Affairs (DFA), the Philippines and Philippine Mission website press releases, etc. I also made extensive use of the ubiquitous Briefing Paper. In my Mission, my officers have mastered the art and science of writing a Briefing Paper, a diplomatic tool that contained the issues to be discussed, the backgrounds of these issues and the Philippine position and stance for each issue, depending on our national interest which are determined in consultation with Philippine agencies and NGOs. In addition to this usual format, we added names of those who were opposed and who were supportive of our positions, what their specific problems and attitudes were and the possible reasons behind their positions and their stance, what they said and what they did not say, etc. It even mentioned personal idiosyncrasies of the diplomats I dealt with and their relationship with their home offices.

A Word About Reflexivity

The projection of the self as the active participant all throughout this representation of experiences is collectively called reflexivity in autoethnography. But which self? The constant struggle between my diplomat/negotiator self or the researcher/storyteller bedeviled me throughout the conceptualization, writing and re-writing of this study. I needed to demarcate clearly and make prominent the autoethnographer in me as the diplomat/negotiator self tends to dominate the internal conversation in my heart and mind. Therein lies the conflict of my story.

I have to start this narrative with a confession. In all my professional life, I have been what Andrew C. Sparkes (2000) called an intellectual imperialist, someone who disdained any kind of study that did not have statistical data in it or is not a clinical, objective, pure science analysis of empirical data. Sparkes labelled "intellectual imperialism" the insistence of so-called scholars to apply the same criteria used on the works of pure science to those using the autoethnographic approach. His autoethnographic work, "The Fatal Flaw", about his experiences from being a healthy, sporty, and strong person to one whose body was paralyzed by an accident, evoked a plethora of criticisms, ranging from admiration for the unique narrative to vitriolic attacks doubting its legitimacy as a serious sociological study. In a critique to his critics, Sparkes defends autoethnography as an appropriate method of arriving at the truth given that qualitative research allows different epistemological and ontological assumptions.

As a Foreign Service Officer for over forty-one years and a negotiator trained to advance, protect and defend Philippine interests abroad, I believed only in the objective, the realistic and the rational in my writing, never allowing my personal views, emotions and impressions to interfere with my work of carrying our relations between my country and others, be they allies or hostile entities opposed to my country's national interests. Indeed, to flow with the ebb of my circle of diplomats and IR practitioners, I subscribed to what Brigg and Bleiker (2010) described the state-of-play in international relations and international studies by saying that "the most prominent approaches in political and international studies have gone out of their way to distance the self from the topic". As a female diplomat coming from the Global South (in earlier times we were called developing country or third world), I had to project a strong, non-emotional persona, especially on "macho" issues like terrorism, cybersecurity, chemical and nuclear weapons, the conflict in the South China Sea, the Korean Peninsula issue, etc. so that I would be taken seriously by others in the diplomatic circles I circulated in. Being the Chair of ASEAN mechanisms in Jakarta and now the head of the political/security branch of my ministry exacerbates this need to project a strong rational image. Despite the many inroads women have made in the world of diplomacy, it is still a man's world out there. It has to be expressed and approached in a masculine voice, which according to Jones, Adams and Ellis (2016), quoting Geertz (1973), is traditionally regarded as objective, in control, and predictable, in contrast to the "feminine traits" of autoethnography—subjective, uncertain and emotion-based, traditionally gendered as insufficient, weak and irrational (Jones, Adams and Ellis 2016, quoting Keller 1995 and Pelias 2011). Before autoethnography, I thus developed a reportorial/memorandum style in all my communications—direct, concise, objective texts devoid of any human or subjective or literary underpinnings. The literary self I described earlier became a separate persona from the official one. I even exacted the same discipline on my younger colleagues, shunning the first or second person pronouns in all communications and correspondences. But when introduced to qualitative methods, particularly autoethnography as an alternative, perhaps a better way of arriving at a truth, I started to mellow. My conversion was slow. Even after reading the masterworks of the autoethnographic gurus of our time, including Carolyn Ellis, Tony Adams, Arthur Bochner, Leon Anderson, Andrew Sparkes, etc., I became even more convinced that such a distinction should be made between "serious" diplomacy and international relations on the one hand and on the other, naturally emotive topics like sexual violence, incest, adoption, lesbian, gay, bisexual, transgender, queer and intersex (LGBTQI), suicide, death, illness, drug addiction, communication, health, education, etc., which were the topics included in the exhaustive list of their collection of autoethnographies. In such cases, the intimate human experience would be nearer the truth as opposed to listening to other people recounting the lived experiences of others. But diplomacy as an autoethnographic topic? No way! Not even the staunchest of these autoethnographic champions dared include it among their pantheons of issues. While I recognized that certain stories fit the ethnographic method, diplomacy, international relations, indeed ASEAN Centrality, should be treated with the same seriousness, objectivity and matter-of-fact approach as that accorded to high science.

Some Ethical Considerations

While the self is at the core of this reflexive discourse, it cannot be helped that the researcher has had to include the participation of others with whom she interacted in the socio-political milieu that she was moving in. This is exacerbated by the fact that these "others" were co-protagonists in the ASEAN drama, either as people representing allies or states that were hostile to the interests of ASEAN and the Philippines, no matter what their avowed support for it was. This set-up would naturally call for a tone of "they versus we" in the narration of vignettes, which could possibly result in causing harm to the autoethnographer and the others. Herein lies another dilemma in choosing autoethnography as a research method. But such risks exist as this cannot be totally avoided in autoethnography. Tullis (2016) provides a logical solution through her introduction of the concept of justice in ensuring that risks and benefits are distributed equally among the participants in the community I write about. As mentioned, this story must be told to help expand the study of ASEAN diplomacy and autoethnography and to help students and diplomacy practitioners have a deeper understanding of ASEAN while minimizing the risks taken to balance the representation of the delicate incidents recounted.

Thus, for ethical reasons, I endeavoured to minimize causing harm to myself and others by hiding my characters' names under pseudonyms (Country X, Y, Z, etc.), obscuring their gender and even the circumstances around the stories, according to the ethical guidelines provided by Tullis. However, there are cases where I thought that such countries or persons would rather have their names mentioned, such as when I share the Best Department of Foreign Affairs Office accolade with my extended selves, the Philippine Mission to Jakarta Team, and mentioning Indonesia as a leader in ASEAN. I also minimized the dramatic contrast in the "they versus we" dialogue even if in real life, the substance of our existence in Jakarta was debate and argumentation as the tool in getting our respective country's national interests covered in the agreements, declarations and action plans we were negotiating. For ethical considerations and the biggest irony of this whole exercise is my decision to delay publication of this manuscript although the urge is great because I want diplomats and students of ASEANology to benefit from it as expeditiously as possible and for my story to be known to many people.

Nature and Sources of Data

As a person directly involved in the practice of ASEAN diplomacy, I had access to materials which I used in this book:

   a. Briefing Papers which contain official and personal information of Ambassadors and their delegations as described in the review of literature;

b. Texts of EAS, ASEAN Plus Three, ASEAN Plus One Statements, Summaries of meetings, Joint Communiques, etc. in three stages—from the raw draft, to their versions midway into negotiations and the final texts (as published in the ASEAN Secretariat website and other sources);
c. Personal calendars, press releases and my personal social media posts and those from the Philippine Mission and DFA websites, the ASEAN Secretariat website and other relevant platforms to substantiate the narrated experience;
d. Sample agendas of the different mechanisms;
e. Diagrams/Photographs of the Meeting Format;
f. Selected non-confidential memos;
g. Speeches/Presentations/Lectures as Speaker or Panelist in various events, footages of TV shows; and
h. Seminal documents such as the ASEAN Charter, the Treaty of Amity and Cooperation, the various Plans of Action as well as Declarations, Statements and Joint Communiques negotiated and concluded with external partners, and works published by scholars of ASEAN studies, and Terms of Reference (TORs) of the different ASEAN mechanisms.

3

ASEAN DIPLOMACY AND ASEAN CENTRALITY

Insistence on ASEAN Centrality an Offshoot of Post-Colonialism and Cold-War Stigma

I believe that there is a historical explanation of why Member States which make up ASEAN have acquired an almost obsessive desire to insist on ASEAN Centrality in their dealings among themselves and their external partners. Wary of their past colonial experience of being dictated on in what they can and cannot do, say or think, and having become the arena on which major powers have flexed their military and political muscles in the not-so-distant past, ASEAN has used the principle of centrality as some kind of a mantra or antidote against repeating this bitter part of their colonial past. However, the awareness of insisting on ASEAN Centrality has not found itself in the 1967 Bangkok Declaration, except for a general reference to the avoidance of "external interference" in a preambular paragraph. It was only much later, after forty years, that it was spelled out and became preeminent in the ASEAN Charter which was adopted in 2007, particularly as a response to ASEAN Member States' growing self-consciousness of weaning themselves away from foreign influence in the post-Cold War era. I can attribute this to the fact that in 1967 when ASEAN was established, the Cold War was still raging and the original ASEAN 5, although trying hard to remove the vestiges of the

Cold War stigma that has divided them in earlier attempts at regionalism, have not yet totally weaned themselves from these predispositions. Still in the infancy of their regional experiment, they had not yet discovered their unique brand of multilateralism which, they would discover later on, could serve as an alternative to the push-and-pull pressure of their former colonial masters and the big powers that are raring to once again use this arena in flexing their political and military muscles. In recent times, with a long queue of external partners desiring to engage it, ASEAN has found its niche and has tried to shake off these vestiges of colonialism and Cold War by insisting on ASEAN Centrality as a foundational principle of its existence and a guaranty of its sustainability and relevance in the web of complex power-play in the region.

Kamasa (2014) reinforces this view in discussing ASEAN's role in Asia's Regional Architecture, stressing that ASEAN's insistence on national sovereignty despite engaging in multilateralism is a result of how ASEAN Member States gained their independence from Western colonizers. While conscious of their huge differences in colonial and cultural backgrounds, ASEAN is projecting its unique identity in a brokering role to push its economic agenda and keep the peace and stability in the region in the midst of big power rivalry in its backyard. This is the ambiguity that many critics of ASEAN are unable to understand, why ASEAN is unable to come to a common position on certain issues like the South China Sea due to differing national perceptions of their interests towards the issue while projecting a united stand to solve and manage the disputes to preserve regional peace and stability.

Stubbs (2008) ascribes ASEAN's attitudes on centrality and consensus to their experiences under colonization, thus colouring their views of relations with other countries. "Colonialism and, following the post-Second World War period of decolonization, the vagaries of the Cold War years had a profound impact on how most Southeast Asian leaders view their relations with other countries", he argues. In my experience dealing with fellow ASEAN diplomats, national colonial experiences might have two extreme results—negative in the sense that the psychological fear of the "white man" would intimidate him/her to accept the latter's positions or the other way around which is for the ASEAN diplomat to always be wary of the intentions and modalities of their external counterparts, thereby making regional cooperation difficult, if not impossible. The third alternative is for ASEAN to be wary of losing its centrality but at the same time, identify and push for regional initiatives that would benefit its Member States.

In almost every important ASEAN document, the theme of centrality is emphasized. It is, of course, an underlying principle embodied in the ASEAN Charter and in the Treaty of Amity and Cooperation. All leaders of ASEAN make it their central theme and all ASEAN Summit documents contain it. While attending the opening ceremonies of the 51st ASEAN Summit in April 2018, I remember well Foreign Minister Balakrishnan's precaution in handling ASEAN's many challenges ahead. He said: "Whilst we celebrate these achievements, it is also important for us to take a reality check and to appreciate the many challenges which lie ahead; and for us to remember that we need to remain anchored on the core principles of ASEAN unity and Centrality." He quotes Prime Minister Lee Hsien Loong's reply to the Foreign Minister's query: "What do we make of unity and Centrality?"—basically, how do we implement it?, to which the Prime Minister highlighted the need for "unity first before we can achieve and aspire to Centrality".

The Chairman's Statement of the 31st ASEAN Summit hosted by the Philippines on 13 November 2017 stresses this point in paragraph 21:

> We stressed the importance of maintaining ASEAN Centrality and unity in our engagement with external parties and in responding to regional security challenges. We, therefore, applauded ASEAN's efforts to preserve its centrality through effective and timely response to emergency situations in the region, projecting a unified position on issues of common interests, and ensuring that ASEAN's collective interests are not compromised. On this note, we underscored the vital role of all the ASEAN-led mechanisms as platforms to promote confidence building and foster dialogue on a wide range of security issues of common interest and concern. We further encouraged all relevant ASEAN Sectoral Bodies and Organs to implement the revised Work Plan on Maintaining and Enhancing ASEAN Centrality that serves as a strategic guideline to ensure ASEAN's central role in the evolving regional architecture.

This insistence is repeated in paragraph 131:

> We reaffirmed the importance of maintaining ASEAN centrality and unity in shaping the evolving regional architecture built upon ASEAN-led mechanisms, including the ASEAN Plus One, ASEAN Plus

Three, East Asia Summit, ASEAN Regional Forum, ASEAN Defence Ministers' Meeting Plus, and in further deepening our engagement with external parties to address existing and emerging challenges as well as strengthen development cooperation in ASEAN.

Once again, in recent times, the Asia-Pacific region finds itself in a flux, with the major powers jostling for position to have a say in determining the regional political security architecture. ASEAN must ensure that it is not forced to take sides just as it was made to do in the past. ASEAN should astutely navigate these treacherous waters and remain in the driver's seat. ASEAN Centrality must do its job of sustaining ASEAN's primacy in shaping the regional political, economic and socio-cultural architecture.

What They Say About ASEAN Diplomacy

A number of scholarly studies, books and articles discuss the state of the art in ASEAN diplomacy, a topic of research that this book also wants to examine. However, none of these studies uses the autoethnographic method that I employ.

No student of ASEAN diplomacy should miss out on former Foreign Minister Marty Natelagawa's book, *Does ASEAN Matter?: A View from Within*, which contains matter-of-fact prescriptions on how ASEAN can maintain its relevance at present and in the future. Natalegawa recounts his personal involvement in some of the most defining moments of ASEAN's recent history, including his mediating role in the settlement of the incendiary Cambodia-Thailand dispute over the Preah Vihear Temple, the heated debates on the creation of the East Asia Summit (EAS), the crafting of the Bali Concord II, and the diplomatic impasse on the non-issuance of the 2012 Joint Communique because of disagreement on the text of the paragraphs pertaining to the South China Sea. On ASEAN centrality and leadership, he says that ASEAN "should not just respond or react to unfolding developments, but also to strongly mould them in a positive manner"—the same precept I advise in my study.

Deepak Nair's ethnography (2019) comes closest in terms of methodology when he theorizes on the origins, manifestations and results of "face-saving" practices and attitudes in ASEAN diplomacy. As a scholar looking in at the community of ASEAN diplomats based in Jakarta, Nair concludes that the concept and practice of face-saving has been under-theorized in international relations, and which, he says, had been relegated to studies of cultural traits in the past. He comes out with a theory on the origins, effects and variations of face-saving practices and tests this theory against his observations of ASEAN diplomats in Jakarta whom he interviewed and observed in 2012. I believe that Nair's approach is correct since much of the dynamics in Jakarta is based on face-saving practices that the diplomats have developed over the years, as described in my book.

In a theory-based study, Katsumata (2004) examines the reasons for the evolution of ASEAN diplomacy, placing particular focus on Member States' interpretations of the ASEAN Way. The study uses both the rationalist and constructivist perspectives in an attempt to explain changes in ASEAN diplomacy, especially their interpretations and views on non-interference. Employing these theories, Katsumata posits that actors pursue their own interests instrumentally and rationally and ASEAN diplomacy becomes "seen as efficient and as following a course which leads inexorably and relatively quickly to a unique equilibrium". He uses ASEAN's behaviour in the 1997 financial crisis and pollution haze as a rational, constructivist response to non-traditional security threats confronting the region. Indeed, adversity is the mother of invention and as ironic as it sounds, the common threats that ASEAN Member States and their external partners face constitute some of the strongest ties that bind them together.

Again using theoretical frameworks in explaining ASEAN diplomacy, He (2006) takes three different IR theories (neorealism, neoliberal institutionalism, and constructivism) and looks at the ways scholars have applied these to ASEAN. He dismisses neorealists' claims that states are too centred on their own survival that multilateral cooperation is, therefore, almost impossible. He says that neorealists fail to explain why ASEAN and other outside powers join multilateral institutions. He favours more the neoliberals who argue that multilateral institutions can "provide information, reduce transaction costs, make commitments more credible, establish focal points of coordination, and in general facilitate the operation of reciprocity". Of constructivists, Mr He agrees with their argument that ASEAN is an emerging "nascent security community", in which the "we feeling" changes the self-regarding and self-help behaviour of states to other-regarding or prosocial behaviour.

I find Professor Sylvano Mahiwo's (2014) meta-nation paradigm a useful tool in understanding ASEAN diplomacy. ASEAN Centrality practised at the intra-nation and supra-nation channel of interaction as discussed by Prof Mahiwo is what I refer to here as the relations of ASEAN Member States interacting with one another and with their external partners, respectively. I provide a glimpse into these two dimensions or stages of ASEAN diplomacy, first as a set of meta-nation interaction among Member States and then their interaction as a group vis-a-vis external partners. I described the setting provided by Prof. Mahiwo by examining my role as a Filipino diplomat in interacting with my fellows in the political and socio-cultural milieu based in Jakarta. The principle of centrality I wish to define here fits the description propounded by Prof. Mahiwo of ASEAN possessing a unique DNA or identity in dealing with entities in the meta-nation level, with a focus on the areas of policymaking and negotiations.

Many scholars dismiss ASEAN as a useless and ineffective regional organization. Donald Emmerson (2008), in particular, derides ASEAN diplomacy as weak and lacking in clout in comparison with the European Union (EU) with its supranational institutions and legally binding arrangements. He blames the ASEAN Way as a great obstacle to the development of ASEAN as a regional institution. It is not surprising that many people share Donaldson's views which regard ASEAN from the perspectives of an entirely different regional grouping with a different set of norms and objectives.

In contrast, Acharya (1998) studied ASEAN multilateralism and praises its benefits, which, according to him, emerged not only from the principles of inter-state relations agreed to by the founders of ASEAN, but also from a subsequent process of interaction, socialization, compromise and adjustment which has allowed ASEAN to develop a culture of diplomacy quite different from the "regulatory" nature of other regional organizations such as the EU. This brand of diplomacy, Acharya rightfully claims, has become part and parcel of ASEAN's corporate identity, having acquired a "constitutive effect", quoting Katzenstein (1996). I can agree with this view because although statements, declarations and other documents agreed upon by ASEAN are not legally binding, they are regarded as serious sources of normative behaviour and become precedents in addressing problems and in the development of ASEAN as a regional organization.

Peter Drysdale's analysis (2017) also approximates my view of ASEAN as a viable regional organization. He said that ASEAN's secret formula in attaining success in its relations among its own Member States and vis-a-vis the world is surprisingly the concept most maligned by many: consensus. I have often time quoted his contention that it is because of consensus that ASEAN can claim ownership of the many initiatives and concepts that it espouses and there is a greater rate of their implementation because of the considerable amount of commitment to the consensus. He claims that criticism of the consensual brand of ASEAN diplomacy arises from "being told through the prism of a post-colonial commentary that has its own axe to grind and dignity to maintain". The account by a Filipino diplomat like myself, rather than by such critical writers who are not from the Member States of ASEAN, answers Drysdale's call for a more reliable, more realistic assessment of ASEAN's relevance and achievement.

What They Say About ASEAN Centrality

The need to "maintain the centrality and proactive role of ASEAN as the primary driving force in its relations and cooperation with its external partners in a regional architecture that is open, transparent and inclusive" is enshrined in Article 1 of the ASEAN Charter. The idea of centrality is not clear-cut and definite. Multiple scholars—both critics and proponents of ASEAN—have given their own definitions and views on what ASEAN Centrality is and what it should be. I wish to mention a number of writers who have propounded their view of ASEAN Centrality although I must point out that not one of them used the subjective approach, much less the autoethnographic method in arriving at their concept or definition of ASEAN Centrality.

The research of Tan (2017) is not based on a subjective approach in defining ASEAN Centrality but is, in fact, an analysis of his compilation of five definitions of ASEAN Centrality already advanced by other social scientists, namely: (i) ASEAN being a regional leader; (ii) ASEAN as a regional convener; (iii) ASEAN as a regional hub; (iv) ASEAN as a regional driver of progress; and (v) ASEAN as a regional "convenience". Tan does not choose what he considers the best definition from among these expositions but merely objectively describes them and provides examples for each.

Likewise, Acharya (2017) uses objective analysis in looking into the existing definitions of ASEAN Centrality, some of which, he claims, are based on myths and are fallacious. He dismisses claims that ASEAN Centrality was an invention of ASEAN, that it is about ASEAN, and that it is being proffered as a model of regionalism for other groups to emulate. He says that ASEAN Centrality is not an ASEAN creation but is the natural fabrication of the dynamics of great power relationships obtained in the region. ASEAN merely accepted its role in the middle of this geopolitical milieu. He discusses a number of current developments which he considers having an eroding effect on ASEAN Centrality, including the inability of ASEAN to arrive at a common position on the South China Sea citing the failure of the group to issue a Joint Communique in 2012, the "China-centric" attitude of China in the region, the growing burden for what he considers an institution with limited capacity and the decline of the US pivot in the regional architecture. Some of Acharya's claims might be valid including the role of great powers exacerbating the political/security challenges in the region but as will be shown in my study, failure to arrive at a common position on the South China Sea issue does not translate into a lack of ASEAN Centrality. In my study, I show that the failure of ASEAN to reach consensus (or what some Member States, including the Philippines and Viet Nam, wished they could include in ASEAN statements) does not prevent ASEAN from fulfilling its avowed objective to maintain peace and stability in the Asia-Pacific architecture by managing their own bilateral disputes and from turning the region once again into a theatre for major conflict. On Acharya's claims concerning the attitudes of China and the United States, this is the reality of international politics and relations, as shown in my study. Each country will fight assiduously for what they consider to be their national interests but will engage in regional cooperation if they see it advantageous to their cause, as is expounded by constructivist theoreticians. While it is true that ASEAN Centrality is also a reaction to major power rivalry, ASEAN makes ASEAN Centrality happen, as shown in my study, which focuses on how diplomats actually conduct ASEAN diplomacy. I agree with Acharya who advises that for this centrality to be sustained, "ASEAN centrality means that ASEAN lies, and must remain, at the core of Asia (or Asia-Pacific) regional institutions, especially the ASEAN Plus Three (APT), ASEAN Regional Forum (ARF) and the East Asian Summit (EAS). ASEAN provides the institutional 'platform' within which the wider Asia Pacific and East Asian regional institutions are anchored." And most of all, ASEAN does not aspire to be a model for regional cooperation just as it does not relish being compared to other regional organizations like the EU.

Caballero-Anthony (2014), while using a behavioural method like I do in defining ASEAN Centrality, i.e., the social network method of analysis (SNA), defines centrality from the perspective of an outsider looking in, as if by a clinical technician objectively studying the behaviour of the regional organization in relation to its responses to its environment, in contrast to my study of someone inside a system looking around her surroundings and noting down observations of the behaviour and attitudes of both herself and the other inhabitants of the political, socio-cultural community that make up ASEAN in Jakarta and drawing conclusions from therein. The SNA approach, she says, explains the creation of ASEAN Centrality by the "close and dense ties with other actors in the network of institutions in East Asian regionalism and most importantly, by acting as the node that bridges these networks". She echoes Acharya's enumeration of challenges to ASEAN Centrality including its alleged failure to reach consensus, inability to carry out collective action and failure to achieve its stated goals. She offers an alternative definition of power from what is traditionally understood as material and ideational sources. SNA, she says, confers on ASEAN the power or ability of ASEAN to connect the other actors in the international system it finds itself in, thereby providing it with the ability to shape or influence what is happening in that region. She concludes that ASEAN has been able to achieve a position of centrality with the tacit approval of the major powers by being in the middle of a network of mechanisms and processes in the region. She may not have intended this effect but to me, this sounds like ASEAN Centrality appears to have been achieved accidentally, a state of being in a "high-betweenness" caught in the middle of a web or regional networks connecting multiple stakeholders in the region. There seems to be little conscious effort by ASEAN to assert its centrality in this instance, a condition that is strongly refuted in my study when ASEAN itself proved capable of setting the agenda, tone, processes, etc. in a very purposeful, deliberate and even insistent manner.

The security perspective of ASEAN Centrality provided by Rolls (2012) earlier reiterates Caballero-Anthony's premise, stating that ASEAN finds itself in the middle of major power-play in ensuring stability in the region as exemplified by the establishment of the ASEAN Regional Forum and the ASEAN Defense Ministers' Meeting Plus. He traces the evolution of ASEAN Centrality being manifested and practised over the years, from its creation in 1967, to the ways it has responded to the different security and political challenges it has been confronted with as well as non-traditional security threats like terrorism and disaster response. He said that ASEAN has evolved in its ability to expand cooperation with other regional actors through several platforms that included other regional players. Rolls' concept of ASEAN Centrality is not derived from a subjective approach but is a result of his comparison of other scholars' concept of the term.

Stubbs (2014) shuns the subjective approach in discussing ASEAN Centrality by analysing how it has catapulted ASEAN to a leadership position when interacting with other states through: (i) facilitation of problem solving in an issue area; (ii) leading the establishment of infrastructure for regional consultation; (iii) influencing or shaping the way issues are discussed. However, his focus on the comparison of ASEAN with other regional groupings like the EU and the North American Free Trade Agreement, is rather misplaced, as if measuring the success of ASEAN Centrality on the standards, institutions and objectives set by these extraneous regional organizations, especially the EU. Again, studying the historical development of ASEAN from an objective point of view, Stubbs' view on the organization's role in the region clearly indicates that the leadership role attached to ASEAN Centrality is justified.

From the economic perspective, Dr Rebecca Santamaria (2019) decries the lack of ASEAN Centrality in the failure to reach consensus to finalize the Regional Comprehensive Economic Partnership (RCEP), blaming the Member States' varying degrees of economic development, national interests and cultural backgrounds for this debacle.[1] This implies that centrality for some scholars means that ASEAN must always arrive at a consensus on important issues like the RCEP or as, suggested by other writers, the issues revolving around the South China Sea. What others perceive as the failure to reach a common position on such major issues is, therefore, construed as a failure of ASEAN Centrality.

Jones (2010) derisively and sarcastically portrays ASEAN's "central role" in managing inter-state relations while exposing their inherent weaknesses and inability to agree among themselves in reaching a consensus among themselves on major issues. Jones basically dismisses ASEAN's capacity to lead in mechanisms such as the EAS and the ARF, being caught in-between the web of big-power flexing of diplomatic muscles and achieving no substantive results in these mechanisms. One can easily surmise that the method employed by Jones is from the perspective of an outsider looking in, trying hard to sound objective and neutral but in fact, shows a basic lack of information on what actually transpires inside these mechanisms and how "chaos" and "rivalries" are translated into cooperative activities to maintain the peace and stability and economic prosperity of the region, as I do in my study.

Tay's and Tan's policy brief (2015) does not use the subjective approach in arriving at their concept of ASEAN Centrality but instead, again from the perspective of objective researchers, examine what has been said about ASEAN Centrality by academics, critiques and outside observers and posit that ASEAN Centrality is lodged in the regional group's ability to use its de facto role of managing big power rivalries and utilize this to maintain peace and stability in the region. They advise ASEAN to maintain a multiplex, rather than a single regional architecture, develop a common voice or consensus on key issues and maintain its normative-setting functions in an inclusive manner. Indeed, this study is a response to their urgent call for ASEAN's policymakers to articulate to their external interlocutors in no uncertain terms what they mean by ASEAN Centrality and exercise it, or they would be sidelined in the stream of a rapidly changing political security architecture. They suggest that for ASEAN to achieve centrality, it must have a consensus on key issues and act successfully as a central actor and influencer of events among others in Asia and proceed to suggest how to reform the EAS mechanism to achieve this. Most of their suggestions have been carried out after the policy brief was published, including the stock take of the achievements and future directions of the EAS as the Leaders-led strategic forum in the Asia-Pacific region and the enhancement of the influence of ASEAN to set the agenda and participation of the EAS, as discussed in this study when ASEAN insisted on setting the agenda, tone, processes and direction of the EAS. For example, the inclusion of maritime cooperation in the key priority issues of the EAS, upon the insistence of ASEAN and which was initially strongly opposed by some EAS participating countries, is a good example of this agenda-setting role by ASEAN in this major regional forum.

What I Say About ASEAN Diplomacy and ASEAN Centrality

The stories, sense of identity, points of view and even biases I recall in the following pages have helped me shape a definition of ASEAN Centrality that is based on the reality of my experience. My participation in the different settings of my unique community has also shaped the kind of diplomat I have become, making my stint as Philippine Ambassador to ASEAN the most memorable and productive part of my life as a Foreign Service Officer of the Republic of the Philippines.

In this book, I explored four dimensions of ASEAN Centrality based on my experience as a diplomat interacting with diplomatic agents of other Member States and external partners of ASEAN and as an agent of my country. These are:

1. ASEAN Centrality as an expression of ASEAN Leadership in regional cooperation as demonstrated in ASEAN chairmanships;
2. ASEAN Centrality as a principle applied in diplomacy in the Member States' interaction among themselves in the Jakarta Channel;
3. ASEAN Centrality in ASEAN's interaction with its external partners where ASEAN plays a dominant part; and

4. ASEAN Centrality as an aspiration to raise the level of awareness about ASEAN, thereby helping to create an ASEAN identity.

Note

1. ASEAN and its RCEP partners minus India, finally got to conquer their differences when the Leaders of the 10+5 attended the historic launch of the RCEP during the ASEAN Summit held virtually in November 2020.

4

ASEAN CENTRALITY AS AN EXPRESSION OF ASEAN LEADERSHIP IN THE REGION: THE PHILIPPINE CHAIRMANSHIP OF ASEAN IN 2017

1 January 2017 is a day forever etched in my memory. At the age of sixty-two and with thirty-six years of foreign service experience behind me, I was as excited as a wide-eyed first-year college student on her first day in school. A member state gets to become the Chair of ASEAN only once every ten years, and for a diplomat like me, a once-in-a-lifetime privilege to head ASEAN on its 50th founding anniversary. Chairmanship of ASEAN is a rare opportunity for the Chair to show leadership in the region by delivering important initiatives close to its heart and to advance an agenda which it believes should help shape the political and socio-economic landscape of the region that is facing a great number of challenges. The expectation is even heightened when the Chair is one of the founding members of ASEAN. I was excited and at the same time apprehensive. I was going to become the Chair of ASEAN, specifically the six ASEAN mechanisms based in Jakarta. The task entailed bringing

together to a consensus ten disparate and diverse countries, as well as their ten dialogue and other external partners who have their own agenda and interests to push and protect as well.

Autoethnography provides me the platform to describe this unique political and socio-cultural setting that I belonged to as well as to narrate the experience I had with the people I related punctuated by my feelings, behaviour and disposition at the time of my chairmanship. I was going to assume the responsibility of bringing together to a consensus the varying, sometimes conflicting, interests of the most senior and astute diplomats from ASEAN Member States (AMS) and ASEAN's external partners, in addition to my primary responsibility of assuring that Philippine and ASEAN interests are protected, promoted and defended. This unique cultural community of Jakarta-based diplomats is made up of representatives coming from different backgrounds and motivations. One has to intently study these backgrounds and motivations to determine whether they are allies or adversaries in advancing one's own objectives. Behind the corny jokes and endless karaoke sessions that we jokingly referred to as prerequisites to becoming an Ambassador to ASEAN are individuals transformed into the fiercest and most tenacious combatants on the debating arena when their national interests are at stake. One of my favourite corny jokes in this setting is that so-and-so is my friend in Agenda Item 3 but my worst enemy in Agenda Item 5, which may not be a joke after all when you examine the debates and negotiations we carried out in our daily lives here. The diplomats' personal traits, either positive or negative, can also add to the drama and dynamics of the relations. For example, there was one European diplomat whom we suspected of not really carrying out instructions from their government but was, of their own nature, the haranguing, hectoring, I-am-superior-to-Asians type of partner. Such diplomats from Dialogue Partners were dreaded or avoided by many of my colleagues. Some colleagues seemed helpless dealing with such external partners and merely acquiesced to their hectoring. They made impossible demands, threatened to collapse the talks and oftentimes doused our enthusiasm whenever we were nearing consensus. Their absurdity even turned to the comical, meaning ridiculous and illogical, especially as we moved nearer the end of our negotiations. On the other hand, another diplomat who had to convey a rather nonsensical position from their Headquarters which we could not accept, was not so disliked by many because of their very convivial attitude. They were always smiling, even when delivering a very difficult message. I gave such diplomats a wide degree of allowance to accommodate their position, but not to the detriment of my national interest. I also had to contend with different linguistic idiosyncrasies and tried to go beyond the literal meanings of the words being uttered (I would advise countries to send delegations adept at oral and written English to go to multilateral posts like ASEAN and the United Nations). For example, one diplomat who did not have a good command of the English language called my intervention "emotional" instead of "impassioned" but since I understood what they meant, I did not take offence. With so many different personalities to contend with and with a variety of different sometimes diametrically opposed positions, I literally cajoled, explained, threatened, and bargained endlessly to achieve consensus and deliver our assigned tasks.

Weeks earlier during the traditional handover ceremony from Laos of the chairmanship of the Committee of Permanent Representatives (CPR) held at the ASEAN Secretariat, I outlined the many goals and objectives that my Mission ambitioned to accomplish during our term as Chair in 2017. The key objectives were numerous and ambitious but my Mission, in conjunction with the other members of the CPR, vowed to accomplish them. "But these are merely tasks", I emphasized in my acceptance speech in January 2017, outlining the initiatives I wanted to accomplish during my term as Chair. "We, the CPR, need to see the bigger picture, the vision or the dream of a better ASEAN for our peoples. A shared vision will put the wind in our wings to enable us to contribute to making the lives of our people a little better", was my exhortation to my fellow ASEAN Diplomats and the ASEAN Secretary General Le Luong Minh at the turnover ceremonies.

I was going to assume the chairmanship of six important bodies that are based in Jakarta—what would henceforth be known as the Jakarta Channel. It was like being the conductor of a motley orchestra composed of the best musicians of the world who wanted their respective musical instruments to stand out, and our job was to produce a harmony that would hold the peace, bring prosperity and engender socio-economic development to our audience, the peoples of ASEAN. The five ASEAN bodies are the following:

1. ASEAN Committee of Permanent Representatives (CPR);
2. ASEAN Connectivity Coordinating Committee (ACCC);
3. ASEAN Plus Three Ambassadors (APT);
4. EAS Ambassadors Meeting in Jakarta (EAMJ); and
5. ASEAN Institute of Peace and Reconciliation (AIPR), later to be called ASEAN-IPR.

In addition, I also assumed Co-Chairmanship of the ASEAN-China Centre Joint Council and the ASEAN-Canada Joint Cooperation Committee as well as the Chairmanship of the ASEAN Foundation on 1 January 2018. I was also a member of another Jakarta-based body, the Initiative for ASEAN Integration (IAI) Task Force, but its chairmanship only rotated among the CLMV countries—Cambodia, Laos, Myanmar and Viet Nam—and never among the older six AMS.

The so-called Jakarta Channel would become my home community, with its unique setting, characteristics, language and manner of discourse, format, and agenda, for a period of more than six years (13 March 2013–30 April 2019). In 2017, it has become the nerve centre of ASEAN's day-to-day operations and relations with her external partners since all AMS, ASEAN's Dialogue Partners (DPs) and one Sectoral Dialogue Partner (SDP), Norway, have sent dedicated Ambassadors to ASEAN as well. That means that the Ambassadors are not accredited to the Indonesian government but are sent there solely to represent their respective countries to ASEAN. There are more than 100 Jakarta-based Ambassadors to Indonesia who are also accredited to ASEAN. AMS Ambassadors are called Permanent Representatives (PRs) and are full-fledged Ambassadors, sometimes even among the most senior ones from their respective countries. I am fortunate to count as my predecessors two eminent Filipinos, former Senator and Defense Secretary Orlando Mercado (2009–2011), who was our first PR since the establishment of the CPR in 2009, followed by former ASEAN Deputy Secretary General for Political and Security and former Dean Menito Villacorta (2011–2013). I have been called many different wrong names such as

Permanent Representative to Jakarta or Permanent Ambassador to the Philippine Mission, etc., indicating how very little is known about these bodies and about ASEAN in general, compared to the level of knowledge by ordinary citizens about the United Nations or even the European Union. For the record, my title was Permanent Representative (PR) of the Philippines to ASEAN. We present our credentials to the ASEAN Secretary General; in my case, to Secretary General Le Luong Minh in March 2013. Many outsiders mistakenly say we present our credentials to the ASEAN Secretariat or that we work for it.

By 2017, my view was that ASEAN has become regarded as one of the major regional organizations in the world and the high-level meetings that it convenes are watched closely by observers. Many analysts refer to this as the convening power of ASEAN, and the agenda, conduct and initiatives of these meetings are very much influenced by the Chair. ASEAN Centrality has also come to mean that ASEAN Chairs during their turn, endeavour to deliver important results and accomplishments, which to them, are based on the implementation of the ASEAN Vision 2025 document and its predecessors, and other documents and blueprints. Centrality is the ability of ASEAN, especially by the Chair, to set the agenda in order to influence the regional, and even global political/security, economic and socio-cultural landscape. These priorities and accomplishments are meant to address the challenges faced by ASEAN at any given time. During the chairmanship of Malaysia in 2015 and Laos in 2016, important deliverables were launched, including the establishment of the ASEAN Community in Kuala Lumpur in 2015.[1] The Philippines aimed to leave behind the legacy of a chairmanship which will not be easily forgotten. Thus, its officials had to work double time to achieve this ambition.

Prior to its assumption of the chairmanship of ASEAN, the Philippines had spent over a year preparing for this huge responsibility. I joined other Heads of Philippine diplomatic posts from around the world, particularly those posted to ASEAN capitals and the capitals of its Dialogue Partners in several brainstorming sessions organized by the Department of Foreign Affairs (DFA) to discuss the theme, priorities, goals and deliverables of its chairmanship, in all the three pillars of the ASEAN Community, in substance and in form. Consultations were also made with civil

FIGURE 4.1
Logo of the Philippine Chairmanship of ASEAN

society organizations to give the department a better picture of what its priorities should be. At the helm of these preparations was the Office of ASEAN Affairs of the DFA, headed by the then Assistant Secretary, now Ambassador to Australia, Hellen de la Vega, serving as the National Secretariat of the Philippines, under the supervision of the Undersecretary for Policy, Ambassador Enrique Manalo. Both these offices and diplomats have their own autoethnographies to write, I am sure, but for this account, I will focus on my own experiences. Of course, these decisions had to have the *imprimatur* of the Secretary of Foreign Affairs, then Secretary Perfecto Yasay, followed by Secretary Alan Peter Cayetano, with the approval of the President. After several of such consultations, the DFA had decided on the following theme for its chairmanship: "Partnering for Change, Engaging the World" (see Figure 4.1) which I would learn by heart and preach to all who would care to listen. The two main ideas in this theme were:

Partnering for Change—The change that was aimed for is a positive change in the lives of the ordinary peoples of ASEAN. The Philippine chairmanship had wanted to introduce initiatives that will strengthen the capacities of micro, small and medium enterprises, promote and protect the welfare of migrant workers, women and children, ensure social protection for the vulnerable sectors of society, and secure the future for the succeeding generations by promoting the protection and sustainability of the environment.

Engaging the World—The Philippines wanted ASEAN to strengthen its interaction with the international community. During the Philippine chairmanship, ASEAN's importance was highlighted to both the region and the rest of the world. ASEAN wanted to continue advancing mutually beneficial arrangements and also tackle traditional and non-traditional issues affecting the peace, stability and prosperity of the region and the other parts of the world. It wanted to show that ASEAN was ready for the World Cup of international relations.

The Philippines' ASEAN chairmanship had six thematic priorities, namely:

1. A people-oriented and people-centred ASEAN;
2. Peace and stability in the region;
3. Maritime security and cooperation;
4. Inclusive, innovation-led growth;
5. ASEAN's resiliency; and
6. ASEAN as a model of regionalism and a global player.

Among the more significant deliverables of the Philippine chairmanship were giant documents representing the three pillars of the ASEAN Community, namely the Framework Agreement on the Code of Conduct on the South China Sea which has been in the pipeline for over a decade (for the ASEAN Political and Security Community—APSC), the Consensus on Migrant Workers (for the ASEAN Socio-Cultural Community—ASCC), and the Regional Comprehensive Economic Partnership (RCEP) (for the ASEAN Economic Community—AEC), which, although reaching a level of much improvement from its earlier text, unfortunately did not get consensus of the ASEAN Plus 5 (China, Japan, Republic of Korea, Australia and New Zealand) and was not launched in 2017.[2] The Philippine chairmanship had to content itself with the launch of the ASEAN-HK Free Trade Agreement instead.

Framework Agreement on the Code of Conduct in the South China Sea

By the time the Philippines assumed chairmanship of ASEAN in 2017, all hopes on the peaceful management of the unsettling situation in the South China Sea were pinned on the possible issuance of a Code of Conduct (COC). Many people have hoped that it would become a set of norms that will guide the behaviour of claimant states in the region. It had been a by-word among Member States and Dialogue Partners and no meeting, whether formal or informal, was held without a mention of the desire for the COC to be concluded as it had taken a long time before any shadow of concrete agreement to even start negotiations could take place.

The news that the eleven countries (ASEAN plus China) had, in August 2017, indeed adopted a framework agreement, was met with excitement, cautious optimism and skepticism by observers of ASEAN's long standing saga in the South China Sea. Ian Storey (2017) provides an objective anatomy of this important document, explaining the parts of the framework including its principles, basic undertakings and legal basis and correctly interpreting it as a conflict management measure not intended to resolve the issue of who owns what in the disputed areas but to achieve the objective of managing the disputes peacefully.

The framework is now being used by the negotiators of the COC in their arduous task of completing their negotiations which were made even more problematic by the long delay in convening face-to-face talks arising from health protocols required to contain the pandemic.[3] A Single Draft Negotiating Text that has passed its First Reading has been agreed on and the next step is to come up with a Second Draft Negotiating Text. The road ahead is formidable and long while unsettling facts on the ground such as militarization, artificial island fortifications, harassment of ordinary fishermen and illegal patrols by China continue. The Philippines had invited negotiators to a face-to-face meeting in a controlled "bubble" environment but they had not been able to come. Virtual meetings had been conducted only on administrative aspects of the negotiations since they believe that the more sensitive sections should be discussed face-to-face. The Philippines had vowed to shepherd the talks further until the expiry of its country-coordinatorship in August 2021.

The Consensus on the Protection and Promotion of the Rights of Migrant Workers

In November 2017, the Leaders of ASEAN issued the Consensus on the Protection and Promotion of the Rights of Migrant Workers, during ceremonies to mark the 50th Anniversary of ASEAN. This landmark agreement is considered by the Philippines as its major achievement in its chairmanship of ASEAN. It had been ten years after another landmark agreement on migrant workers was issued—the 2007 ASEAN Declaration on the Protection and Promotion of the Rights of Migrant Workers (Cebu Declaration on Migrant Workers)—which was also spearheaded by the Philippines.

The promotion, protection and advancement of the rights and welfare of migrant workers is a flagship issue for the Philippines in ASEAN and in the United Nations. It is a difficult agreement to negotiate since Member States have varying interests in it: some are receiving states, others are sending and still others are both sending and receiving, which entails different sets of responsibilities and obligations on all sides of the spectrum. The views of receiving countries like Singapore, Malaysia and Brunei Darussalam clashed with those of sending countries like the Philippines and Indonesia, while the rest (CLMV countries and Thailand) which are both sending and receiving countries had to pick which provisions favoured or disadvantaged them. Among the most contentious issues were on the legal nature of the instrument, on whether or not it should cover undocumented workers (which Singapore and the other receiving countries viewed as an invitation for undocumented workers to flood their countries) and whether or not it should cover the families of migrant diasporas (which could spell huge socio-economic costs to the host countries who would be obliged to provide medical benefits and other social protection facilities to the OFWs and their families). Sending countries had argued that they, too, had human rights and must be protected and assisted.

In the end, a Consensus was forged stipulating the general principles, fundamental rights of migrant workers and members of their families, specific rights of migrant workers, and obligations and commitments of AMS. While not a legal instrument, it is a much improved version of the 2007 Cebu Declaration. Among others, it provides for better migrant protection policies and mechanisms including providing decent work for OFWs, a better quality of life for ASEAN migrant workers through strengthened social protection, publication of a compendium of safe migration information material from AMS (a Philippine initiative), reintegration programme for returning migrant workers, and the conduct of several activities, studies, workshops and cooperation to better protect migrant workers.

The Consensus is a demonstration of the political will and strong commitment of ASEAN Leaders to safeguard the rights of migrant workers who have contributed to the growth and development in the region.

The Philippine Mission has also raised the issue of promoting and protecting migrant workers as a regional concern in the different Jakarta mechanisms. On one occasion during our chairmanship, the CPR was negotiating a Work Plan with the Gulf Cooperation Council (GCC) countries where most Southeast Asian migrant workers, mostly from the Philippines and Indonesia, are deployed. Some of my fellow negotiators, particularly those coming from countries which receive migrant workers, refused to include it in the five-year Work Plan we were negotiating, citing that it was not among those identified as a major focus area in an earlier ministerial meeting held by ASEAN Ministers with those of these Middle Eastern states. One ASEAN diplomat advocating this point was particularly very vocal in their opposition, using this technical/administrative argument. They said in his intervention, "How can we be more forward than our Ministers who had not thought it appropriate to include it as an area of cooperation with the GCC? Agreeing to this proposal (the Philippines, supported by Indonesia) would set an undesirable precedent that we can transcend the authority of our seniors." They were technically correct. But I believed that their real objection was that highlighting the promotion and protection of the rights and welfare of migrant workers might exact more responsibilities on their own countries which are similarly situated. I beseeched my fellow ASEAN diplomats to not be pharisaic in our approach because our people are suffering under unfair and difficult conditions in those countries. "Just because the issue of migrant workers had not been included in the ministerial joint communique does not mean that we can close our eyes to the miserable sufferings of our fellow ASEAN human beings", I pleaded. Verging on *argumentum ad misericordiam*, I gave examples of how migrant workers from AMS, particularly those from Indonesia and the Philippines, have been mistreated in these countries and that all of us should rally behind these workers for the sake of ASEAN unity and respect for the welfare of vulnerable sectors of our community. There was natural resistance from receiving ASEAN members and a lot of active support for my intervention from Indonesia. I was disappointed that the other sending countries were quiet and did not lend their agreement. I persisted, and after an hour of debate, all my colleagues upheld this position with some caveats and the Work Plan was completed with the welfare of migrant workers among the focus areas.

I have also seen to it that the promotion and protection of migrant workers is included in the Plans of Action that we negotiate with our external partners. Canada, Australia, New Zealand, and Japan have been our strongest supporters along this line.

During the same year, the milestone ASEAN Convention on the Trafficking in Persons (ACTIP) entered into force when I deposited the Philippines' Instrument of Ratification on 7 February to Secretary General Le Luong Minh in the ASEAN Secretariat. Although I received from my Headquarters the Instrument of Ratification a few days earlier, I had purposely waited and chosen a date exactly thirty days before 8 March 2017, which is, of course, International Women's Day, for it to become enforceable. Under ASEAN norms, an Agreement becomes enforceable when at least six of the ten Member States have ratified it; the Philippines was the sixth. The ACTIP, which specifically applies to Women and Children, became enforceable on International Women's Day in 2017, its anniversary being celebrated annually as part of commemorating this important day. I think that my being a female diplomat accorded me with this unique perspective not normally inherent among male colleagues. It is also interesting to note that two Leaders' Statements championing the role, rights and empowerment of women, namely the ASEAN Declaration on the Gender-Responsive Implementation of the ASEAN Community Vision 2025 and Sustainable Development Goals, and the Joint Statement on Promoting Women, Peace and Security in ASEAN. We take pride in the fact that the Philippines has always ranked high in global efforts in these initiatives, being the first Asian nation to come up with a National Action Plan on the United Nations Security Council Resolution 1325 on Women, Peace and Security (WPS), the first in gender representation in government offices, and as described in another part of this book, the champion of the cause to enhance the role of women and the protection of their rights especially during conflict situations.

A number of other important documents were also issued during the Philippine chairmanship including those on cybercrime, gender mainstreaming, WPS, culture of prevention, climate change, antimicrobial resistance and others, which the Philippines championed and obtained consensus on with the help of its ASEAN colleagues and partners. At least twenty-nine major documents were adopted, issued or signed. It took several months and the close participation of experts and sectoral bodies to finalize the negotiation of these documents and statements. The complete list appears in Annex A.

The Philippine Mission to ASEAN and the Philippine Chairmanship

As mentioned, I also viewed that being Chair entailed me taking on a leadership role in the ASEAN community in Jakarta and this I carried out with the support of the Philippine Mission to ASEAN (JPM) which I headed. JPM is purely a multilateral post. Multilateral diplomacy presents quite a different challenge from that found in bilateral posts. Unlike many other Philippine diplomatic posts scattered around the globe, JPM does not have consular functions nor does it undertake economic diplomacy or cultural promotion per se, the usual three pillars of Philippine diplomacy. These functions are performed by the Philippine Embassy in Indonesia, which has its own separate Ambassador and staff and is located in separate physical quarters.[4] My job was to represent the Philippines in ASEAN under its various areas of cooperation in the three pillars of the Community, leading in the CPR's task in overseeing the operations of the ASEAN Secretariat; ensuring that all agreements and commitments made by me are in line with Philippine national interests and at the same time advancing the objectives and principles of ASEAN. My function as Chair of six ASEAN bodies based in Jakarta was to ensure that all parties in ASEAN undertakings are brought together towards a consensus and in that consensus, ASEAN Centrality should be practised and achieved and Philippine interests are promoted, protected and implemented.

Throughout 2015–2016, I had primed my lean team of five officers and a few administrative staff to brace themselves for the huge responsibility. The Home Office had refused to hear my plea for additional officers. I needed more personnel support on account of the ambitious goals our Mission had set during our chairmanship. I felt let down by officials of the DFA Human Resources and Management Office who were only counting numbers (our Mission did not even have the ideal staffing pattern of seven officers) and did not grasp the importance of such milestone occasions as the Philippine chairmanship of ASEAN. Fortunately, I have been blessed with the best officers any Head of Post could ever wish for, although all of them with the exception of my Deputy, were junior officers (Third Secretary is the lowest diplomatic rank). My officers and staff were well motivated, had discipline and had the competence to handle any challenge I would hurl in their way, for I was a strict Head of Post, demanding only the highest form of excellence from my staff. Like all diplomatic posts in the world, the Mission had a nickname, JPM (Jakarta Philippine Mission), and we in the JPM were keenly aware of the huge expectations of our colleagues in the department and other agencies of the Philippine government. My officers had honed their multilateral diplomacy skills to the highest caliber. They were not scared of the daunting task; they were ready. My Deputy Permanent Representative (DPR), Noel Novicio, a former journalist turned topnotch diplomat, was not only ready, he was eager to take on the big tasks. He chaired the CPR Working Group that "cleaned" the first versions of documents, negotiating the easy parts under the direction of the CPR. The others, Cecille Lao, Jan Wenceslao, Ma. Angella Alfafara, and John Paul Samonte, had willingly and gladly performed multi-tasking assignments which many other officers would balk at. One officer had to handle at least eight desks or responsibilities at a time, sharing among five of them only three staff employees as their assistants, the latter being the best non-diplomatic employees of the service and with the necessary skills and correct attitude for the most difficult tasks. The administrative staff all played their parts with professionalism and dedication despite my strict governance. Figure 4.2 is a typical assignment slip of our Mission in 2017 which shows the various tasks handled by only a few people.

FIGURE 4.2
Routing Slip of the Philippine Mission

PERMANENT MISSION OF THE PHILIPPINES TO ASEAN

ROUTING SLIP

Date: _____ Control No.: _____

[ ] **NOEL M. NOVICIO**
Deputy Permanent Representative and Planning Officer
APSC Pillar, CPR and CPRWG Meetings, ASEAN-Canada, ASEAN-China, ASEAN- Japan, ASEAN-ROK, ASEAN-US, ASEAN-UN, EAS, APT, WPS/SCS, APSC Blueprint 2025, ASEAN Charter, Negotiations of Outcome Documents, Oversight of Administrative and Fiscal Matters

[ ] **CECILLE JOYCE Y. LAO**
Third Secretary
SCDC, SCB, SCT, ASEC Operations, AAC, ASEAN-Russia, ASEAN-Norway, ASEAN-Switzerland, ASEAN-Germany, ASEAN-Pakistan, ASEAN-Turkey, ICF, ASEAN Projects, Assistant: CPR & CPRWG Meetings, Disposal Committee Chair

[ ] **JAN SHERWIN P. WENCESLAO**
Third Secretary and BAC Chair
AEC Pillar, ACCC, ASEAN-Australia, ASEAN-EU, IAI, Assistant: APT and EAS, ERIA

[ ] **ANGELLA GILBERTO L. ALFAFARA**
Third Secretary
ASCC Pillar, Facebook Manager, ASEAN Foundation, AIPR, AICHR, Entities Associated with ASEAN, ASEAN Women's Circle, Assistant: SCDC, SCB, SCT, AAC, GAD Focal Person

[ ] **JOHN PAUL T. SAMONTE**
Third Secretary and Administrative Officer
Regional Organizations, ACTCs, NAAAs, ASEAN-India, ASEAN-New Zealand, Assistant: ASEAN Charter, OPCRF, ASEAN Agreements, BAC Vice Chair

[ ] **NIHAYA T. MACARADI** - Finance Officer

[ ] **NILO JAY G. DE GUZMAN, JR.** - Communications and Records Officer, Website Administrator. Assistant to Mr. Novicio and Mr. Wenceslao

[ ] **MARC JOSEPH O. JAUCIAN** – Protocol and Security Officer, ASEAN Agreements and Projects, ICF, Assistant to Ms. Lao

[ ] **JAZMIN A. LUNA-JAUCIAN** – Assistant for ASCC Pillar, Assistant to Ms. Alfafara

[ ] **MARIA CECILIA P. WENCESLAO** – Administrative Assistant/ Alternate Communications Officer, Cultural Officer, Alternate GAD Focal Person, OPCRF/IPCRF Point Person, BAC Secretariat, Assistant to Mr. Samonte

[ ] **MARICRIS M. BAUTISTA** – Property Officer, Assistant (substantive) to Mr. Samonte

[ ] **CARINA B. GAURANA** - Secretary to the Ambassador

[ ] **AAN HERDIANA** - General Assistant/ Receptionist, Telephone Operator

[ ] For Action [ ] For Information/File [ ] For Comment/ Recommendation

Remarks:

ELIZABETH P. BUENSUCESO

4. ASEAN Centrality as an Expression of ASEAN Leadership

I am also grateful to their spouses and families. Being without a spouse in a post where social functions are numerous can be a disadvantage but I overcame this by enlisting the help of my Deputy's wife, Doris,[5] who is a writer in her own right but did not mind helping me showcase the best of Philippine cuisine and cultural traditions. She teamed up with Karen, Wilma, Maria and Mic, who quietly worked in the background seeing to it that the food was good, the programme appropriate and the dinner venue was perfect for us not just to be fed and entertained but also had the correct environment to carry out our tasks. It served as our informal negotiation setting as well, where we discussed and reached agreements on many issues. With such partners and motivation, I had set out the following ambitious goals:

1. Chair at least twenty (20) CPR meetings, and several meetings of all the CPR-based mechanisms based in Jakarta, i.e., APT, ACCC, AIPR, EAS and ASEAN Plus One, accomplishing previously agreed upon work plans and a rolling agenda for each. Chairing meant preparing and negotiating the agenda, looking into the contentious issues and finding ways to reconcile them, and moving the agenda forward to the next level (usually the Senior Officials, the Foreign Ministers and the Leaders, or closing the issue at our level). It also meant close coordination with the ASEAN Secretariat to ensure that all preparations for the meeting had been made.

2. Undertake to organize six commemorative activities to be funded by ASEAN or by Dialogue Partners. These are:

    2.1. Tribute to the Founding Fathers of ASEAN
    On the Golden Jubilee of the founding of ASEAN, my Mission and I found it fitting to honour the five founding fathers of ASEAN. As mentioned, I made sure that the artist for this painting was Filipino. In a grand ceremony held at the Philippine International Convention Center on 8 August 2017, ASEAN's 50th Anniversary, President Duterte as ASEAN Chair paid tribute to and awarded plaques of recognition to former Deputy Prime Minister Tun Abdul Razak of Malaysia, and former Foreign Ministers Adam

Malik of Indonesia, Narciso Ramos of the Philippines, S. Rajaratnam of Singapore, and Thanat Khoman of Thailand through their descendants/representatives who were present at the said event. I also spearheaded the commissioning of the painting depicting the historic signing in August 1967 of the Bangkok Declaration establishing ASEAN. The painting was unveiled by Secretary Alan Peter Cayetano and Secretary General Le Luong Minh during the opening ceremonies of the ASEAN Ministerial Meeting at the Cultural Center of the Philippines. The commissioning of this painting was paid for by ASEAN. It is a testament to the world of what ASEAN had attained in 2017 from its humble beginnings in 1967.

2.2. ASEAN Heroes of Biodiversity

Biodiversity is another priority area for the Philippines. When the ASEAN Secretariat proposed that we also undertake a biodiversity activity to raise the level of awareness on this area, I enthusiastically agreed. However, the concept paper that the ASEAN Secretariat official handed me focused on the conduct of a Miss Biodiversity contest. Although the ASEAN Secretariat official had meant well, I knew that conducting an event which sounded like a beauty contest would raise not just eyebrows but howls of protests from among our concerned women sectors in the Philippines. I politely asked to take over the project, and personally changed the concept to Heroes of ASEAN Biodiversity, paying tribute to one hero per member state who has contributed in a big way to the preservation, promotion and advancement of biodiversity in the region. Marine Biologist and educator Dr Angel Alcala was the Philippine recipient of this ASEAN award, for his outstanding work in biodiversity conservation, particularly in the establishment of marine protected areas (MPAs) and the discovery, protection and preservation of reptiles and amphibians. The Biodiversity Heroes of other Member States were as follows:

- Eyad Samhan (Brunei Darussalam)
- Sophea Chhin (Cambodia)

- Alex Waisimon (Indonesia)
- Nitsavanh Louangkhot Pravongviengkham (Lao PDR)
- Prof Zakri Abdul Hamid (Malaysia)
- Dr Maung Maung Kyi (Myanmar)
- Prof Leo Tan Wee Hin (Singapore)
- Dr Nonn Panitvong (Thailand)
- Prof Dr Dang Huy Huynh (Viet Nam)

They were honoured in the same grand ceremony as the Founding Fathers of ASEAN.

2.3. ASEAN Rice Science and Technology Ambassadors

I had always wondered why, despite the fact that rice is the common staple food of the AMS as depicted in the ten rice stalks in the ASEAN emblem, the rice scientists and technologists of ASEAN had never been honoured. In one dinner I hosted for then International Rice Research Institute (IRRI) Deputy Director General, Dr Bruce Tolentino, I pointed this out. Over dinner we conceptualized the project and before I went to bed that night, I had written the skeleton of the project proposal which I sent immediately to him. He completed the technical information asked for in the proposal following the ASEAN template for projects requiring funding from ASEAN or its Dialogue Partners. He immediately coordinated with the Philippine Department of Agriculture to complete its conceptualization and eventual implementation. I obtained approval from the CPR for its funding using the ASEAN-China Cooperation Fund as is required of any regional endeavour. I must commend the managers of this Fund for not interfering with the concept and implementation of the project, assuming that the ASEAN proponents knew what they were doing and having the correct objectives in doing so. It can also be interpreted that it is a cooperation area that they agree with and could benefit from. On the 50th anniversary of ASEAN, the rice scientists and technologists of the Member States would get the recognition they deserved. PhilRice Acting Executive Director Dr Sailila

E. Abdula received the Outstanding Rice Scientist Award for his contribution to the development of the rice industry, particularly the development of tungro-resistant rice varieties such as NSIC Rc120 and Rc226 to help manage the disease in Southern Mindanao, while Mr Nemencio J. Concepcion, a farmer from Bulacan, was hailed Outstanding Rice Farmer for his innovative rice-integrated farming systems using best management practices resulting in high yields and disease resistant crops and unselfishly sharing his knowledge with others. The other awardees were:

- Dr Ouk Makara (Cambodia)
- Dr Satoto (Indonesia)
- Dr Phetmanyseng Xangsayasane and Mr Sihong Khottavong (Lao PDR)
- Dr Asfaliza Ramli and Mr Jaafar bin Zakaria (Malaysia)
- Mr U Than Myint and Ms Myint Yi (Myanmar)
- Dr Yin Zhongchao (Singapore)
- Dr Bunmee Surakhot and Dr Jirapong Jairin (Thailand)
- Dr Tran Thi Cuc Hoa and Mr Phan Thien Khanh (Viet Nam)

2.4. ASEAN Youth Social Entrepreneurship Awards

This project was a win-win-win espousing three advocacies at the same time—empowerment of the youth, promoting social responsibility and growing entrepreneurship. The Philippine awardee was Henry Motte-Muñoz of edukasyon.ph, an NGO that aims to reduce education to employment mismatch, and make education accessible to all Filipino students. Other ASEAN awardees were:

- Haji Syed Mohd Yassin (Brunei)
- Sreat Mom Sophear (Cambodia)
- Rizal Fahreza (Indonesia)
- Dr Khamsen Sisavong (Lao PDR)
- Dr Lutfi Fadil Lokman (Malaysia)
- Thet Zin Myint (Myanmar)

- Jamon Mok (Singapore)
- Prawit Kruasarp (Thailand)
- Truong Ly Hoang Phi (Viet Nam)

2.5. Synchronized Lighting of ASEAN Landmarks
Each member state chose one landmark which would be lit on ASEAN Day at an appointed time. It had to be synchronized because of the time differences among Member States. For the Philippines, this was, of course, the Luneta Park.

2.6. Together with ERIA, publication of the five-volume *ASEAN@50: Retrospectives, Perspectives on the Making, Substance, Significance and Future of ASEAN*
As part of the commemorative activities for ASEAN's 50th Anniversary, the Philippine Mission worked closely with the Economic Research Institute for ASEAN and East Asia (ERIA) under the leadership of its President, Professor Hidetoshi Nishimura, on the production of this epic five-volume publication containing essays from former Leaders and Senior Officials of ASEAN, former ASEAN Secretaries General, including such prominent ASEAN luminaries as former Myanmar President U Thein Sein, former Singapore Prime Minister Goh Chok Tong, former Philippine President Fidel Ramos and former Thai Prime Minister Abhisit Vejjajiva.[6]

This multi-dimensioned project also entailed nine outreach activities that were submitted to my Mission on January 2017 by the late ERIA Chief Economist Dr Ponciano Intal, Jr. Although the funding for the publication and the outreach events would come from the Japan-ASEAN Integration Fund (JAIF) whose sole contributor is the government of Japan, ASEAN still required it to undergo the ASEAN-approved project assessment and review process. For example, some of the outreach activities, i.e., the translation of the five volumes into Japanese and the commemorative event in Tokyo, did not meet the regionality criterion of the ASEAN process. I, therefore, asked Dr Intal not to include the two activities for submission to use JAIF funds and advised him instead to use direct Japanese funds for the purpose. ERIA also had to agree to my proposal to contract the co-sponsorship of the events to other ASEAN entities formally because my Mission was not allowed under Philippine regulations to handle funds for which it would be accountable. Thus, the ASEAN Foundation and the Foreign Service Institute of the Philippines were the formal co-sponsors of the giant project. The highlight of this series of activities was the launch on 19 October 2017 of the High-Level Forum on ASEAN@50 attended by the luminaries personalities I mentioned above, Secretary Alan Peter Cayetano and Liberal Democratic Party Leader Toshihiro Nikai, to raise the level of awareness about ASEAN.

2.7 Completion of Negotiations on the ASEAN Staff Rules and Regulations (ASRR) and the ASEAN Secretariat Financial Rules and Procedures (AFRP)

Negotiations on these two ASEAN Secretariat documents had been pending for two years with no end in sight due to the dismal fact that Member States came from different governmental procedures and systems. Budget cycles, for example, differ from country to country; some prepare annual budgets while others have multiple-year allocations. Even the commencement dates of their fiscal years are different. The Philippine team, led by Deputy Executive Secretary Alberto Bernardo and Assistant Secretary Lynn Danao-Moreno, with the able support of my Officer, Cecille Lao, waded through the documents, patiently chaired marathon meetings that went on until midnight until they finally agreed on a final text for both documents. In my over-eagerness to finalize the much-delayed documents, I have hurt the feelings of DES Bernardo by sending him a memo implying that he had interposed too many and excessive requirements that are impossible or extremely difficult to meet, thus delaying the meetings. Realizing my misstep, I quickly apologized for this slip and we continue to be good friends to this day.

The finalized documents were approved in one of the CPR meetings I chaired and have been in effect since.

3. Amend the ASEAN Charter
   I discuss this at length in the next chapter.

4. EAS Mangrove-Planting and Biodiversity Awareness event
   Biodiversity is one advocacy of the Philippines which our chairmanship focused on. My Mission, therefore, embarked on a mangrove-planting activity involving all the diplomatic missions of the Member States and external partners. You should have seen the dignified EAS Ambassadors gingerly wading in chest-high swampy waters planting the mangroves in a farm near the Jakarta airport (see Figure 4.3). The bottom of the swamp was slippery and one had to really keep her balance to avoid slipping. Two female colleagues who were of the natural petite Asian height also bravely plunged in and the taller ones had to hoist them through their armpits to remain above water. I did not know how

FIGURE 4.3
EAMJ Mangrove Planting Event Organized by the Philippine Mission

to swim but had to show a good example, so I whispered to my staff, NJ, to aid me. Later on, when recollecting the incident over an office lunch, I told him that he was mumbling aloud to himself: *"You can do this! You can do this!"* It turned out that he also did not know how to swim and was psyching himself to go on! What a laugh we had! The mangrove-planting event was followed by a lecture on the importance of biodiversity by the Executive Director of the ASEAN Centre for Biodiversity, Atty. Roberto Oliva. I think our efforts and misadventures paid off and there was greater awareness of biodiversity among the diplomatic missions and the young people of Jakarta who participated.

5. Lead in the negotiations and finalization of various Plans of Action, Joint Communiques, Leaders' and Ministers' Statements and Declarations, etc. with AMS and the external partners of ASEAN
6. Work on the accreditation of the ASEAN Disability Forum and the ASEAN Mayors Forum as Charter Annex 2 entities
7. Strengthen the Jakarta Channel mechanisms, especially the EAS Ambassadors in Jakarta
8. Publish a CPR Handbook
9. Develop a strategy to implement the floundering Master Plan on ASEAN Connectivity 2025
10. Operationalize the ASEAN Institute of Peace and Reconciliation (AIPR), which, five years after its establishment, still did not have a Secretariat and an Executive Director, and
11. Set the ground for the launch of a Women for Peace Network under the AIPR.

This list is rather long for a one-year chairmanship but one lesson I learned from pushing your agenda in ASEAN is to be willing to go the extra mile in trying to get approval for your initiatives. I sought allies from within my ASEAN community and from without to accomplish them. I was hands-on in the conceptualization of the initiatives to align them with what I considered the Philippine idea of a caring and sharing community. Rather than go through the circuitous red-tape of waiting for action from the Home Office which was equally burdened with so many responsibilities, I personally collaborated with experts who understood these concepts, including then IRRI Deputy Director General (now Monetary Board Governor) Dr Bruce Tolentino and DENR Undersecretary Jonas Leones, so that we could duly project ASEAN's and Philippine leadership in these fields.

I am happy to note that we accomplished all these goals in 2017. In December of that year, after the last chairmanship event was over, I treated the whole JPM team and their families to a relaxing retreat in the resort city of Bogor. At a worship service that I led, I asked the ice-breaker question: What do you thank God for in the past year of our chairmanship? My stern and normally reserved officer, Cecille, raised her hand and stood up. "I thank God for...." she stammered and broke into an emotional narration. Her father had been in hospital for a life-threatening illness for months during the early part of our chairmanship. Once she started, the dam burst and we all ended up with a good outlet for our pent-up emotions. We poured out our hearts and spilled the grief and issues which we held in check throughout the year we were Chair. While pursuing our tasks and running after the ASEAN Vision throughout our chairmanship, our individual family lives flowed on: one staff member was himself admitted in a hospital. I, myself, suffered throughout the year from hypertension and excruciating back pain having to sit long hours while chairing the meetings. I remember just allowing my lips and tongue to touch my drinking water in the glass and not swallowing it when I was chairing so as to avoid having to go to the lavatory. There were family relationships issues, babies and other children to take care of, and many other concerns which had to be swept aside temporarily to enable us to fulfill our avowed objectives. Many a tear was shed that day, tears of thanksgiving to God for having carried us through the challenging year. The following year, 2018, our sacrifices were rewarded by an accolade accorded to us by the Department of Foreign Affairs: JPM was named the Best DFA Organization of 2017, together with the Office of ASEAN Affairs and the Philippine Consulate General in Dubai. My Facebook post of me cradling the award said that it belonged to all the dedicated officers and staff members of JPM (see Figure 4.4). I write this autoethnography as well to honour these selfless people who became my partners in pursuing Philippine and ASEAN visions during our watch.

FIGURE 4.4
Receiving the Best DFA Organization Award from Secretary Alan Peter Cayetano

Notes

1. Singapore likewise held the banner high for smart cities in 2018 while Thailand took up the cause of Substainable Development Goals (SDGs) in 2019. In 2020, Viet Nam, despite the pandemic, advocated ASEAN's "cohesiveness and responsiveness" across the three pillars, especially in meeting the complicated challenges posed by COVID-19. In 2021, Brunei's leadership is focused on advancing multilateralism in advancing regional recovery from COVID-19.
2. It was also a battlecry for the Singapore chairmanship and Thailand was hopeful it would happen in theirs. Finally, in the midst of the adversity brought about by the COVID-19 pandemic, the landmark free trade agreement was signed, in meaningful albeit, virtual ceremonies in November 2021, under the chairmanship of Viet Nam.
3. At the time of writing this book, I was the Philippine Representative and Co-Chair with China of the Senior Officials' Meeting on the Implementation of the Declaration on the Conduct of the Parties in the South China Sea (DOC), and am unable here to elaborate on the on-going talks which are very sensitive and might jeopardize its chances.
4. In the midst of all the busyness of 2017, we have also had the opportunity to purchase a chancery for the Mission, which became the third building owned

by the Philippines in Jakarta enjoying diplomatic privileges and immunities, a first in the history of our diplomatic relations with Indonesia.
5. Doris represented the Philippines in the cookbook that I produced in March 2019, entitled *Sem Sem But No Sem: A Cookbook of ASEAN Noodle Dishes*.
6. It was the last official public event of Dr Surin Pitsuwan before his demise on 30 November a month after the launch of the publication.

5

ASEAN CENTRALITY AS A PRINCIPLE OF DIPLOMACY AMONG MEMBER STATES

I refer to the word "principle" as a concept that serves as a guide in the behaviour of a system,[1] such as a regional organization like ASEAN. As mentioned, the need to maintain the centrality of ASEAN is enshrined in Article 1 of the ASEAN Charter. For me, this guiding principle should not just remain on paper; it has to be operationalized and employed actively in the daily conduct of ASEAN's relations among Member States and with other partners, collectively covered by the word diplomacy.

The ultimate aim of diplomacy is to promote, defend and advance one's own national interests in relations with other countries and at the same time, to pursue mutually beneficial ends with these countries by undertaking joint activities or championing mutually cherished values and principles. My instructions have always been clear according to this line, and I believe that my colleagues in the ASEAN family also had similar objectives. Now, in order for us to attain this objective, our brand of diplomacy requires mechanisms in which negotiations and discussions are to take place; these discussions should follow certain processes and procedures, its practitioners should employ a certain language or tone in relating with one another, and there should be a set of definite agenda and objectives to be accomplished. The permeating principle breathing into all these elements is ASEAN Centrality. As mentioned in my introduction, the mechanisms should be those led or created by ASEAN, the agenda should be that agreed upon by ASEAN, the participants should be those accepted by ASEAN, the processes and procedures should be those determined by ASEAN and the language or tone to be used should be that preferred by ASEAN. This view of ASEAN Centrality guided me in chairing ASEAN in 2017 and in participating in this Community throughout my tenure.

Conceptual Framework of the Jakarta Platform

For its conceptual framework, this book draws inspiration from proponents of analytical autoethnography, particularly that proposed by Leon Anderson (2006) who listed three characteristics of this conceptual framework whereby the researcher is a (i) a full member in the research group or setting; (ii) visible as such a member in published texts; and (iii) committed to developing theoretical understandings of broader social phenomena. I think Anderson was thinking of people like me when he introduced this brand of autoethnography which veered slightly away from the highly emotional and emotive type propagated by his contemporaries, to open opportunities for "refining and expanding research". This framework is also echoed in McIlveen (2008) who advanced that autoethnography serves to explicate a specific dimension of personal experience, in relation to the author's membership of a specific group (e.g., demographic, cultural, professional), state-of-being (e.g., feeling ill or ecstatic), or event (e.g., career transition). Such characteristics are the very principles which I intend to use in my research.

However, because autoethnographies tend to vary in subject matter from one another owing to the nature of experiences being portrayed, from medical conditions to specific issues of lesbian, gay, bisexual, transgender, queer and intersex (LGBTQIs), and now in this instance being applied to diplomacy or international relations, I intend to modify this framework as shown in Figure 5.1.

The left side of Figure 5.1 shows myself as the focus of the study, as a full member of the community/specific group of diplomats engaged

FIGURE 5.1
Conceptual Framework

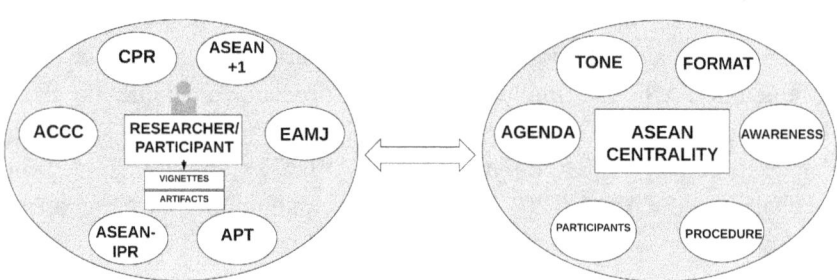

in ASEAN relations being the Ambassador/Permanent Representative of the Philippines to ASEAN for over six years (13 March 2013–30 April 2019). I was an active participant in that community of diplomats that make up the various ASEAN bodies that are based in Jakarta (left side of Figure 5.1), namely the Committee of Permanent Representatives (CPR), the ASEAN Connectivity Coordinating Committee (ACCC), the ASEAN Institute for Peace and Reconciliation (ASEAN-IPR), the ASEAN Plus Three (APT), and the EAS Ambassadors' Meeting in Jakarta (EAMJ), which are tasked to carry out the relations among the Member States of ASEAN and their external partners. There are two more bodies which I was part of—the ASEAN Foundation and the ASEAN-China Centre Joint Council, but these are not included because the dynamics of ASEAN Centrality was not really demonstrated in these two bodies. Some evidence of my participation in this community are recounted through vignettes while some are published or recorded or have manifestations in the artefacts—final texts of documents which were negotiated particularly during the time I was Chair of these ASEAN bodies. The right side of Figure 5.1 shows that my experiences interacting in these bodies allowed me to arrive at an understanding of ASEAN Centrality which I break down into the following elements or manifestations (as shown in the right side of Figure 5.1) as follows:

a. The tone and language that ASEAN uses in its discourse among its own Member States and vis-à-vis external partners;
b. The agenda or subject matter of ASEAN's relations among themselves and vis-à-vis ASEAN's external partners;

c. Participation of diplomats in this community;
d. The procedures of negotiation and policymaking in these bodies;
e. The physical format of these settings;
f. The resiliency of ASEAN to proceed with its agenda despite huge differences and lack of consensus in difficult areas; and
g. The level of awareness about ASEAN by people outside this community.

Thus, by being a "native" of this unique socio-political milieu, I develop an understanding of a higher concept—ASEAN Centrality—a view which in turn also influenced my behaviour while being a participant in it, particularly when I took on the chairmanship of the ASEAN-led mechanisms in Jakarta. I also illustrate my aspiration to raise the level of awareness of ASEAN among its own people and those outside.

I look critically at the culture and practices of the unique community of diplomats and negotiators I found myself in. The conceptual framework details the characteristics, norms, values, processes and practices of this cultural milieu. By treating ASEAN diplomacy as an appropriate subject for autoethnography, I hope to add to the existing body of autoethnographic literature that has hitherto been confined only to the social and behavioural issues. By using what is traditionally labelled a "feminine" method in research, I expose myself to criticism. I even run the risk of this work being dismissed as an entertainment piece good for a Sunday morning read, rather than a serious topic worth the while of aspiring diplomats and even hardened practitioners of diplomacy. By using a story-telling technique and translating the heavily jargoned world of diplomacy and scholarly writing and allowing the audience to participate in the excitement, suspense, apprehension, disappointment, sense of triumph and pride and aspiration of this book, I hope to create a reciprocal relation with the readers of this book.

Jakarta, the Hub of Regional Multilateralism

I must put in a word about multilateralism as a mode in conducting this brand of diplomacy as it has been our *modus vivendi* in Jakarta. With all these important ASEAN mechanisms centred in one place, Jakarta has become a centre of multilateral diplomacy, which for me, is a good environment to practise ASEAN Centrality. I found in this setting the exhilarating beauty of negotiations and dealings with diplomats who have been instructed and trained to fight, defend and promote their own respective national interests and yet are quite cognizant about the need to move forward the regional or multilateral agenda. Critics of multilateralism include those who cite the resurgence of ultra-nationalism and decry the "least common denominator" principle which, they say, may not always be the most efficient means to promote international cooperation (Martin 1992). They also lament what they consider to be ASEAN members' inclination to adopt a policy of "thinking multilaterally but acting bilaterally". This is especially true, according to bitter ASEAN critics, of situations in which bilateralism is seen as a more appropriate, flexible and practical approach to the conduct of regional interstate relations. Donald Emmerson (2008) is among these bitter critics.

As a practitioner of ASEAN diplomacy, I would caution against using such parameters in judging the value of ASEAN as a regional organization. I agree with Institutional Liberalists who assert that although states behave according to the dictates of their national interests (not according to the wishful thoughts of idealists who would rather that states behaved in another more desirable manner agreeable to their perspectives), they still cooperate in regional institutions because they see their interests being pursued through them. ASEAN cannot be judged according to what we wished it did more but with what it purports to achieve, as enshrined in the ASEAN Charter, the ASEAN Vision 2025: Forging Ahead Together, and in many other documents which embody ASEAN's aspirations, norms and principles. Admittedly, there is much to be desired still in achieving the ASEAN vision of a Community, but there has been considerable progress in many areas. I also agree with Acharya (1998) who believes in the benefits of multilateralism which, according to him, emerged not only from the principles of inter-state relations agreed to by the founders of ASEAN, but also from a subsequent process of interaction, socialization, compromise and adjustment which has allowed ASEAN to develop a culture of diplomacy quite different from the "regulatory" nature of other regional organizations such as the European Union (EU). This brand of diplomacy, Acharya rightfully claims, has become part and parcel of ASEAN's corporate identity, having acquired a "constitutive effect", quoting Katzenstein (1996).

While not discounting the efficacy and importance of bilateral diplomacy, having been myself a bilateral Ambassador of the Philippines to four countries earlier in my career, I would also vouch for the accomplishments of multilateral diplomacy, particularly that which I experienced in Jakarta as a living example of its practical value. The job of the Chair, as I learned too well during the Philippine chairmanship, is to find the solution that would help ASEAN and not jeopardize the interest of any of its members, while putting the perspectives of *realpolitik* brought about by the presence of the major powers into the equation.

ASEAN Centrality in the ASEAN Committee of Permanent Representatives (CPR)

I consider the Committee of Permanent Representatives (CPR) of which I was a member and which I chaired in 2017 (see Figure 5.2) as the most distinctive setting to practise ASEAN Centrality. Its physical format, tone and language, agenda and who gets to participate in it are elements

FIGURE 5.2
Chairing a CPR Meeting

of ASEAN Centrality that I wish to recount in the following sections. Its ability to harness consensus from among members with disparate, sometimes conflicting, national interests and even at times when it is unable to achieve consensus, provided me with one of the most exciting, productive and meaningful platforms in my career as a diplomat.

The CPR is a Charter body; its creation was specified in the ASEAN Charter under Article 12. It is the nucleus around which all the other ASEAN bodies based in Jakarta revolve. These other bodies include the EAMJ, the APT, JCC, etc. Among its functions, which I will be recalling in succeeding anecdotes, are:

1. Strengthening relations with ASEAN's external partners;
2. Administrative direction and support to the ASEAN Secretariat;
3. Monitoring and implementation of decisions made by Leaders, Ministers and Senior Officials;
4. Substantive support to the ASEAN Coordinating Council (ACC), which is composed of Ministers of ASEAN Member States (AMS);
5. Cross-pillar coordination among the ASEAN Political-Security Community (APSC), the ASEAN Economic Community (AEC) and the ASEAN Socio-Cultural Community (ASCC); and
6. Engagements with entities outside ASEAN.

Of particular mention here is the fact that the CPR approves the application by entities outside ASEAN, first to use the name ASEAN and to be accredited as entities under Annex 2 of the Charter. In 2017, I spearheaded the move to accredit as such the ASEAN Disability Forum, the ASEAN Mayors' Forum and the ASEAN Council of Chief Justices during my chairmanship in 2017. These two issues are close to my heart, the inclusion of persons with disabilities (PWDs) and local governments into the mainstream ASEAN focus in order to make it a truly caring and sharing ASEAN. Their applications had been pending for a long time and as with any bureaucracy, a little push would go a long way to get the task accomplished. This we did. Immediately after their accreditation, I organized an interface meeting between the CPR and the ASEAN Disability Forum (ADF) (see Figure 5.3) to learn how their agenda can be pushed into the ASEAN system. During this interface,

**FIGURE 5.3
CPR and the ASEAN Disability Forum**

the CPR gave advice to the ADF on how they can mainstream their agenda into that of other bodies, such as the ASEAN Intergovernmental Commission on Human Rights (AICHR), the Senior Officials Meeting on Social Welfare and Development (SOMSWD), and the Senior Economic Officials' Meeting (SEOM) for economic opportunities given to PWDs. I also coached them on how to use the multi-million dollar cooperation funds lodged in the ASEAN Secretariat to fund and implement their projects and initiatives.

However, the CPR was helpless (or perhaps, the other Member States did not deem it expedient to act on it) when dealing with an external entity on its illegal use of the name ASEAN (it called itself the ASEAN Rohingya Association). The name ASEAN is registered with the Intellectual Property Rights Organization and ideally, only organizations authorized by ASEAN may be able to use this name. In fact, there is an established procedure in obtaining this permission. However, this entity espoused advocacies, statements and views contrary to the government of one AMS. Legally and technically speaking, this AMS had all the legal rights to complain and so, with the reluctant support of the other Member States, the ASEAN Secretariat was requested to write to this organization to desist from using the name ASEAN. Nothing came out of the representations of the ASEAN Secretariat; the entity ignored the letter and continued to use this name. The CPR did not pursue further action. To be sure, many other organizations and entities have wittingly or unwittingly used the name ASEAN illegally, but the AMS have no interest in going after them.

The accreditation of the ASEAN Mayors' Forum (AMF) as an entity associated to ASEAN was also a case in the point of disparities in the bureaucratic organizations of local governments in ASEAN. In the Philippines and Indonesia, mayorships are bitterly contested political positions and local governments enjoy autonomous privileges and powers. In other ASEAN countries, mayors or their equivalent are appointed positions, much like local CEOs, given charge to maintain and manage socio-cultural and sometimes economic benefits to the people. They are merely implementors of national government regulations and policies and wield negligible political power. Naming the institution was a primary issue. Was it going to be ASEAN Mayors Association, ASEAN Association of Local Governments, ASEAN Local Government's Forum? Some mayors were even called governors in other AMS. We spent much time debating in the CPR how to realize this accreditation. It was not just a red-tape issue as it had political implications. And yet, I believed that accrediting them to ASEAN was not only technically correct but expedient since they are instrumental in implementing ASEAN community building projects and activities as embodied in ASEAN documents. In some countries, for example, important infrastructure projects as identified in the Master Plan on ASEAN Connectivity are under the power and purview of local governments. Throughout 2017, my Mission worked with the United Cities and Local Governments Asia Pacific (UCLG ASPAC) Secretary General, Dr Bernadia Irawati Tjandradewi, and Taguig City Mayor Lani Cayetano, who was active as head of the League of Cities of the Philippines, to effect this accreditation. Finally, all the issues had been settled and in early 2018, the AMF was accredited as an entity associated to ASEAN.

The CPR is ASEAN's effective focal point which has the ability to make important decisions and serve as the bridge to the different community pillars of ASEAN, to its external partners and to the outside world in general. With these CPR mandates in mind, I utilized this mechanism to the hilt, making it function to benefit ASEAN and push the priorities of my own country.

Strengthening ASEAN Centrality through the CPR and the JCM

The Joint Consultative Meeting (JCM) is a mechanism composed of Senior Officials of the three pillars of the ASEAN Community (APSC, AEC, ASCC), the ASEAN Secretariat and the Committee of Permanent Representatives. It meets at least twice a year.

To strengthen ASEAN Centrality in coordinating the three pillars of the ASEAN Community, the CPR under my chairmanship, had taken the initiative to revise the Terms of Reference (TOR) of the then Joint Preparatory Meeting (JPM). Because of the nature of its function, which was to simply discuss and decide on administrative, logistical and other inane matters preparatory to the ASEAN Summit, the JPM had dwindled into a meeting attended only by Senior Officials from the Ministries of Foreign Affairs of the Member States who were in charge of these matters and not by the other two pillars. I believe the representatives of SEOM and SOCA did not attend because there was no role for them there and they had no speaking opportunities. The discussions focused on drab administrative matters like where translators would be sitting, what attire the Ministers or Leaders were supposed to wear, who were invited to this and that event, the list of outcome documents to be issued, boring reports by Senior Officials of the other two pillars and many other mundane agenda items. By 2016, the JPM had become a moribund mechanism that needed drastic changes. Together with the Philippine Assistant Secretary for ASEAN Affairs, Ambassador Hellen dela Vega, who fits the description of what Anne of Green Gables would call my "kindred spirit" when it comes to ASEAN matters, the Philippines introduced another function to allow the mechanism to become the coordinating mechanism to connect all the three pillars of the ASEAN Community. We also renamed it the Joint Consultative Meeting (JCM) for such a consultative function was direly lacking in ASEAN.

This initiative was motivated by the fact that the three pillars of the ASEAN Community—APSC, AEC and the ASCC—tend to operate like silos having separate trajectories without coordinating with each other. There was also the danger of sidelining cross-pillar and cross-sectoral issues with no clear leader to take the accountability for their implementation. Classic examples of such issues include gender mainstreaming, human rights, disaster risk mitigation and management, empowerment of women, PWDs, connectivity, peace and reconciliation, countering terrorism, and many others which had to be implemented and followed up in their political/security, economic and socio-cultural dimensions.

ASEAN desperately needed a coordinating or consultative mechanism that would harmonize the work of its different pillars or it would lose its centrality in the process. Moreover, the JCM needed to be a problem-solving mechanism that would connect the synergies of the three pillars and obtain ASEAN's objectives as set out in the blueprints.

During the 4/2017 CPR Meeting held on 14 March 2017, I introduced in the agenda our intention to revitalize the then JPM. I conveyed the following points:

1. Cross-pillar coordination is one of ASEAN's weakest links. If we wish to strengthen ASEAN Community-building, we have to discuss how to improve coordination for cross-pillar issues.
2. This is where the JCM could play an important role. Member States could potentially have more frank discussions and make progress on relevant cross-cutting issues through the JCM than if the three Community Councils had to go through the usual steps of writing to each other to decide on pending issues. This can potentially reduce the instances of miscommunications among ASEAN bodies.
3. To facilitate the JCM's work, key cross-pillar issues should be identified and prioritized by all three pillars for discussion. These should be circulated to all three pillars prior to the meeting. During the JCM proper, each pillar should speak on how they intend to carry out their mandate on these cross-pillar issues, what kind of coordination they desire from the other pillars, and the challenges they face in carrying out these tasks. Said issues can range from more general topics such as environmental issues, gender mainstreaming, and disaster management to specific Leaders' Statements, drafts of which originate from the three pillars of the ASEAN Community.

As with any attempt to introduce something new in ASEAN, the proposal had met with opposition or disinterest at first. The other Permanent Representatives (PRs), perhaps, did not want to interfere in the work of their economic and socio-cultural officials or did not want to add to their already heavy burdens. The Philippine Mission and the Philippine delegation to the JCM persisted, especially focusing on the argument that ASEAN was in danger of losing its centrality and relevance because the three pillars did not harmonize with one another. We gained many allies and the amendment happened. The CPR submitted its recommendations to the Senior Officials' Meeting (SOM) which met on 11 October 2017. The JCM that followed the SOM on 12 October took positive note of the revised TOR and requested all the pillars of the ASEAN Community to submit their comments to it. The CPR included these comments and finally, the first JCM held on 8 March 2018 in Singapore adopted the CPR-drafted TOR. This new TOR of the JCM included sections that safeguarded against such deficiencies. The new TOR appears as *Annex B*. In the coming years of ASEAN's evolution, the potential of this body to advance ASEAN's agenda should be exploited.

For example, in 2017, the ASEAN Socio-Cultural Pillar (ASCC), initiated the issuance of a Leaders' Declaration which aimed at fostering a culture of prevention to counter terrorism, radicalization and violent extremism, which of course, fell under the purview of the political/security pillar. And yet, there was logic in taking it up as well under the wings of the ASCC as many believed in the efficacy of using ASCC mechanisms and priorities such as education, moderation, socio-economic well-being, the use of social media and other means to counter these transnational problems. The catch was that the ASCC Ministers had already agreed to issue their original document and the ASEAN Foreign Ministers had no authority to overrule the ASCC Ministers. I have always pointed out a basic flaw in the composition of the ASEAN Coordinating Council which is composed of only the Foreign Ministers and does not include the Ministers of the AECC and ASCC pillars. How can it be a "coordinating council" when its composition is as such? To avert embarrassment and put the Leaders' Declaration in its proper cross-pillar context, we debated this matter in the meeting of the CPR and I brought it to the attention of the Philippine SOM Leader who quietly spoke with the SOCA Leader to accept some amendments to the document which they previously issued so that it would, indeed, reflect the dimensions of the three pillars. The other PRs had also alerted their respective Senior Officials and so, an informal agreement to amend the ASCC document was reached. The differences were discussed and resolved in a JCM prior to the Summit during which amendments introduced by the SOM and the SEOM were incorporated in the document. Thus, the ASEAN Declaration on the Culture of Prevention for a Peaceful, Inclusive, Resilient, Healthy and Harmonious Society was issued in November 2017 under the framework of the ASCC but contained provisions encompassing the APSC and AEC pillars.

Format of the CPR Meeting

The CPR usually meets in the main ASEAN Hall of the ASEAN Secretariat Headquarters (since the transfer to the new premises in late 2019, their meeting venue has transferred to the spacious Nusantara Room). In 2014, under the chairmanship of Myanmar, the CPR had published an ASEAN Protocol Handbook which details the seating and standing arrangements of countries participating in ASEAN meetings. This format provides order in an otherwise confusing situation, assigns roles to each participant and therefore, establishes the sense of identity of the body.

In a CPR format, the Chair takes the lone seat in the front part of the hall facing the locked doors. To their left sits the incoming Chair, who in my time as Chair, had been Singapore. From Singapore, following a clockwise order, are the rest of the AMS in alphabetical arrangement and not by order of precedence, i.e., the date of their arrival in Jakarta, as is normally the case for bilateral seating arrangements. Thus, Brunei Darussalam would come next, followed by Cambodia, Indonesia, etc. to signify that all participants are not there in their personal capacity but to represent sovereign states. To my right sat the representatives from the ASEAN Secretariat. Our Deputy PRs would normally sit beside us and the rest of our delegations would take the seats behind their respective PRs. Table flags are also arranged in the same order. Figure 5.4 is a typical CPR format, which is also the same arrangement followed in the meetings of the ASEAN Institute for Peace and Reconciliation (AIPR), the ACCC, and the ASEAN Foundation.

FIGURE 5.4
Format of the CPR Meeting

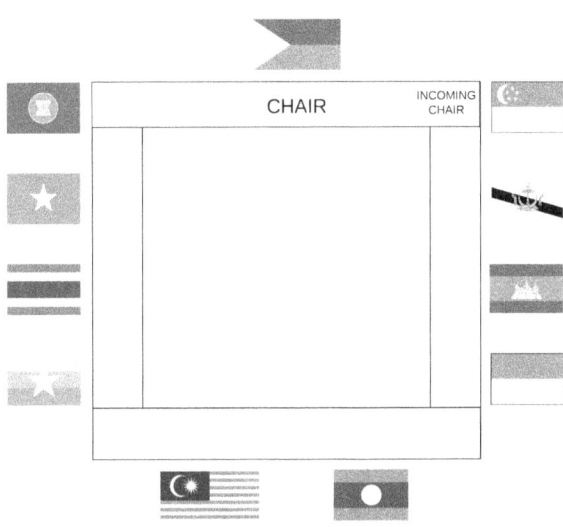

Who Participates in the Meetings of the CPR?

ASEAN Centrality is also manifested in the determination of who gets to participate in ASEAN-led mechanisms and who does not. The Jakarta-based mechanisms decide on who they meet depending on their perception of whether this interaction would be beneficial to ASEAN or not.

Each of the ten AMS sends an Ambassador to ASEAN who is technically called a Permanent Representative (PR). Their tours-of-duty may last an average of three years, depending on the internal practice of each AMS. At the time of my chairmanship, there were four female PRs (Brunei Darussalam, Myanmar, Philippines and Thailand) and six male ones. Of the ten, I have developed deep professional and personal friendships with the PR of Myanmar, U Min Lwin who became a Deputy Minister and that of Singapore, Tan Hung Seng (now Permanent Representative to the World Trade Organization) who, together with me and despite our respective country's huge differences and therefore diverging positions, understood what we could achieve if we upheld ASEAN through thick and thin. This community of diplomats, although locked in bitter debates inside negotiation rooms, have developed a certain camaraderie and oneness of pushing the ASEAN agenda together. As practitioners of multilateral diplomacy, we have developed certain patterns of behaviour and perspectives quite unique from those of other diplomats. We are experts of the so-called "alphabet soup", referring to the many acronyms and abbreviations that ASEAN denizens have developed.[2] Working in tandem with the CPR is the ASEAN Secretariat which is usually represented by the Deputy Secretary General for APSC or his Directors and other officials in CPR meetings to assist in the proceedings. Sometimes, the Secretary General himself attends CPR meetings. The role of the ASEAN Secretary General has also been the subject of many debates between those who wish that they would be more of a General than a Secretary or those who lament that they are a mere Secretary and not a General. The truth is that the ASEAN Secretariat provides much-needed coordination work among the three pillars of the ASEAN Community, being able to attend all their meetings. They assist as resource persons and provide records of all ASEAN meetings.

The CPR conducts regular meetings with ASEAN's Dialogue Partners (DPs) and Sectoral Dialogue Partners (SDPs). They sometimes meet with Civil Society Organizations by invitation, such as when I organized in 2017 an interface with the ASEAN Disability Forum and the eighty-or-so Ambassadors of various countries to Indonesia based in Jakarta and who are also accredited to ASEAN. Of particular mention are the meetings of the CPR with High-Level Officials from ASEAN's external partners who come to visit Jakarta or when the CPR goes on overseas trips to meet with them as a group, since these are high-level interactions and are particularly mean to elevate bilateral relations between ASEAN and the countries these officials represent.

The Agenda of the CPR

As mentioned, what is not included in the agenda of ASEAN, and in this case, the CPR, is as important as what is. Thus, taboo items would include bilateral disputes as mentioned below, embarrassing or face-losing issues (discussed in the tone and language subsection) and criticisms of each country's government and people. However, in cases affecting regional well-being, such items may be subsumed under a more general topic, or there is common understanding that they would discuss them without itemizing them in the written agenda of the meeting.

The agenda of a typical CPR Meeting would consist of items covered by any of its functions above, particularly those tasks assigned to it by the Leaders, the Foreign Ministers and the Senior Officials, and which are fulfillment of the key objectives mentioned in major ASEAN documents such as the ASEAN Vision 2025.

During the handover ceremonies of the CPR Chairmanship from Laos to the Philippines held on 1 December 2016, I outlined the objectives of my chairmanship of the CPR which I mentioned in the first part of this chapter.

The first CPR Meeting I chaired on 18 January 2017 discussed the following agenda items, among others:

1. Themes and Priorities of the Philippine Chairmanship
2. CPR's Work Plan for the year
   The Work Plan is derived from the matters arising from the previous year's agenda, instructions and tasks assigned by the SOM, the Ministers and the Leaders, and initiatives by the Chair in accordance with the TOR of the CPR.
3. The Philippines' proposed Commemorative Activities to Celebrate the 50th Anniversary of ASEAN
4. ASEAN's External Relations
   It will be noted that this agenda item takes up a lot of time and effort since it deals with the relations of ASEAN with its external partners. The agenda of ASEAN is varied and they are all based on seminal documents such as the ASEAN Charter, the ASEAN Vision 2025 which contains the blueprints for each Community Pillar, the Master Plan on ASEAN Connectivity (MPAC) 2025, the various work plans for each sector, Leaders' and Ministers' Statements and Declarations, etc. The CPR's job is to pursue the fulfillment of these visions and plans in its deliberations among Member States and in their dealings with their external partners. Very little attention is focused on the myriad of issues where ASEAN has found convergence on and vowed to implement. On such issues of common concern, there will be little debate in the

deliberations of the CPR. This would happen when championing principles like sovereignty and non-interference in internal affairs, already enshrined in ASEAN documents such as the ASEAN Charter, the Treaty of Amity and Cooperation, ASEAN Vision 2025, etc., plus specific issues like Technical and Vocational Education and Training (TVET), biodiversity and climate change, poverty alleviation, narrowing the development gap, the fight against terrorism and radicalization, disaster risk reduction and management, Sustainable Development Goals (SDGs), and the like where ASEAN Member States would immediately find consensus among themselves.

Moreover, certain national "favourites" would be espoused by particular Member States for inclusion in the agenda of the CPR. Having spent more than six years in Jakarta has provided me with an almost instinctive discernment on the particular inclinations of my colleagues in the CPR. Singapore would always bat for free trade and liberalization of investment regimes and air connectivity. The Philippines and Indonesia would always support each other on matters concerning the promotion and protection of the rights and welfare of migrant workers and human rights. Indonesia was always looking for opportunities to include Illegal Unreported and Unregulated Fishing (IUUF) and ASEAN Centrality in the Indo-Pacific in any work plan. The CLMV countries (Cambodia, Laos, Viet Nam and Myanmar) are always seeking to include the narrowing of development gaps in ASEAN Plans of Action even if Viet Nam has already surpassed some "older" Member States in SDG indexes. The Philippines and Viet Nam are always insisting on strong language on the South China Sea as reflected in documents being negotiated. The Philippines is the champion for women's economic and political empowerment, TVET and biodiversity. Thailand is the standard bearer for the promotion and implementation of SDGs. Malaysia, before the election of Prime Minister Mahathir, had always sought to highlight the role of the Global Movement of Moderates (GMM) as a strategy to combat terrorism. (However, Malaysia had retreated from this advocacy in recent times due to the alleged involvement of the GMM Foundation officials in some irregularities). Many more such national advocacies would find support eventually in ASEAN's agenda, or at least, the CPR would be able to find language that would gain the support of all on these issues.

On the other hand, when it deems it not beneficial to its own agenda, the CPR would not agree with the agenda of its external partners as discussed in other sections of this book.

ASEAN Centrality In Spite of Conflicting Bilateral Disputes

Like many regions in the world, ASEAN Member States have been racked by bilateral disputes natural to close-door neighbours and those with huge differences in religious, cultural, economic and political backgrounds. Such issues as the sovereignty claims of the Philippines over Sabah, the dispute between Cambodia and Thailand over the Preah Vihear Temple and its immediate grounds, the Batu Puteh issue between Malaysia and Singapore, the Miangas issue between the Philippines and Indonesia, the conflicting claims between Thailand and Myanmar over three islands in the Andaman Sea, between Brunei and Malaysia over Limbang and a certain portion of the South China Sea, and several issues between Indonesia and Malaysia, are all substantial and critical, but they do not appear in any ASEAN meeting agenda. The mediating role of former Foreign Minister Marty Natalegawa in the settlement of the Preah Vihear Temple dispute which was then already exacting loss of lives was not done as an agenda item in ASEAN but was conducted in its sidelines and using the friendly good-neighbourly atmosphere that ASEAN engenders. Therefore, although bilateral disputes had reached critical levels in the past, ASEAN had not allowed these bilateral differences to get in the way of regional cooperation. Severino (2001) explains:

> ASEAN, bilateral issues—whether they have to do with boundaries, borders or the movement of people—are managed bilaterally, without being complicated by unnecessary regionalization or internationalization. As in the case of many other regional organizations, ASEAN's insistence on consensus ensures that the association takes no action that threatens the vital interests of any member.

When I assumed office in March 2013, I remember calling on the Ambassador of Malaysia as a routine practice for newly-arrived

Ambassadors in a post. At that time, the Lahad Datu incident[3] was still hugging the headlines and the issue of the ownership of Sabah is a raw irritant for both countries which they have managed peacefully so as not to disrupt relations. The Malaysian Ambassador and I vowed that we would not discuss the matter in ASEAN and that we would not let our respective country's claims be a hindrance in the pursuit of our regional goals. During my entire tour of duty of six years, we have never brought up the matter in any ASEAN meeting. We left the discussion on this sensitive issue in the appropriate bilateral forums and under the appropriate framework of the United Nations.

The absence of this type of agenda in ASEAN deliberation and its confinement to bilateral platforms, using peaceful means and the rule of law in the management and resolution of disputes and conflict is a strong sign of ASEAN Centrality as it contributes to the strengthening of the regional spirit of cooperation and unity.

ASEAN Centrality through ASEAN Consensus or Without

As earlier mentioned, criticism of ASEAN Centrality has been based on ASEAN's inability to reach consensus on vital issues, including the South China Sea, the Northern Rakhine, the RCEP (there seemed to be a deadlock at this time), and the Korean Peninsula issue. I would like to discuss three instances in this book which happened during my watch as Chair of the CPR, where some kind of consensus was reached despite the difficulties facing the Member States or the resilience of ASEAN when consensus cannot be attained. These are the negotiations on the paragraphs concerning the South China Sea, IUUF, mention of the VX sarin chemical when negotiating the ASEAN text of the EAS Leaders' Statement on Chemical Weapons and the Amendment/Update of the ASEAN Charter.

ASEAN Consensus on the South China Sea Issue

In almost every document that the CPR is tasked to negotiate, inclusion of paragraphs on the South China Sea inevitably leads to prolonged and heated debate. The employment of strong language espoused by myself and the representative of Viet Nam, such as in the following paragraph would characterize any negotiation on the issue:

> We reaffirm the importance of maintaining stability, and security, freedom of navigation and overflight in the region, including in the South China Sea. We emphasise the need to enhance mutual trust and confidence, exercise self-restraint in the conduct of activities and avoid actions that may complicate the situation, ***including militarisation and threat or use of force as well as artificial island building.*** We reaffirm the peaceful resolutions of disputes, in accordance with universally recognised principles of international law, including the 1982 United Nations Convention on the Law of the Sea (UNCLOS). In this regard, we support the full and effective implementation of the Declaration on the Conduct of the Parties in the South China Sea (DOC) in its entirety and look forward to an early conclusion of an effective and meaningful Code of Conduct in the South China Sea (COC), consistent with international law.

The contestable element in this proposed paragraph is the phrase, "*including militarisation and threat or use of force as well as island building*" which some AMS find too confrontational, unnecessary and does not enjoy consensus. There was a time when some AMS would attempt to include the phrase, "*artificial island building*" as shown above. Of late, however, Member States who had wanted to include its mention had backed down from this position because of apprehension that it might create the impression of accepting a status quo, i.e., that the artificial islands created would attain the status of "islands" which under the UNCLOS, imply other entitlements to those who own or control them although the Permanent Court of Arbitration (PCA) Award to the Philippines was very specific that such artificial activities do not change the natural characteristics of those features in the Spratlys.[4] My Deputy, Noel Novicio, and I would make the rounds of Member States at the sidelines of meetings to reach a consensus. In the end, Member States opted to adopt a more positive and pragmatic view but still expressing concern. Thus, the final paragraph appearing in the Chairman's Statement of the 31st Summit appears as follows:

> We likewise reaffirmed the importance of maintaining and promoting peace, security, stability, maritime safety and security, rules-based order and freedom of navigation in and overflight above the South China Sea. In this regard, we further reaffirmed the need to enhance mutual

trust and confidence, emphasized the importance of non-militarization and self-restraint in the conduct of all activities by claimants and all other states, including those mentioned in the DOC that could further complicate the situation and escalate tensions in the South China Sea, and stressed the need to adhere to the peaceful resolution of disputes, in accordance with universally recognised principles of international law.

On the other hand, the Philippines and other AMS had insisted on the phrase, *"full respect for legal and diplomatic processes"*, found in another section of the statement, despite the attempt by some members to remove it arguing that they had nothing to do with the arbitration procedures initiated by the Philippines against China in 2013 and its concomitant decision. Cambodia has always insisted that it was not a member of the UNCLOS under whose framework the arbitration case was filed by the Philippines and so, could not associate with this language. In 2017, ASEAN had to find consensus and avoid the stalemate of 2012 when no Joint Communique was issued on account of the Philippine insistence on strong language on the South China Sea issue. In ASEAN circles, *"full respect for legal and diplomatic processes"*, specifically referred to the arbitration proceedings resorted to by the Philippines under the UNCLOS. During one such meeting, I gave the following intervention:

- The principle of "full respect for legal and diplomatic processes" has been affirmed as a fundamental ASEAN norm, as reflected in the Joint Communique of the 49th ASEAN Ministerial Meeting held on 24–25 July 2016 in Vientiane.
- The inclusion of the principle into paragraph 2 of the Joint Communique enshrines "the full respect for legal and diplomatic processes" as a core ASEAN value, alongside the principles of ASEAN unity and centrality and adherence to the rule of law.
- The Philippines underscores that the reference to full respect for legal and diplomatic principle governs all activities of the ASEAN Community as well as ASEAN's relations with its Dialogue Partners, including efforts to peacefully resolve disputes in the South China Sea.
- This is not a Philippine position but an ASEAN position.
- The Philippines shall continue to advance its strong advocacy for the peaceful resolution of disputes and adherence to the rule of

law, and international law, including UNCLOS, to maintain peace and stability in the region.
- The Philippines is further ready to engage all parties in order to enhance mutual cooperation in political, economic/investment and cultural activities, parallel to and supportive of efforts aimed at the peaceful resolution of the South China Sea disputes.

After a long deliberation, Member States finally agreed with the above arguments and this is how the paragraph now appears in the 2017 Chairman's Statement of the 31st ASEAN Summit:

> We reaffirmed the shared commitment to maintaining and promoting peace, security and stability in the region, as well as to the peaceful resolution of disputes, **including full respect for legal and diplomatic processes**, without resorting to the threat or use of force, in accordance with the universally recognized principles of international law, including the 1982 United Nations Convention on the Law of the Sea (UNCLOS).

It must also be clarified that ASEAN indeed has consensus on the South China Sea issue, although it is not what the Philippines and Viet Nam would have wished. The consensus is that ASEAN does not take sides on who owns what in the contested areas but that ASEAN's common interest is to prevent the escalation of conflict in the region and that the rule of international law must prevail. They also have a consensus on the full and effective implementation of the DOC and the push for the adoption of a COC for the South China Sea, which is envisioned, not as a dispute settling mechanism, but as a confidence building strategy to manage tensions and avoid miscalculations which could lead to conflagration. They are lodging their full support to international law, including the 1982 UNCLOS, for the settlement of the South China Sea disputes.

I remember one ASEAN Foreign Ministers' Retreat when the Philippines was trying to harness the support of ASEAN to endorse the arbitration process and victory of the Philippines in the PCA where it filed its case against China on the matter of the South China Sea. In a rare frank discussion, one Minister said that this was not the consensus. They could not endorse the arbitration win because the Philippines did not seek the consent of ASEAN when they went to the tribunal in 2013. It was a unilateral decision by the Philippines, he said, and that the Philippines cannot expect the whole of ASEAN to endorse it. He cited the fact that when their own country had bilateral disputes with another AMS, they went straight ahead to the International Court of Justice (ICJ) and did not seek ASEAN endorsement of nor permission for their action. He concluded that the ASEAN consensus on the matter was that the peace and stability of the entire region of the South China Sea held primordial importance and that "bilateral disputes" should be discussed in separate venues. His view was supported by another Minister. The others held their strategic silence. Thus, the Philippines did not get the support of ASEAN to own the arbitral victory as its collective achievement. To be sure, the most common view held by AMS and many external partners before the arbitral award of the Philippines was that the South China Sea disputes were bilateral issues between the Philippines and China and should not be endorsed by multilateral forums although members can also discuss them in their interventions. At an Asia-Europe Meeting (ASEM) I attended as Philippine SOM Leader in 2012 (before we filed our arbitration case), I had sought the support of ASEM countries to include in the Chair's Statement paragraphs pertaining to the South China Sea. The debate on this issue was held around 4 a.m. Before this the negotiations had been going on since 8.30 a.m. the day before and we had no breaks except for a thirty-minute respite each for lunch and dinner. I made an impassioned intervention to which one Asian delegate vigorously replied saying that the ASEM was not the appropriate venue to raise the South China Sea issue. His intervention was so intense and emphatic that something funny happened—his microphone which he had been pounding to emphasize his point, fell from its brace support! Other AMS were quiet, perhaps agreeing with the Asian delegate that while it was an important issue, Europe which is far away geographically from the South China Sea region, should not get involved in it. The other Asian members had their own maritime disputes and did not want to confuse those with the Philippine issue. I did not get any support from Asian or ASEAN members, save one brief intervention by Viet Nam. Ironically, it was the EU-dominated structure of the ASEM that I have always complained about that enabled me to insert my paragraph, albeit a heavily watered down version. The UK, Germany, France and the EU supported my proposal, agreeing with me that the peace and stability and freedom of navigation and overflight in the region straddled by the South China Sea is a concern that affected us all. For the first time in the history of the ASEM, a paragraph that obliquely refers to the South China Sea because it was placed under the chapeau of "Regional Issues" was added. Paragraph 45 of the Chair's Statement of the 9th ASEM Summit says:

> Leaders exchanged views on the recent developments in Asia and Europe on the basis of equal partnership, mutual respect and mutual benefits. They recognised ASEM partners' efforts to maintain peace, security and stability and to settle disputes by peaceful means in accordance with UN Charter and international law.

Small victory one might say but never before has the issue of the South China Sea disputes been discussed or placed in a Leaders' approved ASEM Statement. This just goes to show that despite assiduous efforts by the Philippines' diplomats, the issue of the South China Sea had not been provided the appropriate venue it deserved before it won its arbitration proceedings against China which is now permanently part of international law. Still, such lack of support before the 2013 filing by the Philippines of its PCA case had not hindered the progress of ASEAN to accomplish the goals of the ASEAN Community in fostering peace and stability in the region.

ASEAN Member States are united in their view that the rule of law, particularly the 1982 UNCLOS and the principle of peaceful settlement of disputes should be the bases in managing the South China Sea issue. They have also espoused the non-use of force or the threat to use force in settling their differences. They are united in the full and effective implementation of the DOC and are all looking forward to the completion of the COC in the South China Sea between ASEAN and China.

ASEAN Consensus on Illegal Unreported and Unregulated Fishing (IUUF)

Another issue hotly debated in the CPR was the inclusion of IUUF in the Chairman's Statement for the 30th ASEAN Summit and other documents, such as the ASEAN-Australia Plan of Action. Indonesia had wanted to make a big issue of this by giving it a prominent focus in the Chairman's Statement. Earlier, there were reports about the controversial manner with which the fiery former Minister for Fisheries of Indonesia, Ibu Susi Pudjiastuti, had burned, later scuttled fishing boats from Viet Nam, Thailand, Malaysia, and the Philippines caught poaching in Indonesian waters. Many people in Indonesia had approved of Minister Susi's non-conventional manner of highlighting the issue of IUUF. Indonesia had wanted to include IUUF in a paragraph together with other non-traditional security issues like terrorism, trafficking in drugs and persons, etc., in order to give it the same prominence and importance and thereby giving the issue political colour. Their original formulation read as follows:

> We will comprehensively address cross-sectoral concerns, including non-traditional security issues and transnational challenges, such as illicit drug trafficking, trafficking-in-persons, terrorism, and violent extremism; as well as other transboundary challenges such as disaster management, emerging infectious diseases and illegal, unreported and unregulated (IUU) fishing. We will further strengthen our efforts to address key regional and global challenges in collaboration with the international community.

In this context, IUUF was equated with the other serious security threats as mentioned above, to which most AMS were opposed because putting it in that context raised its level of contentiousness. On the part of the Philippines, we could not deny that IUUF also posed a grave threat to ASEAN's economic security even if Philippine fishing ships had been among those burned or scuttled and the Filipino crew of those ships had been detained for illegal poaching. The Philippine Consulate General in Manado exists for the purpose of assisting these Filipino fishermen. IUUF was also contrary to our advocacy to prevent illegal poaching in our own waters involving other foreign fishing vessels. Thus, as Chair, I offered a compromise whereby it is mentioned, not alongside other serious political security threats but in a separate paragraph of its own under the general heading of Economic matters, not co-equal with grave issues like terrorism and trafficking in persons and illicit drugs. The final paragraph appearing in the Joint Communique reads thus:

> We noted that challenges of Illegal, Unreported and Unregulated (IUU) Fishing remain and have become even more complex in the region. We are therefore committed to expanding regional cooperation to address this issue, including through supporting the effective implementation of the relevant international law and instruments. We noted with satisfaction that there are initiatives taken by ASEAN-led mechanisms to discuss and address the challenges of IUU fishing.

ASEAN Consensus on Use of the Name of the Chemical Weapon "VX sarin" in the ASEAN Text of the EAS Leaders' Declaration

Before a text is negotiated with ASEAN's external partners, ASEAN must first come up with an ASEAN-agreed text. One of the contentious issues that came up during the negotiation of this ASEAN version was the use of the words "VX sarin" in paragraph 7 of the Declaration. The proposed paragraph looked straightforward enough—it said:

> Denounce the chemical weapons incident involving the nerve agent VX against a national of the Democratic People's Republic of Korea (DPRK) in Kuala Lumpur that posed great risk to public safety and security;

However, for some reason, two AMS would not agree to the above formulation which specifically mentions the name of the nerve agent. How ASEAN resolved the issue and preserving its unity in the process employing the face-saving technique mentioned in the beginning is recounted in detail in the section on the EAS of this study, but needless to say, the ASEAN compromise was retained in support of ASEAN Centrality.

ASEAN Centrality Despite Inability to Amend/Update the ASEAN Charter

One of the most controversial topics the Philippines introduced in the CPR during this period was the review or update of the ASEAN Charter. In

2017, the Philippines had considered it the opportune moment to revise the landmark document as it contained some basic errors and needed to be updated to reflect realities that have emerged ten years after its issuance in 2007. The Charter itself provides for its review every five years. Armed with instructions from my Home Office and a Philippine discussion paper, I introduced the topic at the first CPR Meeting I chaired on 18 January 2017.

Immediately, the proposal drew varied, sometimes even critical responses from the other PRs. Some AMS questioned whether or not the context of the proposed scoping is in line with Article 48 (Amendments) or Article 50 (Review); others said that there was no need to amend the Charter since any operational changes could simply be annexed to it. Still others maintained that as the ASEAN Charter provides the legal and institutional framework for ASEAN and serves as the constitution of the association, it is important that frequent amendments should be avoided. However, I argued that it is high time the Charter should be amended due to the aforementioned errors and the significant changes ASEAN has undergone since the Charter's issuance. At the end of that meeting, the CPR agreed to recommend to the SOM whether or not such an amendment should take place, the scope or which part of the Charter needed to be updated. The meeting also provided justifications for the update and which appropriate body was going to undertake the actual review of the Charter.

After receiving the mandate and instructions to undertake a scoping exercise (to determine which sections should be amended) from the SOM and the Ministers during their retreat in Boracay in February 2017, my Mission endeavoured to push the updating of the Charter in every opportunity, a prerogative of being the Chair of the CPR. At the end of March, the CPR was ready to endorse to the SOM the following proposed amendments (see Figure 5.5) to the Charter.

We also believed that Article 10 entitled ASEAN Sectoral Ministerial Bodies and Annex 1 were inconsistent since the latter contained names of entities that were not formal mechanisms of ASEAN like the ASEAN Foreign Ministers' Meeting (AMM), such as the inclusion of the ASEAN-Japan Centre and the ASEAN University Network. We proposed changing Article 10's title to add the phrase "and Other Bodies", which would then

FIGURE 5.5
Proposed Amendments to the ASEAN Charter

PROPOSED ARTICLES AND SECTIONS TO BE UPDATED IN THE ASEAN CHARTER

ARTICLE	CURRENT TEXTS	PROPOSED TEXTS
ARTICLE 12. COMMITTEE OF PERMANENT REPRESENTATIVES TO ASEAN	ARTICLE 12. COMMITTEE OF PERMANENT REPRESENTATIVES TO ASEAN (2)(e) perform such other functions as may be determined by the ASEAN Coordinating Council.	ARTICLE 12. COMMITTEE OF PERMANENT REPRESENTATIVES TO ASEAN (2)(e) perform such other functions as may be determined by the ASEAN Coordinating Council (ACC), and in accordance with the terms of reference as approved by the ACC.
ARTICLE 14. ASEAN HUMAN RIGHTS BODY	ARTICLE 14. ASEAN HUMAN RIGHTS BODY 1. In conformity with the purposes and principles of the ASEAN Charter relating to the promotion and protection of human rights and fundamental freedoms, ASEAN shall establish an ASEAN human rights body. 2. This ASEAN human rights body shall operate in accordance with the terms of reference to be determined by the ASEAN Foreign Ministers Meeting.	ARTICLE 14. ASEAN INTERGOVERNMENTAL COMMISSION ON HUMAN RIGHTS 1. In conformity with the purposes and principles of the ASEAN Charter relating to the promotion and protection of human rights and fundamental freedoms, each ASEAN Member State shall appoint a representative to the ASEAN Intergovernmental Commission on Human Rights (AICHR). 2. AICHR shall operate in accordance with the terms of reference approved by the ASEAN Foreign Ministers Meeting.
ARTICLE 40. ASEAN ANTHEM	ARTICLE 40. ASEAN ANTHEM ASEAN shall have an anthem.	ARTCILE 40. ASEAN ANTHEM The ASEAN Anthem appears as Annex 5.
ARTICLE 44. STATUS OF EXTERNAL PARTIES	ARTICLE 44. STATUS OF EXTERNAL PARTIES 2. External parties may be invited to ASEAN meetings or cooperative activities without being conferred any formal status, in accordance with the rules of procedure.	ARTICLE 44. STATUS OF EXTERNAL PARTIES 2. External parties may be invited to ASEAN meetings or cooperative activities without being conferred any formal status, in accordance with the rules of procedures and the Guidelines for ASEAN's External Relations.

read as: ASEAN Sectoral Ministerial and Other Bodies, or to remove from Annex 1 those bodies that were not ministerial bodies to make these two parts consistent with each other.

However, after seven months of hard work, to my great dismay and that of most of my colleagues who laboured hard to complete our assigned task, one member state suddenly made the sudden announcement that it could not agree to any amendment of the Charter. I wonder what the real reason for this member state could be, but I suspect it had something to do with the debacle they would be facing defending such meagre amendments in their legislative body. There was also the fear by some that opening up the Charter for amendment then would also open up amending other provisions that would expose ASEAN to bitter disagreements because the Charter itself took years to negotiate and finalize. As Tommy Koh, one of the framers of the Charter remarked, "While ASEAN watchers point to the lack of political appetite to review the Charter, the reality is that ASEAN leaders do not see a need to undertake this laborious and politically tricky endeavour."

Wanting to save the opportunity to essay another attempt at revision in the future, the Philippines tried to salvage the situation by inserting this paragraph in the Chairman's statement of the 31st ASEAN Summit:

> We noted that the CPR had undertaken extensive deliberations on updating certain articles and sections of the ASEAN Charter, entailing substantive discussions on its implementation, which would serve as a basis for the review of the ASEAN Charter in the future. We remain committed to promoting a rules-based ASEAN Community in adherence to the purposes and principles stipulated in the existing ASEAN Charter, which sufficiently confers ASEAN a legal personality and provides an institutional framework for ASEAN to realize its goal of lasting peace, shared prosperity, security, stability, sustainable economic growth and social progress.

The Philippines, with the concurrence of the other nine also managed to allow the ASEAN Secretariat to rearrange the list in Annex 1 into categories so that the ministerial bodies are not mixed up with the other entities. Annex 2 was also amended without the necessity of revising the whole Charter to include only those entities that were still active and include new ones which wanted to be accredited.

Although the whole exercise failed to reach ASEAN consensus, ASEAN Centrality was still exercised in the process and it did not deter them from moving forward with other important issues and the matter was conducted in the usual consultative, non-confrontational manner that ASEAN is noted for. Looking back now, I believe that our failure to reach a consensus did not present any major setback in the performance of the work of ASEAN and the attainment of its objectives. I am optimistic that there would be another opportune time to revise the ASEAN Charter, especially as we look to the next visioning exercise for ASEAN in the next ten years after 2025.[5]

The Tone and Language of the CPR

The tone and language of ASEAN are non-confrontational, friendly and familial. In fact, the word "family" has become a common term to refer to their unique community; oftentimes referring to it as the ASEAN family. Although different from each other in their national interests owing from diverse backgrounds in governmental systems, level of economic development, cultural and religious backgrounds, etc., and even if their debates and discussions last long into the night, the meetings of ASEAN shun away from acrimonious, naming and shaming and accusatory language that those outside it are wont to use.

The tone and language of ASEAN are very much shaped by *musyawarah mufakat* (non-confrontational consensus-building), a basic principle of the "ASEAN Way". ASEAN has not confined the practice of the ASEAN Way among its own members only but insists that this be adhered to by its external partners especially when interacting with ASEAN in ASEAN-led mechanisms such as the ASEAN Regional Forum (ARF), ASEAN Plus Three, ASEAN Plus One, and the EAS.

As mentioned earlier, the ASEAN Way has been derided by critics as an ineffective, weak and slow system that has delayed or prevented ASEAN from arriving at solutions to important issues and which has allowed human rights abuses to thrive in ASEAN Member States. However, it is this oft-maligned ASEAN Way that has allowed the regional grouping to accomplish what it had despite enormous differences among them and in their relations with outside partners. This view is supported by former Secretary General Rodolfo Severino (2001), who attributed ASEAN's singular achievement to ASEAN's approach to the conduct of relations among members, which he says is characterized by putting a premium on dialogue and consultation in place of posturing and confrontation and prefers quiet discussions and eschews "megaphone diplomacy" and "feel-good diplomacy". "It considers mutual respect and understanding—understanding by each member of another's situation and difficulties—as vital to the peace and stability of the region and to the future of the association itself", he concluded when assessing the accomplishments of ASEAN at 40.

A believer in the constructivist theory of international relations, Koga (2010) also defends the ASEAN Way as an effective tool developed by ASEAN in its diplomacy within and among Member States and in relating with the world. He says:

> According to social constructivist theory, ideational factors in international relations promote the formulation of identities and interests through interaction among actors and between actors and structures. In this sense, institutions are regarded as a relatively stable collection of practices and rules defining appropriate behavior for specific groups of actors in specific situations. Because ASEAN Way consensus decision-making does not oblige member states to restrain their behavior, but rather to seek cooperation, the ASEAN Way was internalized within ASEAN and beyond through the Cold War and the post–Cold War eras.

Indeed, despite the fact that the ASEAN Way is not the legalistic framework that other more rigid organizations such as the EU subscribe to, the Statements, Joint Communique and other informal documents emanating from ASEAN's interactions become the basis for their future actions and cooperation. These decisions become translated into specific activities that are all aimed at promoting, defending and advancing the interest of ASEAN.

As mentioned earlier, Nair theorizes on the origins, manifestations and results of "face-saving" practices and attitudes that constitute a large part of the ASEAN Way and that ASEAN has utilized this concept to avoid conflict and to serve as a "mode of accountability that contrasted with rational legal organizational formulas with participants valuing heightened concern for the feelings and faces of its participants".

One such face-saving incident during my chairmanship was with regards to the continued delay in the approval of the ASEAN Secretariat Annual Budget which the CPR had the responsibility to approve and endorse to the Ministers. Unlike the Philippines which could always revert to the budget of the previous year to continue funding its important expenses, the ASEAN Secretariat had to have a budget approved by the Foreign Ministers during their annual AMM. However, perhaps due to internal misunderstandings on the part of officials of a certain member state, the PR of this member state had continued to express reservations on important items like new allocations for funding the hiring of critically-needed personnel needed especially to monitor the progress of the three community pillars and strengthen its legal services, repair in the buildings of the Secretariat and the residence of the Secretary General and other important items. The entire budget was at stake as decisions could not be taken piece-meal but were included in the entire budget proposal. As the date of the budget submission (sometime in early July) was nearing, I was becoming frustrated and angry because the delay did not come from the inability of that member to contribute to the ASEAN Fund but by some simple red-tape involving their high ranking officials. Instead of venting these frustrations openly in the meetings, I quietly sought the help of a Senior Minister of that member state to help sort out the difficulty without blaming or accusing anyone. The Minister understood the situation and shortly thereafter, the member state gave its approval and the Secretariat enjoyed an increased budget for the following year.

Another such instance was when the non-confrontational approach proved a big help to me when experiencing a prolonged debate on certain issues we were negotiating. This was because one member state had not sent a regular Ambassador to the discussions and those representing that country were either too shy or ill-prepared or did not feel confident they could make quick decisions for their country, so they kept on making reservations or even objecting to even the simplest non-controversial issues. This delayed the conclusion of many documents we were negotiating and the mounting pressure added to my anxiety as Chair. Instead of openly accusing these junior officers, I quietly sent a communication to their senior official to send someone who had the appropriate credentials and mandate to negotiate. The member state appreciated this no-shaming approach, sent an Ambassador-level representative and my work as Chair was facilitated thereafter.

There is tremendous pressure for AMS to adopt a more confrontational approach among themselves especially on issues that involve human rights, the South China Sea and the Northern Rakhine issue. ASEAN has not succumbed to these pressures to resort to name-calling and confrontation. It does not mean, however, that these issues are ignored altogether. ASEAN discusses these difficult issues in a manner consistent with the ASEAN Way. Nobody calls these interventions interference in the internal affairs of any member state. Instead, the Philippines always refers to the Philippine saying "*ang sakit ng kalingkingan ay dama ng buong katawan*" (the hurt of the small finger is felt by the entire body), when discussing difficult issues such as mentioned above.

I attended a ministerial retreat whereby some AMS have called on Myanmar to do something concrete to address the situation of the refugees from the Northern Rakhine state. On the other hand, AMS had acceded to the request of Myanmar to not call these people Rohingya, as most western countries are wont to do, because the word Rohingya in itself denoted that they were entitled to Burmese citizenship, which, of course, is one of the main issues of contention in this matter. Instead of accusing Myanmar of human rights violations as is the practice outside ASEAN, Member States inquired from Myanmar what they could do to help ease the conditions of the refugees and for Myanmar to address their concerns. I do not know if it was the result of this discussion but shortly after this, Myanmar engaged in bilateral discussion with Bangladesh to address core issues on the refugees and allowed ASEAN to undertake some interventions including allowing the Secretary General to send an assessment team there. Still, I believe that Myanmar will have to do a lot more to help the hapless people of their Northern Rakhine state.

ASEAN Centrality in the ASEAN Connectivity Coordinating Committee (ACCC)

Another ASEAN body based in Jakarta where ASEAN Centrality was practised is the ASEAN Connectivity Coordinating Committee (ACCC) which I was a member of for six years and which I chaired in 2017. It is also here where ASEAN Centrality was put to the test, both in terms of achieving ASEAN consensus in its implementation and in its relations with external partners. This mechanism is composed of the Permanent Representatives to ASEAN or any other special representatives appointed by ASEAN Member States. It is tasked mainly to coordinate the implementation of the MPAC 2025 and in so doing, cooperate with ASEAN's external partners. The TOR of the ACCC appears as *Annex C*.

MPAC 2025, is composed of five strategic areas, namely, (i) Sustainable Infrastructure; (ii) Digital Innovation; (iii) Seamless Logistics; (iv) Regulatory Excellence; and (v) People Mobility; with a total of fifteen key initiatives under these strategic areas. It is clear to see that this is another cross-pillar ASEAN programme that needs the cooperation and implementation by the three pillars of the ASEAN Community, particularly that of the AEC.

ASEAN Connectivity is a paradox. It is either an orphan with no parent community pillar claiming it as its own or that it has too many parents as its coverage encompasses all three ASEAN communities. The first ten-year Master Plan on ASEAN Connectivity was called MPAC 1 and was issued in 2007. However, it has had a limited rate of success (over 38 per cent), due to several reasons, including lack of ownership of its plans and projects by its intended users. Thus, when we negotiated the successor Master Plan, several colleagues and I had insisted on a plan that would command its ownership by all Member States, and would, therefore, have a higher rate of implementation than its predecessor. This meant that the projects and programmes must be realistic and that it should not be a wish list of things we had wanted to happen without ensuring that they are doable and that the different sectors are willing to implement them. Still, the successor document, MPAC 2025, initially suffered a huge setback and proved to be a difficult ASEAN programme to undertake. First of all, it is not under any specific pillar since its key initiatives and projects are multi-pillar and multi-sectoral in nature. That means to say that not one ASEAN body is in the lead, and because of the silo tendency of the pillars to focus on their respective work plans, as discussed earlier, the MPAC is oftentimes sidelined because not one mechanism owns it. While it was issued in November 2016, by the beginning of 2017, there was still very little buy-in from among its stakeholders, or the people who were meant to implement it. Most of these ASEAN officials, such as the Senior Economic Officials, ASEAN Finance and Central Bank Deputies, Senior Transport Officials, etc. have their own work plans or blueprints in their respective mechanisms and did not want to be burdened by another plan not produced by them.

To overcome this lack of enthusiasm from implementing agencies, the previous ASEAN Chair, Laos, had planned to convene a forum to socialize the plan among the various ASEAN bodies meant to implement it. While preparations for its conduct were made during the Laos chairmanship, the event, entitled MPAC 2025 Workshop on Initiatives and Project Concepts was set to be held in February 2017, which fell under my chairmanship. However, by the beginning of January 2017, only one ASEAN body had agreed to attend the forum. The Director of ASEAN Connectivity in the ASEAN Secretariat, Mr Lim Chze Cheen, and my Officer, Jan Wenceslao, were despondent. I called them and other people concerned to a brainstorming meeting and rethought our strategy. We agreed to reschedule the event to July 2017, and to take steps to ensure that all stakeholders attend the forum. This involved negotiations with the two funding partners of the MPAC, the Economic Research Institute for ASEAN and East Asia (ERIA) and the Australian Government through the ASEAN-Australia Development Cooperation Program II (AADCP II). Our strategy was to hold the annual Connectivity Forum organized by ERIA back-to-back with the MPAC Forum sponsored by the AADCP II, to allow more participants to join since they would already be there for the other event. However, because of the strict guidelines followed by the funds of these two organizations, it was difficult at first to combine their resources for the back-to-back events. There was also the issue of ownership of the events as these two partner organizations had, of course, to account for their funds. However, as a result of adroit negotiations we undertook with the representatives of ERIA and AADCP who have exercised flexibility because they, too, shared our objective to enhance ASEAN Connectivity, the desired effect was achieved. In a very rare opportunity, multiple stakeholders, including representatives of the ten Member States from the different ASEAN mechanisms involved in transport, finance, immigration, education, trade and industry, tourism and other sectors attended and got to contribute their inputs in the formulation of specific key initiatives and projects under the three pillars of ASEAN Connectivity. During the forum held in July in Alabang (see Figure 5.6), the delegates, as subject matter experts, particularly those concerned with the respective initiatives, provided technical inputs to the prepared draft

FIGURE 5.6
8th ASEAN Connectivity Symposium

project concepts to help address challenges in ASEAN Connectivity and identify the steps forward in implementing MPAC 2025.

One remaining issue needed to be addressed—the fact that ASEAN had no sectoral body that was responsible for Physical Infrastructure. Each Key Initiative in the MPAC 2025 had to have a Lead Implementing Body (LIB) that would oversee its implementation. Because no such ASEAN mechanism exists, the SEOM had been designated the LIB for Physical Infrastructure, since the ASEAN Economic Ministers' Meeting (AEMM) to which the SEOM reports, is the overall coordinator of the sectors under the economic pillar which includes a host of many concerns including, finance, transportation, communication, science and technology, agriculture, etc. However, the SEOM categorically stated that they did not want to become the LIB for this area, burdened as they were already with implementing their own AEC Blueprint. In fact, during their meeting in Boracay in February 2017, the SEOM agreed that they would not be involved in the implementation of MPAC 2025 and that they should focus only on their own master plan. The ACCC made a decision to address this issue the ASEAN Way. Under my chairmanship, the ACCC adopted a strategy to avoid a confrontational scenario with the SEOM. First, Director Lim and I went to the SEOM meeting in Bangkok in March 2017 to explain to them what the MPAC 2025 is all about and their role in implementing it. I tried to persuade them that the ACCC was their partner and that their function as LIB was not that complicated and difficult and most important of all, that we were all in this together. The goodwill earned by this gesture was considerable because a PR would normally not go out of their way to attend SEOM meetings but I did travel all the way to Bangkok and patiently waited for my time slot to make a presentation. After this, later in the same month, I sought an informal bilateral meeting with the Chair of SEOM, Ms Ann Robeniol of the Philippine Department of Trade and Industry, and offered a four-point solution, namely:

a. To define the term "Lead Implementing Body" which can be reflected in the Summary Record of the JCM. This definition would remove from SEOM the sole responsibility of implementing the Key Initiative but would simply require them to coordinate its implementation. Such a solution would encourage SEOM to participate in the MPAC 2025 implementation.

b. For action lines outside SEOM's mandate or purview, SEOM would not be expected to implement the measures, but would only play an overall coordinating role where relevant. The ACCC Chair will write to the Implementing Bodies under Seamless Logistics to urge them to cooperate with SEOM.

c. In addition, the ASEAN Secretariat will play a supporting role in coordinating the outputs under MPAC 2025. The ACCC and ASEAN Secretariat will prepare a project concept and proposal to undertake a consultancy project with funding from Dialogue Partners or other external parties. The role of SEOM is to provide supervisory inputs to the project development and implementation.

d. The ACCC and ASEAN Secretariat will also engage with sectoral bodies implementing MPAC, by inter-alia participating in sectoral meetings, to cooperate with Lead Implementing Bodies.

While at that time not yet offering full agreement, the SEOM Chair softened her stance and after the Joint Consultative Meeting that ensued the following day, the SEOM finally agreed to be the Lead Implementing Body of Key Initiative 1 on Physical Infrastructure.

Moreover, ACCC succeeded in enrolling the area of connectivity as a permanent or regular agenda item in the JCM, which became the venue for formalizing the new definition of Lead Implementing Body for Physical Infrastructure. It is important for Connectivity to be included in a joint pillar mechanism so as not to be sidetracked by the silo mentality that I feared ASEAN was leading to because of how the Vision 2025 was structured.

ASEAN Centrality in the ASEAN Institute for Peace and Reconciliation (AIPR)

The ASEAN Institute for Peace and Reconciliation (ASEAN-IPR) is another Jakarta-based ASEAN body composed of at least eight CPR members and two representatives (normally Indonesia and Thailand) from capitals. Its TOR lists its functions as follows:

a. Serving an ASEAN institution for research activities on peace, conflict management and conflict resolution
b. Promoting of activities agreed in the ASEAN Political-Security Community (APSC) Blueprint, and additional activities as agreed by ASEAN Member States

The TOR of AIPR appears as Annex D

An instance when ASEAN Centrality was achieved through the arrival at a consensus despite the huge differences among the Member States concerned my proposal to establish an ASEAN Women Mediators Network under the framework of the ASEAN-IPR. I had always wondered why ASEAN did not have its own ASEAN Women Mediators group while other regions of the world had established their own groups, such as the FemWise-Africa, the Mediterranean Women Mediators Network, Nordic Women Mediators Network, Women on the Frontline Mediation Network, Women Mediators Across the Commonwealth, and of course, the Global

Alliance of Regional Women Mediator Networks, all living proof of the important role women play in peace processes and reconciliation. Being a former Ambassador to Norway, I was also familiar with the Nordic Women Mediators Network[6] which was launched in Oslo in 2015. I, therefore, undertook personal initiatives to consult with the Norwegian Ambassador to ASEAN, Morten Hoglund, and other officials from Norway who had agreed to support the formation of a similar network in ASEAN. I wanted to establish a similar group in ASEAN, composed of women who come from varying expertise in the field of peace and security including conflict mediation, peace talks facilitation, peacebuilding and negotiations. These are women who know how to conduct mediation, ceasefire arrangements, constitutional reform, civil-military relations, international humanitarian law, human rights, communications and inclusive strategies in peace and reconciliation.

I knew that AMS have women of this caliber and expertise but that not many know about them and what they are doing in the field of peace processes and reconciliation efforts. Indeed, all over the world, there is very little representation of women in an area where they can contribute most.

The proposal to form a similar ASEAN Mediators Network was also a direct result of a symposium my Mission organized in Cebu in December 2015[7] which recommended that a network of women peacebuilders involved in peace processes and reconciliation be organized. One of the most prominent speakers in that forum was an Indonesian mediator, Shadia Marhaban, a former child combatant in the Free Aceh Movement (GAM) who became a member of GAM's negotiating team in the Helsinki talks that ended the thirty-year conflict. She has since gained a reputation as an international mediator. Another stalwart speaker in this symposium was Professor Miriam-Coronel Ferrer who then headed the Philippine panel of the peace negotiations with the Moro Islamic Liberation Front (MILF). She was the first woman negotiator who had signed a peace agreement that is being actually implemented. Our feminist premise was that if women were more involved in such roles as negotiators, mediators, facilitators or even peace-keepers, then much progress would be achieved in bringing peace and reconciliation to conflict areas in the Member States of ASEAN, including the Philippines, Myanmar and Thailand.

I introduced the idea to my colleagues at the ASEAN-IPR meeting that I chaired in April 2017 through a Concept Note which was the procedural way of attaining consensus to do a project together in the name of ASEAN. However, the proposal did not get immediate ASEAN endorsement because of the simple fact that there were not enough qualified women mediators in all the Member States, although there were many good ones concentrated in a few AMS like the Philippines, Indonesia and probably, Myanmar. Under ASEAN guidelines, any ASEAN body must have representations from all Member States, or at least have the tacit approval of all ten. Not all AMS, like Singapore and Brunei Darussalam, are engaged in peace processes, nor do they face internal insurgency issues, and so, it is natural that they have not developed this kind of expertise among their women. And so, it was a no go for our project. My officer in charge of AIPR matters, Gibb Alfafara, and I were undaunted. We changed the proposal to the simpler ASEAN Women Experts on Peace and Reconciliation, which changed the membership requirement to women practitioners or experts in peace processes and negotiations. Still, this revised version did not receive consensual endorsement because not all Member States felt that they had such expertise. Moreover, some Member States had insisted that we could not establish such a mechanism until we had operationalized the AIPR and had appointed an Executive Director, another major hurdle which required the negotiation among us of the TOR of the AIPR Secretariat and its Executive Director. After months of deliberations we were able to complete these requirements and in October 2017, at the sidelines of the AIPR Symposium on International Humanitarian Law that the Philippines organized, I announced the appointment of Ambassador Jenie Rezlan as the first AIPR Executive Director. Finally, my third proposal met with unanimous endorsement (although one Member State reluctantly did so). I called the network of women experts the ASEAN Women for Peace Registry (AWPR), and envisioned that it would include women representatives from all Member States who were, in one way or another, working on peace, security and reconciliation. They could be mediators, negotiators, facilitators, peace and reconciliation academics or teachers or simply advocates of this area of cooperation in their respective countries. This easing of the requirements on who could be nominated to this body

FIGURE 5.7
Launch of the ASEAN Women for Peace Registry

was acceptable to all Member States. Gibb was happy. She feverishly prepared for the launch of the group.

On 13 December 2018, three years after the Cebu Symposium that launched this dream, in cooperation with the Ateneo de Manila represented by Dr Jennifer (Apple) Oreta, and with funding support from Norway, the Registry was inaugurated in the same city it was conceived in (see Figure 5.7). A last-minute attempt by one member state to prevent its launch was averted by a lot of diplomatic manoeuvrings between myself and the Ambassador of that country. They have not been able to designate their AWPR representatives and so, they had indicated their preference not to launch AWPR but agreed to carry on with the symposium.[8] This member state has also traditionally been diverting the agenda of AIPR away from civil conflicts to other non-traditional security threats like cybersecurity because I suspect that it did not want to expose its own insurgency threat to foreign interference. In fact, this AMS had been very careful about including speakers from their country to talk about the security threat they face from their own insurgency groups because they claim that doing so might aggravate and complicate their situation. But a rather embarrassing scenario was prevented and the launch proceeded.

The keynote address was by no less than the Secretary General of ASEAN, Dato Lim Jock Hoi. It was the first time that a Secretary General of ASEAN himself came to address a symposium on women, indicating the importance he accorded this particular advocacy. "There is no doubt that collective actions are crucial for mainstreaming women's rights and gender equality in peace and security", he said in his Keynote Address. "In this regard, the establishment of an ASEAN Women Peace Registry (AWPR) is an important initiative towards addressing this issue and to build the capacity of women as peace-builders and to encourage a more gendered approach to peace and conflict in the region", he added.

I gave the group the nickname "Awesome AWPR". At first, two Member States had not been able to identify their representatives but the others, like the Philippines, Viet Nam and Laos sent high-level representatives. Today all countries have sent in the names of their representatives who are prominent women negotiators, mediators, peace studies scholars and teachers, peace and reconciliation advocates, etc. from the ASEAN Member States. The AWPR is meant to take stock of its women experts in the field of peace and reconciliation pursuant to the mandate of the ASEAN-IPR, and in accordance with the purposes and principles of the ASEAN Charter, as articulated in its TOR, as well as the relevant action lines of the APSC Blueprint 2025. It also aims to contribute to the implementation of the "Joint Statement on Promoting Women, Peace and Security in ASEAN", which was adopted by the ASEAN Leaders on 13 November 2017 during the 31st ASEAN Summit which encouraged the integration of gender perspectives in all conflict prevention initiatives and strategies. While some of the women peace workers are already actively involved in peace and reconciliation efforts in their respective countries, my dream is for them to be harnessed by Member States whenever and wherever their expertise is needed.

I put a lot of hope in the potential of this network of women to build, keep, and create peace in the region fraught with so much conflict and misunderstanding. The AWPR held its first informal meeting in Phnom Penh in September 2019 at the sidelines of the Regional Symposium on Implementing Women, Peace, and Security (WPS) Agenda held in

Phnom Penh on 22–23 August 2019 and was poised to hold a more formal getting-to-know-you and mapping meeting in Jakarta in March 2020 which was postponed due to the COVID-19 pandemic. Hopefully, in the near future, ASEAN leaders and other officials would be able to employ the expertise of these ASEAN women peace practitioners. Like a mother following the gingerly steps of her baby, I follow the progress of AWPR.

Notes

1. HarperCollins (2019).
2. This prompted the CPR to publish a handbook of ASEAN acronyms and abbreviations in 2017 under my chairmanship.
3. In February 2013, a group of people, calling themselves the Royal Army of Sulu and who are members of the Kiran clan of the Philippines, occupied Lahad Datu, a remote area in Sabah, demanding recognition of their claim as the rightful owner of Sabah. After a brief standoff which has caused anxiety between the Philippines and Malaysia, an attack on the group was staged by Malaysian police resulting in the death of two Malaysian police officers and twelve of the Royal Army and the wounding of several others.
4. See PCA Award, 56–57, paras. 145–48.
5. In 2020 under the chairmanship of Viet Nam, ASEAN embarked on a review of the ASEAN Charter but the focus of the initiative is to monitor and assess the implementation of its provisions and not to amend its text.
6. Peace Research Institute Oslo. (2015), Nordic Women Mediators, https://www.prio.org/Projects/Project/?x=1725.
7. AIPR Workshop on Strengthening Women's Participation in Peace Processes and Conflict Resolution, 18–19 March 2015.
8. At the time of this writing, all Member States have designated their representatives. The Registry may be accessed through the ASEAN-IPR website.

6

ASEAN CENTRALITY AS A PRINCIPLE OF DIPLOMACY WITH ASEAN'S EXTERNAL PARTNERS

Everywhere I spoke about ASEAN, I have always been asked about its importance, and even its relevance, in the face of its perceived failure to address at least three major issues—the South China Sea, the Northern Rakhine (Rohingya) problem and human rights. One of the quickest ways to counter arguments against the charges of the irrelevance of ASEAN is the fact that it has formal partnerships with all the major powers in the world—the United States, China, Russia, Japan and the European Union (EU) and many more are waiting in the queue. This is despite the long and arduous process of applying to become an External Partner. Even the seemingly simple act of signing the Instrument of Accession to the Treaty of Amity and Cooperation (TAC) follows the same long and sometimes cumbersome process that takes several months to complete. If ASEAN were irrelevant, I would say, why would these external parties go through all this? Obviously, the answer lies in their perception that indeed, ASEAN matters and that, of course, they would want to benefit from ASEAN's growing economic and political/security importance as well as push their own agenda into that of ASEAN. The dynamics of how this happens will be the subject of this section, using the autoethnographic framework I described earlier.

ASEAN has not indicated any ranking or category of hierarchy for its external partners but it is generally understood that such a hierarchy exists. Among the Dialogue Partners (DPs), nine are sub-classified as Strategic Dialogue Partners (SDPs) while Canada has also indicated its desire to become one.[1] This de facto categorization is reflected in Table 6.1.

The growing interest by other countries in ASEAN is also reflected in the number of applicants waiting to be accepted as external partners

TABLE 6.1
Matrix of ASEAN's External Partners (as of February 2021)

Dialogue Partners	• Australia • Canada • China • European Union (EU) • India • Japan • Republic of Korea (ROK) • New Zealand • United States • Russia
Sectoral Dialogue Partners	• Pakistan • Norway • Switzerland • Turkey
Development Partners	• Germany • Chile • France • Italy
Regional Organizations	• Gulf Cooperation Council (GCC) • Economic Cooperation Organization (ECO) • Pacific Alliance • Mercado Común del Sur (MERCOSUR) • Community of Latin America and Caribbean States (CELAC) • South Asian Association for Regional Cooperation (SAARC)
International Organization	• United Nations (UN)

of ASEAN. These are: Bangladesh, the UK, Morocco, Fiji (Observer Status), Ecuador, Egypt, and Mongolia.

The TAC issued in 1976 is a fundamental peace treaty that all members, external partners and observers of ASEAN must accede to. Thus, countries and regional organizations desiring to apply for formal relationships with ASEAN regard it as their first step towards their acceptance for any category of external partnership. To date, there are 43 High Contracting Parties (HCPs) to the TAC, comprising 10 ASEAN Member States (AMS) and 30 non-ASEAN HCPs, including the Permanent Members of the United Nations Security Council and one regional organization, the EU. The recent accessions are Bahrain (2019), Germany (17 August 2020), and Colombia, Cuba, and South Africa (10 November 2020).

The following applications have received concurrence from AMS and accessions are to be signed at the sidelines of a major ASEAN meeting: the United Arab Emirates, Qatar, Kingdom of the Netherlands, the Hellenic Republic. The following applications are being considered: Belarus, Kingdom of Denmark and Venezuela.

The deliberations on the desirability of establishing these partnerships are heavily debated in the Committee of Permanent Representatives (CPR). Among the criteria for acceptance, aside from their readiness and ability to conduct substantive relations is the establishment of diplomatic relations with all Member States. Thus, when Israel, informally indicated its desire to be accepted as a DP of ASEAN in 2015 which the Philippines was inclined to support because of the potential of this country to contribute to the economic development of ASEAN, the request was not considered because at least three Member States do not have diplomatic relations with her. On the other hand, when Turkey started their campaign for a sectoral dialogue partnership, you can imagine which countries were favourably endorsing them during these debates.

The ten DPs—Australia, Canada, China, the EU, India, Japan, Korea, New Zealand, Russia and the United States—have annual meetings with ASEAN in its different mechanisms, depending on the level of representation of all participants. Thus, there is an ASEAN-US Senior Officials' Meeting (SOM), ASEAN-China Ministerial Meeting, and so forth. It will be noted that when referring to these bilateral meetings, the name of ASEAN appears first, for example, ASEAN-Japan, while the DP would refer to them as Japan-ASEAN meetings in their own documents and when they speak.

In Jakarta, the CPR has a formal mechanism in conducting relations with external partners. With full DPs, they are called Joint Cooperation Committees (JCCs) while those with SDPs are called Joint Sectoral Cooperation Committees (JSCCs). ASEAN's relations with these countries are shepherded by a designated ASEAN member called Country Coordinator. The ASEAN Secretariat acts as the Coordinator for SDPs and other partners. In addition, some DPs also participate in other Jakarta-based mechanisms, such as the ASEAN Plus Three (APT) and the East Asia Summit (EAS). Of the ten, only Canada and the EU are not members of the EAS, although both of them have indicated their desire to join this premier strategic body. To this date, the decision to include the two to the EAS has yet to be resolved on account of several reasons, not the least of which is the possible complication of the EAS agenda which the EU would inexorably bring with them if they are allowed membership.

The presence of dedicated DP Ambassadors in Jakarta provides for intimate, focused discussions of issues of importance to both sides. Norway is the only SDP which has sent a dedicated Ambassador. The officials of Norway intimated to me that although they are not yet a full DP, they will act and cooperate like one. Having been Ambassador to Norway once, I know that Norway is fully qualified to be a DP of ASEAN.

The Sectoral Dialogue type of relationship differs from full Dialogue Partnership in that they do not have bilateral SOM, Ministerial or Leaders'-Level meetings with ASEAN but they do have annual meetings with the CPR in Jakarta. Meetings of the CPR are also held with Ambassadors representing the Economic Cooperation Organization (ECO) composed of Afghanistan, Azerbaijan, Iran, Kazakhstan, Kyrgyzstan, Pakistan, Tajikistan, Turkey, Turkmenistan and Uzbekistan, the Gulf Cooperation Council (GCC) composed of Saudi Arabia, Kuwait, Qatar, UAE, Bahrain and Oman, the Pacific Alliance (PA) composed of Brazil, Argentina, Uruguay and Paraguay, and the Mercosur made up of Brazil, Uruguay, Paraguay and Venezuela.

ASEAN Centrality in the CPR Interface with High Level Officials of External Partners

Apart from the regular meetings, officials outside the CPR who wish to interface with it need to seek the approval of the latter, depending on the necessity of having the meeting, the substance of the agenda and the nature of the persons/groups requesting for the interface. ASEAN Centrality is exercised when the CPR could decide on the agenda, format and objectives of the meeting. As a rule, the CPR welcomes interactions with officials of ASEAN's external partners, except in one case when it was detrimental to ASEAN's interest to do so.

The CPR met Australian Prime Minister Malcolm Turnbull and Foreign Minister Julie Bishop in May 2017, with Vice President Michael Pence in April 2017, Chinese Vice Minister of Commerce Qian Keming in September 2017, Moroccan Secretary of State for Foreign Affairs and International Cooperation Mounia Boucetta in February 2018, Norwegian Deputy Minister for Foreign Affairs Laila Boukhari in January 2017, with Chinese Vice Premier Liu Yandong in November 2017, and with Chinese State Councilor and Foreign Minister Wang Yi and Alibaba Founder Jack Ma in September 2018. The CPR also holds annual interface meetings with the UN usually represented by Assistant Secretary General for Political Affairs Mr Miroslav Jenča and other UN officials.

External parties wishing to be granted formal status with ASEAN must follow an established process, starting with the endorsement of the CPR and the ASEAN Secretariat. Thus, during my tenure as Chair, the CPR also met with Deputy Undersecretary of the Ministry of Foreign Affairs of the Republic of Turkey Ümit Yardim and Moroccan Secretary of State for Foreign Affairs and International Cooperation Mounia Boucetta who sought meetings with the former in order to make presentations of their country's applications to become a SDP of ASEAN. The CPR acted favourably on their requests and made the appropriate recommendation to the Ministers of ASEAN via the SOM.

The CPR also visited some external partners to strengthen ASEAN's external relations. They visited India 1–7 July 2018 as part of the ASEAN@50 and ASEAN-India 25th Anniversary and to prepare for the New Delhi Summit in January the following year. They met with many Indian officials, including Secretary of State EAST Preeti Saran who proposed the conclusion of a number of documents for the Delhi Summit. Here are the CPR's responses to Secretary of State EAST Saran:

1. New Delhi Declaration to be issued by the leaders of India and ASEAN. The CPR agreed to negotiate this in Jakarta with the Ambassador of India to ASEAN Suresh Reddy;
2. Joint Statement on Counter-Terrorism which the CPR cautioned, should be coordinated and negotiated with the appropriate ASEAN body—the Senior Officials Meeting on Transnational Crime (SOMTC);
3. Joint Statement on Biodiversity—this has been one issue identified to be a shared interest of both sides;
4. Agreement on Maritime Cooperation—The CPR politely declined to issue a separate Joint Statement on this and proposed instead that the issue of maritime cooperation, as well as air and sea connectivity, be included inside the Delhi Declaration, citing lack of material time to negotiate such a huge document. I wonder if the real reason was the fact that ASEAN considered issues like the South China Sea complicated enough among the current major players and adding one more player into the equation would further add other bones of contention into the soup; and
5. Memorandum of Understanding (MOU) on ASEAN-India Centre—This matter has presented a rather annoying albeit insignificant irritant amidst the robust relations between the two sides. ASEAN had complained that the Centre had been using the name of ASEAN without the permission of ASEAN and operating outside the parameters and participation of ASEAN. Its Executive Director had been issuing statements and conducting activities outside the purview of ASEAN, unlike other centres that carried the name of ASEAN, such as the ASEAN-China Centre, the ASEAN-Korea Centre, the ASEAN-Japan Centre and the ASEAN-Russia Centre whose projects and activities are agreed upon by both ASEAN and their respective DP. The CPR had insisted that the so-called "ASEAN-India Centre" should also come under the purview of ASEAN. Thus, after long discussions

and negotiations, an agreement in principle was forged to sign an ASEAN-India MOU on the establishment of the Centre. However, citing internal administrative complications, India never got around to fulfilling its part of the deal and the MOU remains pending to this day. The CPR told their Indian counterparts that minus the MOU, the so-called ASEAN-India Centre does not have the legal standing to bear the name ASEAN.

The CPR visited Beijing, Nanning and Hangzhou in 2017. They met with various Chinese officials, as well as State Councillor and Foreign Minister Wang Yi (see Figure 6.1). A number of issues were discussed considering the many facets of the strategic partnership between ASEAN and China. Speaking on behalf of ASEAN, I explained to Minister Wang, among other issues, the importance of respecting ASEAN Centrality in view of the emergence of various concepts that seek to define the current regional architecture. I expressed appreciation for the many different areas of cooperation between ASEAN and China and enjoined China's support in strengthening ASEAN-led mechanisms,

FIGURE 6.1
CPR Meeting with Foreign Minister Wang Yi

including the EAS, ARF and APT. I said that any discussion of a regional security architecture would have to take into account ASEAN Centrality as a foundation.

Minister Wang Yi assured the CPR that China has always regarded ASEAN in high esteem. "China will continue to place ASEAN in an important position of China's diplomatic situation and the priority direction of neighboring diplomacy", Wang said. He called on ASEAN and China to work together and firmly uphold multilateral rules, common interests and regional security, and emphasized that ASEAN Centrality should be upheld to maintain the stability of the East Asia region, and major countries' rivalry should not be allowed to undermine ASEAN Centrality. He emphasized that ASEAN and China should work together to uphold multilateralism and maintain a rules-based international order. He said that if rules are no longer upheld and the international system is no longer respected, the small- and medium-sized countries would be the victims. Therefore, China needs to work with AMS and other countries to further promote multilateralism, international rules, and free trade regime with the World Trade Organization as a basis, he maintained. He also said that ASEAN and China should uphold their common interests in maintaining peace and stability in the region. He underscored that China could not accept the geostrategic competitions played by some major countries from outside the region, which is a common theme of China when addressing the issue of the South China Sea. I responded that ASEAN considered China a major and important partner and that the peaceful rise of China was an important ingredient in maintaining peace and stability in the region. I emphasized our commitment to the peaceful resolution of our differences based on international law, particularly the 1982 UNCLOS. I repeated to him ASEAN's desire for peace and stability in the South China Sea and the need to substantiate our commitment to this principle with the facts on the ground.

During this visit, the CPR also met with Alibaba Founder Jack Ma who gave practical advice on how technology can be used to allow ASEAN to acquire the most benefit of the fourth industrial revolution. My friend, Ambassador Min Lwin, remarked that in the past, old people taught their juniors. Here we were, most of us in our senior years, being given a lecture by young executives, some in their late twenties, on the technical nuances of cloud computing, and the use of digital technology in Micro, Small and Medium Enterprises (MSMEs). Although not a government official, Jack Ma was an important person to interact with in relation to the economic development of ASEAN. I consider him a modern-day Confucius: he was a practical philosopher. He patiently listened to everyone as though he would learn immensely from our discourse even when I personally thought what some of us said to him did not make sense or were inane.

The CPR visited Sydney and Canberra, Australia, from 27 May to 3 June 2017, at the invitation of the Australian Department of Foreign Affairs and Trade (DFAT), as part of preparations for the ASEAN-Australia Special Summit from 17 to 18 March 2018 in Sydney. Australia also used the visit as an opportunity to underline its continued commitment to ASEAN, and call on both sides to intensify engagement in response to global and regional developments. During the CPR's call on Prime Minister Turnbull, ASEAN Centrality was again a prominent topic. The Prime Minister said that the forthcoming ASEAN-Australia Summit would reinforce ASEAN Centrality in the regional architecture since ASEAN is Australia's strong partner in upholding the rule of law and both sides promote peace and stability in a rules-based order. Australia espouses an Indo-Pacific concept in its foreign policy and has repeatedly vowed its commitment to uphold ASEAN Centrality in the changing political and security architecture. The CPR also met with Foreign Minister Bishop who repeated the same message. As Chair of the group, I responded that Australia is a strong partner of ASEAN and our cooperation in all the three pillars should be continued. I encouraged Australia to support ASEAN's work on women economic empowerment, migrant workers, technical and vocational education and implement the reverse Colombo Plan in all the Member States.

CPR Refusal to Meet with Unfriendly Partners

The CPR has also made known its displeasure to other parties by refusing to meet with them if they felt that they had undermined ASEAN or if they believed that the meeting would not contribute to ASEAN's progress. For example, a certain SDP of ASEAN has been requesting to convene the annual meeting they had enjoyed with the CPR in past years but which had deliberately not been convened for some time. The Ambassador of this country came to pay me a private visit to discuss their country's predicament. They also formalized the said request in letters to the Deputy Secretary General of ASEAN (Coordinator for Sectoral Dialogue relations). Because it was a private visit, I was able to tell them frankly why the CPR had opted to delay the holding of the meeting since late 2016 in large part because of their country's actions at the Non-Aligned Movement (NAM) Summit in Venezuela in September 2016, which ASEAN believed had maligned the organization and undermined their efforts at unity in the face of difficult challenges. They said they were unaware of their colleague's actions at the NAM and that their country had no intention to malign ASEAN. ASEAN has not granted the request to this day.

Invitations for the CPR to undertake visits in capitals of some partners in Europe were also not entertained because the CPR felt that those visits would not be beneficial to ASEAN. This is either due to the unacceptable agenda and motives of the inviting party, which normally would focus on human rights issues, or that they might be pressured to make commitments which ASEAN is not ready to undertake.

ASEAN Centrality in the Relations of the ASEAN Connectivity Coordinating Committee (ACCC) with External Partners

Another example of how ACCC achieved centrality in the area of ASEAN Connectivity was its relations with its DPs. The ACCC also conducted various engagements with ASEAN's external partners, including the EU, Japan, China, etc. on how they can support the implementation of the Master Plan on ASEAN Connectivity (MPAC) 2025.

On 25 July 2017, the ACCC met with Japan, whose delegation was led by their Ambassador. The topic was how Japan could support ASEAN Connectivity. Japan spoke of its own Free and Open Indo-Pacific Strategy (FOIPS) and this is the fulcrum through which Japan was seeking to enhance connectivity within ASEAN and with neighbouring regions. Japan underscored that it is not only physical infrastructure which should be improved but also institutional mechanisms or systems such as customs procedures and flows of peoples. The Mekong-Japan Connectivity Initiative is one of Japan's initiatives contributing to strengthen "vibrant connectivity" in the region through supporting infrastructure, enhancing institutional systems and human resource development. Japan spoke of their Expanded Partnership for Quality Infrastructure which is their initiative to provide infrastructure financing across the world amounting to approximately US$200 billion in the next five years. It also aims to further improve measures for promotion of quality infrastructure investment by improving transparency, streamlining duration between feasibility studies and commencement of construction work, accelerating official development assistance (ODA) loans, and encouraging investment and financing of private companies and public-private partnerships (PPP) through support of Japan International Cooperation Agency (JICA), Nippon Export and Investment Insurance (NEXI), Japan Overseas Infrastructure Investment Corporation (JOIN) and the Japan Bank for International Cooperation (JBIC).

However, ASEAN was informed by the Japanese delegation that the Expanded Partnerships for Quality Infrastructure was not a new financing scheme but a concept emphasizing quality infrastructure (including size of financing and cost effectiveness) following its experience since JICA began its economic cooperation programmes with countries around the world in the 1950s. Funds and procedures to conduct feasibility studies need to be streamlined and made transparent. Under the Expanded Partnerships for Quality Infrastructure, more Japanese agencies are involved. Each agency has its own standards and procedures. In supporting the MPAC 2025, it is important that sectoral experts from Japan interact with the sectoral experts from the respective relevant ASEAN sectoral bodies/lead implementing bodies. It has been applied on a bilateral basis between Japan and individual AMS.

I led the discussion of the MPAC 2025 with the Japanese delegation while my colleagues also spoke on how Japan could help implement it. At the end of the meeting, it was agreed that ASEAN's challenge was how to find synergies between its regional agenda found in the MPAC, in addition to the bilateral projects it has with Japan under the Japanese infrastructure programmes mentioned above. It was important that the

MPAC 2025 not be overshadowed but instead become embedded or connected to the bilateral initiatives.²

The ACCC also met with representatives of China on how they can support MPAC 2025. At the MPAC 2025 Forum on Initiatives and Project Concepts held in Alabang, Mr Yang Weiqun, Deputy Director General of the Asian Affairs Department of the Ministry of Commerce of China spoke on the areas (or 5 "tongs" in Chinese) of President Xi Jinping's Belt and Road Initiative (BRI), namely, policy coordination, connectivity of infrastructure, unimpeded trade, financial integration and closer people to people ties which are common priorities with the MPAC 2025. He said that China was willing to mobilize potential resources and tap into other existing sources such as the Silk Road Fund established in 2014 with $40 billion contribution from China and the $100 billion worth of loans by the Asian Infrastructure Investment Bank (AIIB). In a subsequent ACCC + China Meeting that I co-chaired with Vice Minister Qian Keming of the Ministry of Commerce of the People's Republic of China, this message was repeated with the latter emphasizing that the five tongs were aligned with the MPAC 2025.

Speaking on behalf of ASEAN, I underscored the role of MPAC 2025 as a catalyst in realizing a resilient, inclusive, people-oriented and people-centred ASEAN Community that is integrated with the global economy. I said that this vision of transforming the region into one of opportunities for our peoples, our business communities can only be realized with the support and cooperation of our external partners, including China. However, I emphasized that external support for MPAC 2025 should follow the strategy, objectives, initiatives and projects embedded in the Master Plan and not the other way around, i.e. that ASEAN follows the BRI.

Another specific instance of ASEAN displaying centrality on the matter of connectivity was when dealing with China's proposal, delivered by the Vice Minister, to negotiate an ASEAN-China Leaders' Statement on Further Deepening the ASEAN-China Cooperation on Infrastructure Connectivity, with the BRI at the core of its strategy. The proposal was originally raised at the Senior Economic Officials' Meeting (SEOM) which referred the matter to the ACCC as a cross-cutting issue. However, ACCC believed that they did not have the mandate nor the competence to negotiate the document in Jakarta. I politely delivered this message to the Minister of Commerce Gao Yan who wrote to me earlier to inquire about the ACCC's reply to Vice Minister Qian's proposal. In the end, the proposed ASEAN-China Statement was not negotiated with the ACCC but was later on issued using another method prescribed by ASEAN, i.e., for the document to be negotiated between the Ministry of Commerce (MofCom) of China and the ASEAN SEOM.

I also organized an interface with all other partners of ASEAN at an ACCC Meeting held in July 2017 in Manila with all of ASEAN's external partners, who had, like China, wanted to connect MPAC 2025 to their respective infrastructure agenda and not the other way around. I and my colleagues in the ACCC and the ASEAN Secretariat told them about ASEAN's desire to come up with a rolling list of potential ASEAN infrastructure projects, based on what AMS need, and their viability and marketability, as well as establish a platform to measure sustainable infrastructure and improve existing ones.

ASEAN Centrality in the EAS Ambassadors' Meeting in Jakarta (EAMJ)

The EAS Ambassadors' Meeting in Jakarta (EAMJ) is seated according to ASEAN's protocol with the CPR members sitting around the Plus 8 who are arranged in alphabetical order sandwiched by the AMS. There is no coordinator among the Non-ASEAN Participating Countries (PCs) of the EAMJ and the Chair has to manage the meeting as each Ambassador speaks as an individual representative of their country. The Chair of the EAMJ is always from ASEAN and there is no Co-Chair, which gives ASEAN an advantage because time management, agenda setting, tone and language, number and level of participation, etc., are under the direction and discretion of ASEAN. Speaking slots are by inscription, i.e., those desiring to speak should raise their flags or tap on an electronic recording system to indicate the order of speaking.

The EAS is an ASEAN-led mechanism which has become the most important strategic forum in the Asia-Pacific region as it involves the ten AMS plus major powers including the United States, Japan, China, Russia, Australia, India, the Republic of Korea and New Zealand. Although

FIGURE 6.2
Physical Format of the EAMJ

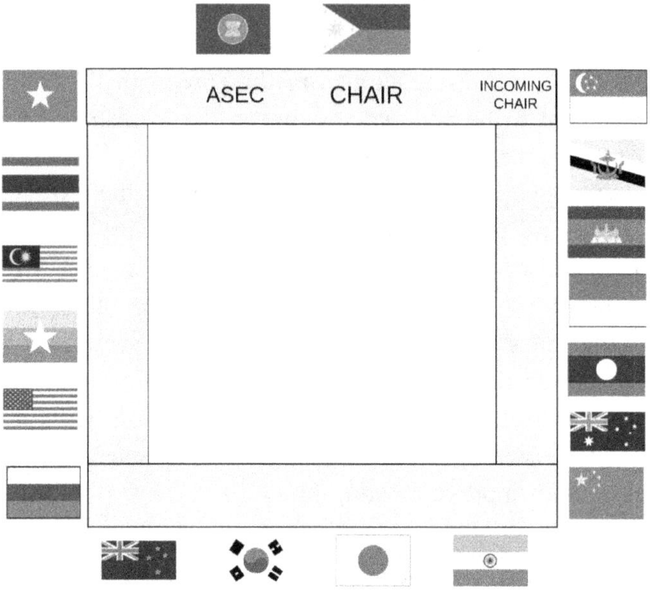

its six priority areas did not include political or security matters before the Philippine chairmanship, it has become the forum where important strategic issues like the South China Sea and the Korean Peninsula issues are discussed by the Leaders and Ministers of the ASEAN Plus 8 PCs, as they are known in ASEAN parlance. It has a Summit-level platform, as well as Ministerial and Senior Officials meetings. However, before 2017, the EAS platform in Jakarta had not yet been established formally, meaning its terms of reference and mandate have not been formally recognized. Its six priority areas (later to become seven during the Philippine chairmanship with the inclusion of maritime security and cooperation): environment and energy, education, finance, global health issues and pandemic diseases, natural disaster management, and ASEAN Connectivity.

2017 would see the transformation of the Jakarta arm of the EAS (later to be called EAMJ) and its meetings becoming the veritable battlefield of ideas and national interests of the eighteen PCs, most of the time conflicting with each other. The Ambassadors of the EAS are all professional diplomats carefully trained to fight for their individual country's national interests but were also aware of the benefits of cooperating with each other in multilateral settings. It was, therefore, with great trepidation when I assumed chairmanship of this body in January 2017. Already, forebodings of controversial debates loomed on the horizon. The year before, under the chairmanship of Laos, a number of vital issues remained unresolved because of the obstacles hurled in the way by the major powers in the meetings. I vowed to resolve these issues during my chairmanship in a manner that ASEAN approved. There was also talk in the beginning of the year that more negotiations would be in the pipeline as non-ASEAN PCs had intended to submit a number of proposals for Leaders' Statements. There was also the task of negotiating a new five-year Plan of Action, a formidable task in addition to the many Leaders' Declarations. All this amidst the lack of clarity in the negotiation process and the seemingly irreconcilable differences among the eighteen PCs. ASEAN had to show leadership to resolve these issues. ASEAN's ability to ward off attempts by major powers to convert the EAS into their diplomatic arena is a graphic test of ASEAN Centrality.

I will have to use pseudonyms so as not to jeopardize relations among the PCs but will make the distinction between AMS and non-AMS PCs to show how ASEAN managed its differences of positions vis-a-vis the Non-ASEAN partners in the EAS, and thereby maintained its centrality in the midst of conflicting interests presented by each delegation during the negotiations and interaction among each other. I would like to cite in this section five incidents/issues when this was demonstrated. These are:

1. Negotiations on the Terms of Reference of the EAS Ambassadors in Jakarta
2. Procedures in the Negotiations of Documents
3. Negotiations on the 2017 EAS Leaders' Statements
    3.1. EAS Leaders' Statement on Chemical Weapons
    3.2. EAS Leaders' Statement on Anti-Money Laundering and Countering the Financing of Terrorism
    3.3. EAS Leaders' Statement on Cooperation in Poverty Alleviation

3.4. EAS Leaders' Statement on Countering the Ideological Challenge of Terrorism and Terrorist Narratives and Propaganda

4. Negotiations on the EAS Manila Plan of Action 2018–2022

ASEAN Leadership in Negotiating the Four EAS Statements

It was literally and figuratively the eleventh hour as we Ambassadors and working group diplomats of the eighteen PCs were confined in a meeting room at the Sofitel Plaza Manila, mired in deep deadlock close to midnight (12 November) before all four documents we were negotiating were going to be adopted by the Leaders (Heads of Governments/Heads of State) of ASEAN and those of the eight PCs. (It was a rare occasion when then President Trump attended an ASEAN Summit). It was a make-or-break situation for ASEAN Centrality and for me personally. Failure to issue the statements meant a loss of face for the host; that ASEAN could not even bring all PCs to a consensus in a so-called ASEAN-led forum. This would be tantamount to a failure of ASEAN Centrality. The Leaders' Statements are tools intended to set norms for keeping the peace and security of the region from traditional and non-traditional threats and without them, the Leaders of the eighteen PCs would be left with nothing but a Chairman's Statement of the proceedings with no tangible accomplishments. Senior officials were not optimistic that we could finalize the negotiations; in fact, it was not in the talking points of the Chair of the EAS Summit that the aforementioned documents would be adopted and issued.

Months before this fateful night, we had held numerous negotiating sessions to meld together the various interests, suggestions and paragraphs or insertions of the eighteen PCs. ASEAN and the other parties had taken a hardline position as a standard negotiating stance; it seemed like no one was going to give in and the nearer we approached the deadline, the harder the country positions had become, which is expected in any negotiation. But I also sensed that all eighteen were eager to finalize the statements. We were all in this together. I recalled one effective technique in negotiations—environmental mapping—which

I proceeded to do by talking to all the interested parties in smaller groups or bilaterally to find out their bottom lines and interests so as to guide me on how to play the mediating role of Chair but at the same time uphold the principle of ASEAN Centrality. I remember sitting in a sunny corner of the Jakarta Raffles Hotel coffee shop where I met secretly with the Ambassadors of EAS countries who had big stakes in the negotiations. I felt like a psychiatrist meeting with her patients one by one to find out what their concerns and anxieties were and how I could manoeuvre the discussions so that the concerns were covered. I also wanted to know their red lines and bottom lines and what compromises they could offer. They came one after another (I instructed my Protocol officer, who was to escort them from the hotel lobby to my corner, to make sure that they do not bump into each other in the intervals). In these intimate one-to-one conversations, I learned about their bottom lines or false bottom lines, where we can compromise, traded QPQs, who sided with whom, etc. They also gave me ideas on how to resolve the impasses.

After months of arguing, bargaining and QPQing, the four documents were cleared except for a few pesky paragraphs which were inserted by non-ASEAN partners and which held the document hostage to one another. The problem paragraphs were from non-ASEAN partners, again a test of ASEAN Centrality. It was all or nothing; we could not release or finalize one document and proceed to the next—we had to clear all of them at the same time. If we released one ahead of the rest, the parties who had inserted the paragraphs or phrases in the other documents would lose their bargaining chip. I jokingly said in the final negotiating meeting that this was like "Gunfight at OK Corral" to which the millennials raised their eyebrows, not being familiar with the old western movie of the same title. But on this historic night, the eve of the EAS Summit, I was optimistic we would finish despite our earlier debacles. At around 11 p.m., I asked my staff to provide food and drinks for all participants and after this repast, all negotiators were in an ebullient mood. We rolled up our sleeves and worked on the following remaining paragraphs which have undergone several permutations in past negotiating sessions. Here is how the paragraphs were eventually resolved employing the principle of ASEAN Centrality in the process.

EAS Leaders' Statement on Chemical Weapons

The three contentious issues left unresolved in this document contained: (i) reference to the mention of the specific chemical substance used in the murder of a DPRK national, Kim Jong Nam who was a half-brother of DPRK Leader Kim Jong-un at the Kuala Lumpur International Airport on 13 February 2017; (ii) the use of the phrase "shared destiny for humankind"; and (iii) the reference to remaining chemical weapons left by a former war enemy in the territory of another.

In the beginning, the ASEAN-agreed text looked like this for the first issue:

> Denounce the chemical weapons incident involving the nerve agent VX against a national of the Democratic People's Republic of Korea (DPRK) in Kuala Lumpur that posed great risk to public safety and security;

However, as mentioned earlier, two AMS back-tracked on their earlier agreement to mention the name of the chemical agent (VX nerve agent) in the attack. This confounded me as the aforementioned AMS did not give any justification to back up their objections, try as I did to extract the reasons. I said that if all AMS had to support their position in consideration of ASEAN Centrality, we should at least know why so that we could defend the position before our non-ASEAN partners. They would not speak. Here was another instance of a face-saving incident. However, I instinctively noticed that the matter was of utmost importance to the national interest of the two AMS and any miscalculation would lead to the detriment of their nationals who had been involved in the assassination. I suspected that specifically mentioning sarin in an ASEAN document might complicate the chance of these nationals from being acquitted from the criminal charges they were facing in relation to this incident. Therefore, we, the whole of ASEAN, had to support them, reason or no reason. ASEAN and two other non-ASEAN PCs moved for the deletion of the entire paragraph, a technique in negotiations to start upping the ante. However, many non-ASEAN PCs could not accept this proposed deletion because in a document issued by the Organization for the Prohibition of Chemical Weapons (OPCW), the name of the nerve agent was already mentioned and the two objecting AMS and their two non-ASEAN PC allies had voted in favour of both issuances in that international body. This was a fact ASEAN could not controvert. To come up with a compromise, we merged the two ideas together without mentioning the name of the nerve agent in our EAS Declaration and quoted instead the relevant provisions of the aforementioned OPCW and UNGA resolutions which mentioned the name of the chemical weapon concerned. The two AMS found this satisfactory. We then offered the compromise to the other non-ASEAN PCs. All eighteen were agreeable to this compromise. The final paragraph in the Statement now reads as follows:

> Note the grave concern expressed by the Executive Council of the Organisation for the Prohibition of Chemical Weapons in its decision EC-84/DEC.8 of 8 March 2017 on the chemical weapon incident according to the statements of the Government of Malaysia;

Another issue of great contention which we had to finalize on that fateful night was the inclusion in all the documents, but particularly in this phrase, "Community of shared future or destiny for mankind", which one non-ASEAN PC had wanted to insert in this and some other EAS documents being negotiated. Now, that would sound like a harmless, even desirable phrase to put in a statement that renounces the use of chemical weapons for the destruction of mankind. But most EAS PCs had objected to the introduction of a phrase that seemed to them an expression of a national slogan or a national concept, rather than reflective of an EAS aspiration. ASEAN's original text in September 2017 was as follows:

> EMPHASIZING the common aspiration to ensure regional and global security and safety, not only for this generation but for generations to come;

But with the proposed addition, it would look like this:

> EMPHASIZING the common aspiration to ensure regional and global security and safety, not only for this generation but for generations to come towards a community of shared destiny for all mankind;

This was non-negotiable for most of the seventeen PCs, particularly those from the non-ASEAN countries. We were in deadlock and no permutation of the shared destiny phrase would be acceptable. Some transpositions offered included "shared vision for all mankind, shared destiny for all humanity", and many other "shared" ideas. Suddenly, a particular Ambassador from Asia, who had been quiet during the meeting, perhaps nodding off for some time, suddenly looked up, raised his flag and asked to be recognized which I quickly did. He said, "Why don't we just adopt the language from the ASEAN Vision 2025—a caring and sharing community?" "'Brilliant!" I exclaimed. "Now, who would not accept ASEAN's caring and sharing community?" I added, and no one did.

Thus, in the final text of the Chemical Weapons statement, the phrase "shared destiny for all mankind" disappeared and the final paragraph was simply put as:

> EMPHASIZING the common aspiration to ensure regional and global security and safety, not only for this generation but for generations to come;

and as a compromise, it appears in Operative Paragraph 11 in the final text of the Poverty Alleviation Statement as suggested by the aforementioned Asian Ambassador as follows:

> REAFFIRMING our recognition that eradicating poverty in all its forms and dimensions, including extreme poverty, is the greatest global challenge and an indispensable requirement for sustainable development with a view to **building a caring and sharing community**;

Still a third contentious issue in the Chemical Weapons statement was the insistence of one non-ASEAN PC to include in Operative Paragraph 4 of the Statement as follows:

> Recall the provision of the CWC that the Abandoning State Party undertakes to destroy all chemical weapons it has abandoned and shall provide all necessary financial, technical, expert, facility as well as other resources, and urge the Abandoning State Party to continue to make the fullest possible effort to complete destruction of chemical weapons

abandoned by Country Y on the territory of Country Z as early as possible; (Proposed by Country Z) from EC-84/2, the Report of the 84th Session of the OPCW Executive Council on March 9, 2017.

Now, the contentious issues here are the mention of specific names of countries and the inclusion of the term, "abandoned by Country Y on the territory of Country Z as early as possible". The major EAS PC objecting to the inclusion of these elements in the paragraph told me that these issues are already being addressed bilaterally and should not be mentioned anymore in an EAS document. Many EAS PCs, including the Philippines, agreed with this position. The latter also told me that this was his country's bottom line. If these elements are mentioned, the objecting PC said that he would not agree with the entire Leaders' Statement on Chemical Weapons, forcing a domino effect whereby all the other Statements would also not be issued, resulting in the collapse of the entire negotiation process. In fact, this paragraph was the motherlode of the hostage-paragraphs as countries started to place stumbling blocks in each other's statements as their bargaining chips in the negotiations. They would release their impossible demands only if they are able to obtain the language that they wanted in the other documents. ASEAN rallied to the call for unity and consensus and finally, after a lot QPQS or horse-trading, the final paragraph minus the offensive element, received consensus. This is how it stands to this day:

> Call on all State Parties to comply with the destruction of their chemical weapons stockpiles, and also express determination that the destruction of all categories of chemical weapons should be completed in the shortest time possible in accordance with the provisions of the Convention and the Verification Annex, and with the full application of the relevant decisions that have been taken;

EAS Leaders' Statement on Anti-Money Laundering and Countering the Financing of Terrorism

There was no major disagreement in the final stage of negotiating this document except for the phrase, once again, on shared destiny which was changed to "shared future for mankind". One EAS PC had originally proposed the paragraph to read as follows:

> EXPRESSING grave concern about the spread of terrorism that threatens global and regional peace and security, which undermines the efforts to **create a community of shared future for mankind.**

We just applied the same formula in finalizing this paragraph, and deleted any reference to the phrase, as mentioned above. The final paragraph now reads:

> EXPRESSING grave concern about the spread of terrorism that threatens global and regional peace and security;

EAS Leaders' Statement on Cooperation in Poverty Alleviation

In this Statement, the remaining contentious paragraph, which was proposed by one non-ASEAN PC, read as follows:

> Encourage governance to promote and strengthen domestic fiscal transparency [including ensuring legislative oversight of budget processes, strengthening the capacity of supreme audit institutions, and ensuring that government budget documents are available, reliable, complete and transparent] to reduce corruption and fraud,

Many AMS and some non-ASEAN PCs objected to the addition of this paragraph which they considered to be an infringement into their national legislative and budgetary procedures and system. Some AMS' budgetary processes did not include legislative participation while in others, the legislative branch of government had the control of the national budgets. Besides, the original ASEAN text did not have this entire paragraph. To resolve the issue, the Chair negotiated some side-bargaining (in exchange for flexibility in some contentious paragraphs in the other Statements), and the resulting final text of the Statement no longer included the above-mentioned proposal, which is, again, a sign of ASEAN Centrality prevailing in discussions to bring together towards a common purpose differing conditions obtained in the participating countries. The nearest paragraph that reflected this original intention is the following final text:

> Promote a whole-of-government approach towards multidimensional poverty eradication through multi-sectoral, multi-stakeholder and community-based approaches that also encourages partnership with civil society organisations and the private sector;

EAS Leaders' Statement on Countering the Ideological Challenge of Terrorism and Terrorist Narratives and Propaganda

The proponent of this Statement was a non-ASEAN PC and the original title they had proposed seemed acceptable enough: *EAS Leaders' Statement on Countering Terrorist Ideologies*. This was later on modified to say: *EAS Leaders' Statement on Countering the Spread of Ideologies Which Encourage Terrorism*, because of the objection of one AMS to the original expression "Terrorist Ideologies". They would not explain the reason for their country's reservation, but I noticed that again, it was an issue of grave concern to their country's people. We, in ASEAN, had understood this AMS's concern and we decided to present this as an ASEAN position. While they had not expressly mentioned it, we could only guess that the reason was the mistaken notion by some people to equate certain religions as espousing terrorist ideologies. I had to sell this idea to the non-ASEAN proponent who balked at first, citing UN Resolutions and other international agreements that used the same terminology. However, I persuaded the proponent to accept ASEAN's reservation to not use the expression "Terrorist Ideology". In return, they wanted to insert a few more phrases to the title to make clear what they meant by terrorist ideology, which we in ASEAN, and eventually the other seven EAS members, allowed. The resulting title is rather a mouthful, but it satisfied all participating countries' interests. The final title of the Statement now reads *EAS Leaders' Statement on Countering Ideological Challenges of Terrorism and Terrorist Narratives and Propaganda*.

Another paragraph which courted controversy was the following:

> Continue to work with the United Nations and other international and regional institutions, including the United Nations Office of Counter-Terrorism, Southeast Asia Regional Centre for Counter-Terrorism (SEARRCT), Jakarta Centre for Law Enforcement Cooperation (JCLEC), Global Movement for Moderates Foundation (GMMF), International Law Enforcement Academy (ILEA) and, when appropriate, other relevant centres in ASEAN and other regions to continuously develop strategies, techniques and tactics to prevent and counter terrorism and terrorism-related threats.

The two unacceptable issues in this paragraph were the mention of the Global Movement for Moderates Foundation (GMMF) and the inclusion in the last part of the paragraph of the phrase "to prevent terrorism-related threats". Some non-ASEAN PCs had objected to the mention of the GMMF because at that time, there were allegations of financial impropriety on the part of the said Foundation[3] and although the concept of moderation was an acceptable, if not desirable, concept to all (in fact, in 2015 there was a Langkawi Declaration on the Global Movement of Moderates (GMM) which outlines measures to help promote moderation and curb extremism throughout the region), mentioning in the document the name of a center which was under a cloud of suspicion was deemed inappropriate. AMS agreed to delete the name of the Foundation but in return had asked the body to also not mention the names of the other counter-terrorism institutions, such as the UN-CTO, SEARCCT, etc. This deal was made because at that time, the allegations were still just unproven whispers and we had to be careful. The final text reads as follows:

> Continue to work with the United Nations and other international and regional institutions and, where appropriate, other relevant centres in ASEAN and other regions to continuously develop strategies, techniques and tactics to counter terrorism and related threats.

There was also objection by most PCs to the last part of the paragraph—prevent and counter terrorism—which was proposed by another non-ASEAN PC. This phrase was also not included because of the fear by some EAS PCs, including all AMS, that it could be used by some countries to justify the curtailment of individual freedoms of their citizens in the name of preventing terrorism.

Negotiations on the Manila Plan of Action on EAS Cooperation with focus on the Regional Security Architecture (RSA)

Another example where ASEAN proved its assertion for centrality was in the negotiation on the successor Plan of Action to the Phnom Penh Declaration on the EAS Development Initiative which was set to expire at the end of December 2017. I had deliberately postponed negotiation of this document till after the ASEAN Summit so as not to have it also held hostage to the deadlock in negotiations of the other four EAS Leaders' Statements discussed earlier.

Three issues in the negotiations of this document are worthy of mention in the discussion of ASEAN Centrality: (i) whether or not to negotiate a new Plan of Action or simply extend the current one which is tied to the issue of the inclusion of maritime security and cooperation as an additional priority area of cooperation; (ii) the title of the document; and (iii) the treatment of the phrase "Regional Security Architecture".

Extended Plan of Action (POA) or a Negotiated New POA and Inclusion of Maritime Cooperation as an EAS Priority Area of Cooperation

The first issue concerning the Manila Plan of Action (POA) was whether to have a new Plan or simply extend the current one. Some non-ASEAN PCs had proposed the latter while many would have none of this proposal. The obvious motivation for an extended POA, instead of working on a new one, was the elimination of the possibility to add additional elements into it. Some AMS, especially the Philippines, had earlier proposed the inclusion of maritime security and cooperation as a new focus area of cooperation, in addition to the existing ones, namely Environment and Energy Cooperation, Education Cooperation, Finance Cooperation, Cooperation on Global Health issues and Pandemic Diseases, Cooperation on ASEAN Connectivity, Trade and Economic Cooperation and Food Security Cooperation. In the beginning, it was also difficult to gain consensus from AMS to support the inclusion of maritime cooperation. I found this contradictory because in recent years, the EAS has become the leading strategic forum to discuss maritime issues like the South China Sea, marine plastic debris and maritime piracy. After painstakingly gaining their agreement, the Philippines had succeeded in gaining support for its inclusion even among the non-ASEAN PCs, as no viable arguments could be presented against it. The only reason for opposing the negotiation of a new POA and for extending the POA had disappeared. During the first meeting of the EAMJ on 12 April 2017, I made the following points in my intervention to finally settle the issue:

- The current POA was already extended before. Another extension will not be in the interest of strengthening our existing cooperation and exploring new areas of partnership in accordance with the Leaders' decisions and proposals.
- The current POA only covers areas up to the 2012 Phnom Penh Declaration on the EAS Development Initiative.
- The new POA will build upon the original POA and include new areas of cooperation in accordance with the Leaders' decisions.
- The Kuala Lumpur Declaration on the 10th Anniversary of the EAS gave us the mandate to draft a new POA because it clearly called to "undertake a periodic review of areas of cooperation, reflecting current priorities, challenges and interests". Cognisant that maritime cooperation has increasingly featured in East Asia Summit discussions, its inclusion as a priority area of cooperation merits further consideration.

Needless to say, ASEAN's insistence to negotiate a new POA prevailed, as this was completed and ratified three days before 2017 ended.

ASEAN Resolution on the Title of the EAS Plan of Action

Resolution of this issue was not very complicated as the question involved only AMS. The title of the preceding Plan of Action was Phnom Penh Declaration on the EAS Development Initiative, as it has been the practice to name important documents after the cities hosting the event that launched them. Because the document was going to be negotiated and finalized in Manila under the Chairmanship of the Philippines, I had thought it appropriate to call it Manila Plan of Action on EAS Cooperation. However, some AMS had deemed it necessary to somehow reflect elements of the original title. I simply proposed a compromise with my fellow ASEAN Ambassador and the issue was resolved quickly. Thus, the compromised title became: Manila Plan of Action to Implement the Phnom Penh Declaration on the EAS Development Initiative (2018–2022).

The second issue concerned the EAS Workshop on Regional Security Architecture (RSA), which was not a regular mechanism of the EAS but was held as an EAS event under the voluntary initiative of any EAS PC. The previous workshop hosts had been Russia, Australia, Thailand, Brunei Darussalam, and Indonesia. Most EAS PCs considered it no longer viable nor useful to continue the series of workshops in the format that it had taken previously which was to invite a large number of participants from all eighteen PCs. They believed that holding such annual workshops did not yield any practical nor concrete results. They had wanted to put a stop to it. However, some insisted that the discussions continue, perhaps seeing value in being included in the equation of the regional security architecture of the Asia-Pacific region which hosts two of the hottest hotspots in the world. The last workshop held in May 2017 in Bangkok proposed a compromise solution which was endorsed by all—to pass the ball to the EAMJ, which had, anyway the mandate to "exchange information on regional development cooperation initiatives and security policies and initiatives". Now, that Bangkok workshop did not specify how the EAMJ would include in its agenda discussion on the RSA, but only specified that capital-based officials may attend it. Many EAS PCs believed that it can include RSA only once in its agenda and that should comply with the instruction, since policy discussions on RSA belonged to the Senior Officials, the Ministers and the Leaders of ASEAN. The main proponents of the RSA forum believed otherwise—that the instructions implied that RSA would become a mainstay or regular item agenda of every EAMJ, the complication is compounded by the objection of some EAS PCs that the EAMJ was not a policy forum but should act only in compliance with instructions from the EAS SOM and perform tasks such as monitoring the decisions of higher ASEAN officials. The insistence of some EAS PCs to obligate officials coming from capitals to attend the EAMJ also presented complications for some because this would entail additional expenses and manpower and argued that Jakarta-based people are deemed sufficient to comprise an EAMJ.

However, a particular non-ASEAN PC thought otherwise, and so had insisted that the EAMJ include "regional security" architecture as a regular feature in the agenda and more than that, to hold workshop-like sessions as a side event to every EAMJ session, with experts and officials based in capitals attending. This PC had taken on a hardline position on this matter as it was under the strict instructions of his capital. He had wanted the phrase to appear as an Operative Paragraph of the document, which would enjoin all parties to implement practical measures to operationalize it. Other non-ASEAN PCs had wanted to remove it altogether, citing that it did not deserve mention in a five-year Plan of Action. ASEAN, caught in-between the opposing sides of this debate posed by the non-ASEAN participants of the EAS, had to offer a compromise solution—mention it as a Preambular Paragraph and not as an Operative Paragraph. This way, RSA remains as a live issue in the EAS, but is not under any obligation to operationalize it or hold actual activities to operationalize it, as would be the case if it were to appear as an Operative Paragraph. The EAMJ accepted ASEAN's solution. Thus, it now appears in the final text as a Preambular Paragraph of the Manila Plan of Action, which reads:

> Given that the EAS is an integral component of the evolving regional architecture with ASEAN a driving force, the EAS will continue these discussions among EAS Ambassadors in Jakarta with optional participation of similarly-ranked officials from capitals as noted in the 12th EAS Chairman's Statement.

However, to fulfill the meaning of the Bangkok EAS RSA Workshop, I led the conduct of an EAMJ activity, a mini brainstorming session, in which EAS members presented their respective Indo-Pacific concepts, strategies or ideas. The United States, Japan, Australia, India and Indonesia presented their respective countries' understanding and strategy in the Indo-Pacific region.

ASEAN Says No to the Continued Delay in Negotiating the EAS Terms of Reference (TOR)

Another contentious issue which had placed ASEAN in the middle of bickering among non-ASEAN PCs was on the Terms of Reference (TOR) of the EAMJ. Two Non-ASEAN EAS PCs had caused undue delay in negotiating this TOR, which the body had deemed necessary in discharging its functions and mandate. For over eight months in 2016, the CPR discussed with the eight other non-ASEAN PCs the proposed TOR of the grouping. The CPR had anticipated that more and more, the body would be tasked to perform important functions by the Leaders, Ministers and Senior Officials, including the negotiation of Leaders' Statements and Declarations. Without a TOR and with such a motley group of varying, sometimes mutually exclusive interests and positions, such tasks would be impossible to undertake. That would mean undermining the centrality of this ASEAN-led mechanism. However, try as it did, the Laos chairmanship failed to finalize this document, due to the objections of two non-ASEAN PCs to formalize the mandate of the EAMJ. I did not want this undue delay to hijack my chairmanship of the group. The proposed TOR was bogged down by a number of issues, not the least among them was the scope of work to be covered by the body. Two non-ASEAN Ambassadors questioned the mandate and ability of the ASEAN Permanent Representatives and Ambassadors of the non-ASEAN EAS to negotiate documents in Jakarta and insisted that such negotiations should take place in the capital of the proponent country, as was the practice in the past. For me and other AMS, this would give undue advantage to the proponent country, usually a non-ASEAN PC, in assuming control and primacy in the negotiations process. The two objecting non-ASEAN Ambassadors also claimed that only the home-based leaders such as the Senior Officials, Ministers and Leaders had the authority to make important decisions on documents being negotiated and important issues being resolved. I remember a heated discussion between one non-ASEAN PC with an ASEAN Ambassador who argued that all of us were Ambassadors Extraordinary and Plenipotentiary, sent to represent our respective countries to ASEAN, and of course, had the mandate to negotiate such documents. This type of debate went on and on for months in 2016. I did not want this issue to be a stumbling block in our anticipated tasks waiting ahead of us during my term in 2017. Finally, at an EAS Retreat meeting held in Surakarta, Indonesia in February 2017, I resolved to put an end to this impasse. ASEAN Centrality cannot be hijacked by this issue.

At an earlier first meeting of the CPR on 18 January, which I chaired, I introduced to my ASEAN colleagues my proposal to no longer pursue negotiating the TOR as we had wasted enough time discussing it. Instead, I proposed that we make an announcement to the other non-ASEAN PCs that even without a formalized TOR, this mechanism in Jakarta will continue to function because of the mandate given to us by the EAS Leaders. I cited the following provisions in previous Leaders' Declarations, which I maintained, were enough basis for the EAS Ambassadors to perform their tasks in Jakarta. These are:

1. In the 11th EAS Chairman's Statement issued in November 2016 in Vientiane, the Leaders said that "we noted with appreciation that the Committee of Permanent Representatives to ASEAN and Ambassadors of non-ASEAN EAS participating countries in Jakarta have convened two meetings since April 2016 and welcomed the establishment of the EAS Unit within the ASEAN Secretariat."
2. In the Kuala Lumpur Declaration on the 10th EAS Anniversary in 2015, the EAS Leaders said that they will undertake initiatives to strengthen the EAS, including, among others, to "establish regular engagement between the Committee of Permanent Representatives to ASEAN and the non-ASEAN Ambassadors of East Asia Summit participating countries in Jakarta to discuss implementation of Leaders' decisions as well as exchange information on regional development cooperation initiatives and security policies and initiatives".

In addition, I cited the fact that the EAMJ has already established the precedence of meeting formally to negotiate outcome documents such as Leaders' Declarations and Statements for submission to the EAS SOM and subsequently to the Ministers and Leaders of EAS. I also proposed that henceforth, the name of this mechanism will be: EAS Ambassadors' Meeting in Jakarta (EAMJ).

My colleagues agreed with my strategy. Moreover, in order to legitimize the CPR decision, I submitted it to the ASEAN SOM, which agreed with the CPR. To prepare for the acceptance of this proposal by the entire membership of the EAMJ, I spoke bilaterally with like-minded non-ASEAN PCs to support the ASEAN position.

Thus, on 12 April at the first EAS Meeting, I made the following intervention:

> In accordance with the mandate given to us by the EAS Leaders, we have the responsibility to further strengthen our engagement in Jakarta and make it an important platform to monitor and even implement some of their key initiatives. We are at the nascent stage of evolving this responsibility and this Chair commits to do its utmost in fulfilling the mandate entrusted to us by our Leaders.

Because time is of the essence, I said, and we have already spent at least eight months debating on the TOR of the EAS mechanism in Jakarta, I announced that we would no longer pursue this discussion and operate in accordance with the mandate given to us by the Leaders, as mentioned above.

The EAMJ had no choice but to agree. To cement its mandate and existence as a regular ASEAN-led mechanism, the Philippine chairmanship endeavoured to insert paragraphs in the EAS Chairman's Statement as follows:

> We welcomed the continued efforts to strengthen the EAS and its work processes with a view to ensuring effective implementation of the EAS Leaders' decisions and initiatives. We expressed support for the important role of the EAS Ambassadors in Jakarta in discussing the implementation of Leaders' decisions and exchanging information on regional development cooperation initiatives and security policies and initiatives, and developing dialogue on the regional security architecture, as provided in the KL Declaration and in accordance with EAS procedures. We commended the contribution of the EAS Ambassadors in Jakarta in finalising the outcome documents of the 13th EAS. We also welcomed the further strengthening of the EAS Unit at the ASEAN Secretariat to facilitate and support EAS coordination and cooperation effectively.

Thus, ASEAN was able to solve the issue through diplomacy and the insistence on its own procedures.

Procedures Employed in Negotiating EAS Documents

Despite the decision to scrap negotiations for a TOR, the EAMJ still needed guidelines on how to negotiate documents assigned to it by Senior Officials and Ministers because even among themselves, there have been no established rules of format to follow. Instead of the EAS TOR, which could have filled this gap, as earlier discussed, the CPR instead negotiated and released an internal document entitled ASEAN Processes and Procedures on the Issuance of EAS Statements and Declarations, which is an "ASEAN-only" document, meaning only AMS were involved in its finalization. This ASEAN-only document, meaning only ASEAN approved it, was issued again to avoid the messy debate in the larger EAMJ. It detailed the procedures and principles to be followed in negotiating EAS outcome documents of Summits, Ministerial-Level or Senior Officials' Meetings. It also contained elements that ensured ASEAN Centrality in the process, format, language and schedule of negotiations. The ASEAN internal document outlined the process as follows:

(i) The Proponent Country will submit a concept note on the proposed Statement;
(ii) The SOM will task the EAMJ to negotiate the proposed Statement;
(iii) The CPR will consult with the relevant ASEAN sectoral bodies for consideration and endorsement;
(iv) After the concept note is endorsed by the ASEAN sectoral bodies, the Chair, with the assistance of the ASEAN Secretariat, will prepare the zero draft text for consideration of AMS; and
(v) After the draft is agreed among AMS, the EAMJ will negotiate and finalize the text.

In the past, initial drafts submitted by proponent countries became the texts used in negotiations. In 2016, for example, a non-ASEAN

PC had put forward a proposal for Leaders to issue two statements on maritime cooperation and nuclear non-proliferation. Because there were no rules or terms that would guide the negotiations, the proponent country undertook to negotiate the documents from its capital. This has resulted in long delays in the process because of the impracticality of negotiating in a venue where parties to the negotiations were not physically there. There were gaps in interpreting the meaning of terms and objectives and so, despite months of negotiations and with only one document being negotiated, the CPR and the Ambassadors of the non-ASEAN EAS had to sit down two nights before the 2016 EAS Summits to finalize the documents.

A big change, which the Philippine chairmanship introduced, in implementing the essence of ASEAN Centrality was to require that all negotiating texts will be ASEAN texts. This is a negotiation technique which ensures that documents begin from an ASEAN perspective in the first place. Therefore, even if non-ASEAN PCs submitted concept notes or draft statements or declarations, ASEAN would convert them into ASEAN texts which would then be used in the negotiations. How this is done follows this procedure: the ASEAN Chair, with the help of the ASEAN Secretariat, prepares a draft text based on the concept paper submitted by a proponent. The CPR then deliberated on the prepared draft and came up with an "ASEAN Agreed" text, which, thereafter, became the basis of the negotiations with the other eight EAS PCs. This move drew an uproar among the non-ASEAN PCs as they no longer had the advantage to control in the process. In one EAS SOM session, one non-ASEAN PC Ambassador and a member of the EAMJ, who represented their country in the meeting, openly accused me of dictating the rules of the negotiations. I asked permission from my SOM Leader to take the floor to respond to this outburst. I said that if ASEAN's external partners truly meant what they claim is their respect for ASEAN Centrality, then there should be no issue if the negotiating text was an ASEAN text. Officials of another non-ASEAN PC also "reported" me to my Home Office officials for "changing the rules" and thus causing delay in the negotiations. My reply to this was that there were no rules or agreed procedures in negotiating EAS documents in the first place, we might as well start with an ASEAN text. My seniors in the Home

Office, of course, replied to the officials of the non-ASEAN EAS that I was right in my initiative and that ASEAN Centrality should be upheld.

Although indeed, the procedure I introduced somewhat delayed the EAS negotiations, I still believe that using an ASEAN-agreed text as a basis for negotiations with the other non-ASEAN PCs was the most efficient process in our task to finish documents on time while ensuring ASEAN Centrality in the final outcome. To this date, this practice is being followed by succeeding Chairs.

ASEAN Centrality in the ASEAN+1 Mechanism

In the ASEAN+1 mechanism, the DP and the Country Coordinator sit as Co-Chairs of the Meeting. The physical format looks like in Figure 6.3. The same physical arrangement is followed when posing for the customary official photograph.

Before the formal meeting with the DP, ASEAN conducts internal ASEAN-only consultations among themselves, called Coordination Meetings. These internal meetings are meant to coordinate ASEAN

FIGURE 6.3
Format of an ASEAN-China JCC Meeting

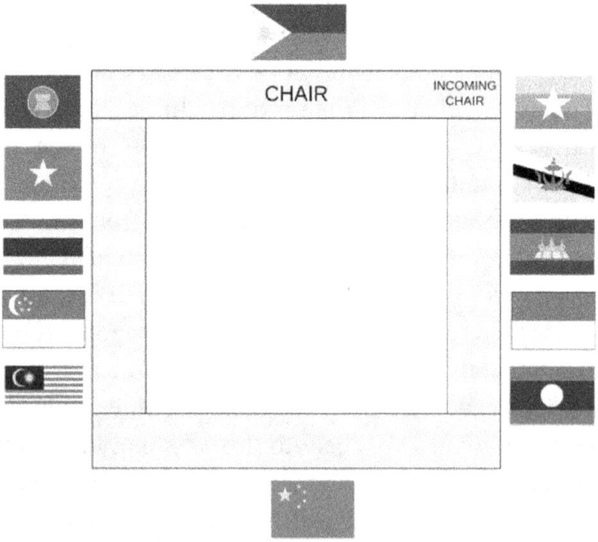

positions on issues to be discussed to ensure that AMS do not contradict one another during the actual meeting. For example, on issues whereby ASEAN has not yet reached a consensus, paragraphs pertaining to such issues are not handed over to the external partners until after an ASEAN position is reached. If there is no consensus on certain issues, the Chair will find a way to convey this to the DP during another private consultation meeting with the latter. The Chair should also ensure that the DP does not introduce issues that have the effect of embarrassing any AMS or sounds like lecturing or criticizing ASEAN.

In some cases when a formal meeting is not warranted or not deemed desirable by ASEAN, an informal breakfast or lunch format is resorted to in order to indicate that the discussions ensuing would be informal; there would be no record of the engagement and that whatever is said there has no binding effect on any of the parties. Such events included lunches or breakfasts with visiting officials from the United States, Italy and Norway.

The JSCC is chaired by the Deputy Secretary General (DSG) of ASEAN in charge of the political and security pillar and the Ambassador of the SDP who sits opposite him as Co-Chair. The Member States are simply arranged in an alphabetical order around the table with the SDP in the middle. They are also allowed to bring representatives from their capital and other line agencies as heads or members of their delegations.

It will be noted that SDPs do not have separate meetings with Senior Officials, Ministers or Leaders of ASEAN. They do have trilateral ministerial meetings, i.e., the Minister of the SDP, the Minister of the ASEAN Chair for that year and the Secretary General who has ministerial rank.

Figure 6.4 shows the prescribed format for the CPR's Meeting with any external partner, be they major, small and medium powers. This format is determined by ASEAN. These meetings are called JCC for full DPs and JSCC Meetings for SDPs. ASEAN has ten full DPs, namely, Australia, Canada, China, the EU, India, Japan, Korea, New Zealand, Russia and the United States. The SDPs are Morocco, Norway, Pakistan, Switzerland and Turkey. Each AMS is designated Country Coordinator for a particular DP for a period of three years while the ASEAN Secretariat

FIGURE 6.4
Format of the Joint Sectoral Cooperation Committee (JSCC)

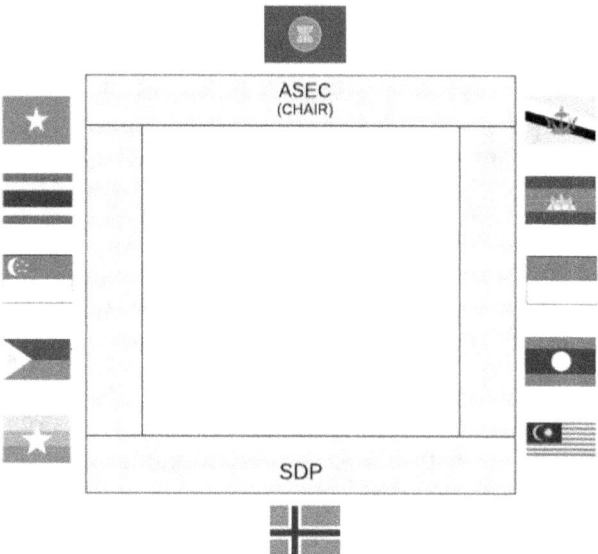

is the Coordinator for relations with SDPs. During the period under review, the Philippines was Country Coordinator for ASEAN-Australia Relations (2012–2015), ASEAN-Canada Relations (2015–2018) and ASEAN-China Relations (2018–2021). These meetings are held once a year but informal engagements also happen especially when negotiating important documents for Ministers and Leaders to issue.

The format of meetings is indicative of the co-equal status of the meeting participants. The number of seats allotted to the external partner is determined by ASEAN. In Figure 6.3, the Head of Delegation of the external partner, in this case, China, is seated opposite the Chair who is the Country Coordinator for these relations. Normally, the chief delegate is the Ambassador but there were times when high ranking officials from capitals also head their delegations, such as when Vice Premier Liu Yandong met with the CPR in November 2017. The DP is surrounded by AMS arranged in alphabetical order, with the exception of the Incoming Country Coordinator (Myanmar) who is seated at the left-hand side of the current Chair/Country Coordinator. The ASEAN

Secretariat is always seated at the right-hand side of the Chair. Two seats are allotted per member state in the front row while four to six seats are given to the DP.

As mentioned, ASEAN has formal platforms for interacting with its external partners who may fall under the classification of full DPs, SDPs, Development Partners, fellow regional groups, the United Nations and civil society.

There are ASEAN+1 meetings among the Leaders of ASEAN and the DPs called Summits, Ministerial-Level or Senior Officials' Meetings and in Jakarta, these are called Joint Cooperation Committees (JCCs). The CPR is oftentimes tasked to negotiate and prepare the documents to be issued or adopted by these high-level bilateral meetings.

ASEAN has ten DPs and AMS take turns acting as Country Coordinator for a period of three years each. A Country Coordinator acts as the shepherd of ASEAN's relations with a DP. This AMS is charged with steering and advancing such relations by coordinating closely with the Ambassador and other officials of the external partner of ASEAN. My turn as Country Coordinator for ASEAN-Canada relations ended in August 2018 and I assumed as Country Coordinator for ASEAN-China relations right after this until I left in April 2019. In 2017, the respective Country Coordinators were:

Australia – Myanmar
Canada – the Philippines
China – Singapore
The European Union – Thailand
India – Brunei Darussalam
Japan – Cambodia
Korea – Viet Nam
New Zealand – Indonesia
Russia – Laos
The United States of America – Malaysia

I would like to discuss here a few instances of ASEAN relations with its DPs and how ASEAN Centrality came to the fore of the processes and the agenda.

ASEAN + USA: The CPR and Vice President Michael Pence

Of particular significance to me personally and to ASEAN in general was the CPR meeting with Vice President Michael Pence in April 2017 (see Figure 6.5). Having coordinated extensively with the US Mission to ASEAN weeks before on the details of the meeting, the much-awaited day finally came. At that time, ASEAN had been apprehensive that the newly installed Trump administration had not yet made a categorical statement on how the United States viewed ASEAN, considering recent speculations of a US retreat in the Southeast Asian region. While the ASEAN Secretariat had allowed the usual meticulous security checks of the ASEAN Secretariat premises performed by the "men-in-black" requisite in any visit by a US dignitary, including choosing which ASEAN meeting room provided the best security cover, the CPR insisted on the

FIGURE 6.5
Co-Chairing ASEAN+1 Meeting with Vice President Michael Pence

format and the manner with which the meeting was to be conducted. It was going to be a meeting of sovereign equals. I chaired the meeting sitting side by side Vice President Pence (the meeting room was small for security reasons), with him as Co-Chair. We each had about the same speaking time but I had to control the time limitation for the other AMS. I told Vice President Pence: "I do not believe in wishes but in prayers because wishes do not come true and prayers do", knowing that he shared the same Christian background as I did. My three prayers were: (i) for the United States to make a categorical, unequivocal statement of where ASEAN stands in the view of the US; (ii) for President Trump to attend the ASEAN-US Summit to be held in Manila in November that year and; (iii) for the United States to send a dedicated Ambassador to ASEAN as the current head of post was a Charge d'Affaires. He smilingly replied that all my prayers have been granted, especially the first one. Right after the meeting, he made a speech before the media at the ASEAN Secretariat, stressing the "value that President Trump places on the US-ASEAN strategic partnership and firm and unwavering commitment to build on the strong commitment we already have" and vowing to redouble US support to keep the peace and stability of the region especially on the South China Sea and the Korean Peninsula issue.[4] Later in the year, President Trump made a dramatic appearance at the Manila Summit where he enunciated the so-called Free and Open Indo-Pacific Strategy (FOIPS) of the United States with the Quad. However, the United States has yet to fulfill its promise to send a full-fledged Ambassador to ASEAN to this date, a situation I do not attribute to a disregard of ASEAN in particular, but is the same predicament around the world where full-fledged US Ambassadors have yet to be appointed in many parts of the world.

ASEAN-China JCC

ASEAN's relations with China are among the most substantive among its external partners as they encompass all pillars of cooperation. They are also the most complex because of the South China Sea dimension. China, of course, is a rising power and ASEAN's strategy is to manage this rise by balancing the thorny issues with the benefits that they may derive out of these relations. This strategy is also based on the belief that ASEAN can encourage China to become a responsible hegemon. The ASEAN-China JCC was more focused on the economic and socio-cultural aspects of the relations and left the political-security part to the SOM and the Ministers, except when negotiating documents concerning the South China Sea, the Korean Peninsula and other traditional and non-traditional security threats.

During the ASEAN-China Summit of 2017, Premier Li Keqiang announced a new ASEAN-China Cooperation Fund with an initial contribution of US$10 million as part of China's growing soft diplomacy to the regional grouping although a lot of these are already being poured in bilateral country-to-country relations. One of my practical tasks as Country Coordinator of ASEAN-China relations was to set the direction on the utilization of this fund, set up an administrative structure whereby ASEAN can participate in disbursing and accounting for it. This entailed the setting up of the ASEAN-China Project Management Team which is composed of representatives from China and ASEAN tasked with appraising and submitting to the CPR for approval of all projects meant to utilize the Cooperation Fund. (Similar arrangements to co-manage development cooperation funds have been established with Australia, Japan, Korea and Norway). ASEAN also saw to it that the CPR would also have a role to play in approving who would qualify for the ASEAN-China Young Leaders Scholarship programme announced by Premier Li in the same speech.

ASEAN Says No to Lecturing by External Partners

The bilateral meetings between ASEAN and its DPs are also occasions for the latter to inject their national agendas in their relations with ASEAN. Two of these bilateral agendas are the Northern Rakhine or Rohingya issue as the West prefers to call it and human rights.

For example, during a JCC Meeting with a western DP which has appointed a Special Envoy on the Rohingya issue, ASEAN has refused to include a separate agenda item on the matter and insisted that the DP should bring up the issue under the general agenda item, Developments in Country X. The DP was also warned that the tone of their discussion

6. ASEAN Centrality with ASEAN's External Partners

should not be in a lecturing mode and that they must be factual in their presentation. ASEAN has also abided by the request of Myanmar to call the issue Northern Rakhine, and not Rohingya, as the West is wont to do, because according to Myanmar, using the term Rohingya already imputes Myanmarish citizenship on these persons, which is still a highly contestable issue in Myanmar with regards to the concerned group of people in the Northern Rakhine state. Many other western DPs of ASEAN, such as the EU, Australia, the United States, and New Zealand, have similar requests to discuss human rights and the Rohingya issue but ASEAN would always insist that if such issues were discussed during bilateral meetings with them, they should be done according to ASEAN's procedures and language.

In another instance, ASEAN said no to a major DP which wanted to change overnight the objective and nature of a document being negotiated which was the ASEAN + Country X Leaders' Statement on Cyber and Digital Economy. From the very beginning, the nature and intention of the document had been economic, i.e., how to prevent attacks on the rapidly growing digital economy. ASEAN and Country X had spent many sessions negotiating the provisions of this document months before and were in the final stretches of negotiations during the last drafting session on 10 November 2017, when suddenly, on the eve of its supposed-to-be issuance by the Leaders of ASEAN+1, Country X had wanted to change the nature of the document to a purely political one. They had introduced several paragraphs that changed entirely what the document meant to address. It had become a political-security document. Now, lest it be misunderstood that ASEAN did not recognize the importance of cybersecurity, especially in the fight against terrorism and other forms of non-traditional security threats, I wish to emphasize here that what ASEAN had objected to was the manner with which Country X had wanted to change directions overnight, catching the Member States unaware and unprepared to make decisions. Thus, when the ASEAN Co-Chair of the negotiating meeting put their foot down, the other AMS and I had to support the Country Coordinator. I remember having made the intervention that Country X could not just change directions and purpose on the eve of the issuance of the Leaders' Statement. I added that in the course of the negotiations in the last few months, we consulted with our economic ministries to determine our positions on every paragraph of the document. To suddenly change the nature of the document at this time had left us no opportunity to consult our political line agencies to accurately reflect our respective national interests in the resulting document. That night, the talks collapsed and the Statement was not finalized, and, therefore, not issued by the Leaders of the two sides. Perhaps, this major DP has been used to having their unreasonable way in the past and when ASEAN said no, it was a cause of a big disappointment for them. The Ambassador of that DP told me later on that I was a bit too heavy in my intervention to "kill" their initiative. I had replied to this Ambassador that although the Philippines and ASEAN valued the topic at hand, there is a time to run away in negotiations when the stakes are too high and you are doomed to lose.

Another example of ASEAN's resistance to a DP's insistence to follow their own process was demonstrated in the application of the EU to elevate ASEAN-EU relations to the level of Strategic Partnership. At the 20th ASEAN-EU Ministerial Meeting held in Brussels in 2014, the Ministers of both sides agreed to work towards upgrading their partnership to a strategic level. Towards this goal, both sides worked on the "Bangkok Roadmap for Elevating the ASEAN-EU Enhanced Partnership" which was meant to be adopted during the 26th ASEAN Economic Ministers' Meeting in October 2016. However, this did not happen because of the insistence of the EU to link this elevation of status to their automatic acceptance into the EAS, which required the express approval of ASEAN. The EU had previously cited their accession to the TAC, scaled up its cooperation with ASEAN, taken part in top-level visits and many other initiatives which they thought qualified them to this elevation in status. To be sure, AMS had no issue in elevating ASEAN-EU relations to a strategic level and I remember that the Philippines had been among the first to endorse this application. Although the Philippines believed that the EU has carried out substantive cooperation with ASEAN especially in the areas of climate change, disaster management, biodiversity, trade and investment, maritime security, and many others, I conveyed disagreement to the linking during the ASEAN-EU JCC held on 30 January 2018. In our CPR meetings, AMS expressed their disagreement with the EU proposal and had found this insistence of the EU a bit high-handed and offensive to ASEAN's sensibilities. Besides, ASEAN has been guarding the gates to EAS membership very assiduously as they believe that letting in more members might complicate an already difficult agglomeration of conflicting interests in the current EAS membership. Thus, the elevation of ASEAN-EU relations to a strategic level did not happen until after six years from the time the EU conveyed their application and not until they agreed to delink it from their acceptance as an EAS participating country.[5]

ASEAN Centrality in the ASEAN Plus Three (APT) Meeting

The CPR also meets regularly (at least once a year but more often when negotiating documents) with the Plus Three countries, China, Japan and the Republic of Korea. The three also rotate among themselves the coordinatorship of their group; the Coordinator then sits in the middle of the space allotted to them. In Figure 6.6, Japan assumed the coordinatorship but this does not mean that the Plus Three coordinate their positions because each speaks purely from his/her national point of

FIGURE 6.6
Format of the ASEAN Plus Three (APT) Meeting

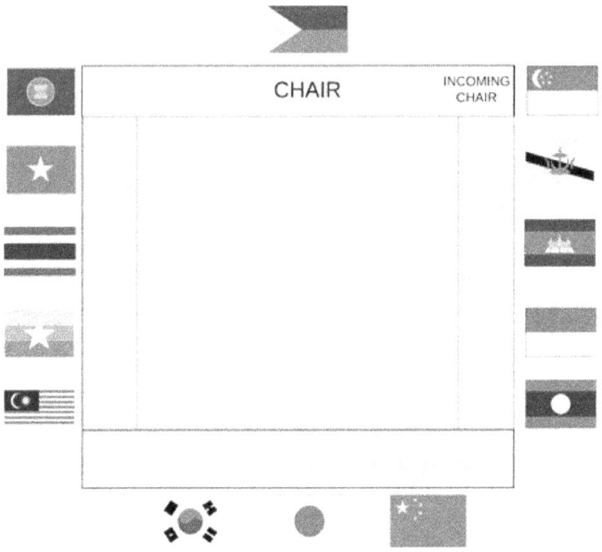

view. The arrangement is solely for the purpose of determining who sits in the middle and who gets to speak first during the Opening Remarks portion of the meeting. All three are invited to give opening and closing remarks during meetings. For the Opening Remarks, the ASEAN Chair speaks first, followed by the Plus Three Coordinator and the other two countries. For the Closing Remarks, all three are given the opportunity to speak but ASEAN, through the Chair, would literally have the last say as they would give the Closing Remarks last and get to formally close the meeting. Figure 6.6 shows the arrangement of seats during the APT Meeting, with the CPR seats positioned as if surrounding the Plus Three.

The ASEAN Plus Three (APT) or CPR Plus Three Ambassadors Meeting is a mechanism that regularly meets in Jakarta, since all participating countries have dedicated Ambassadors to ASEAN based in Jakarta. The Plus Three countries are China, Japan and the Republic of Korea. The TOR of the CPR Plus Three mechanism in Jakarta empowers it to: (i) identify priorities for East Asia cooperation; (ii) coordinate, monitor and review the implementation of relevant documents/decisions; (iii) coordinate follow-up to the decisions of APT Summit, APT Foreign Ministers' Meeting and APT SOM and submit progress reports; and (iv) act as the approving authority for APT cooperation projects funded from the APT Cooperation Fund. The APT mechanism was born out of the 1998 Asian financial crisis that crippled most Asian economies. Its main focus areas of cooperation are finance, connectivity, food security, energy, environment and biodiversity conservation, health and pandemic diseases, culture, tourism, science, technology and innovation, information and communication technology, poverty eradication, disaster management, and youth and education. It is thus focused more on economic, financial and socio-cultural cooperation although from time to time, the issue of the Korean Peninsula comes up, especially in the wake of nuclear missile testing by the Democratic People's Republic of Korea (DPRK). In which case, political-security discussion is allowed by ASEAN, since ASEAN and all Plus Three countries have a large stake in the Korean Peninsula security concern.

ASEAN Centrality did not really come to the test in the APT Forum since most of the topics and key priorities were focused on functional, rather than political security cooperation (unless the DPRK conducts missile tests which would trigger interventions from Japan and the Republic of Korea), except in two minor cases.

All Plus Three countries adhere to the principle of ASEAN Centrality as can be gleaned from the Preambular Paragraph of the 2017 APT Ministers' Declaration on the 20th Anniversary of the mechanism as follows:

> The Ministers reaffirmed the strategic role of the cooperation framework in promoting peace, security, stability and prosperity in East Asia. They cited the central role of ASEAN in the evolving regional architecture and stressed that the APT would continue to support the implementation of the ASEAN Community Vision 2025 to pave the way towards deeper regional integration in East Asia. They agreed that the 20th Anniversary of APT Cooperation this year provides great opportunities of further strengthening existing areas of cooperation and explore potential new initiatives for mutual benefit. In this regard, they looked forward to the adoption of the Manila Declaration on the 20th Anniversary of ASEAN Plus Three Cooperation at the APT Summit in November 2017.

Under the Philippine chairmanship, the CPR to ASEAN and Ambassadors of the Plus Three countries to ASEAN in Jakarta negotiated and finalized the new APT Cooperation Work Plan (2018–2022) which was adopted by the 18th APT Foreign Ministers' Meeting in Manila in August. It was also submitted to the 20th APT Summit in November for the Leaders' notation. The Work Plan will further strengthen APT cooperation through, among others, deepening political and security dialogue and cooperation, and promoting trade and investment, people-to-people exchanges, women empowerment and gender equality and regional connectivity. To mark this milestone, the APT Leaders also issued the "Manila Declaration on the 20th Anniversary of APT Cooperation" after the Commemorative Summit. The Declaration calls for deepening and strengthening political and security dialogue and cooperation, including through high-level visits, dialogues and consultations; strengthening cooperation on traditional and non-traditional security issues; promoting regional integration; and implementing selected recommendations of the East Asia Vision Group II. This document was also negotiated and finalized by the APT mechanism in Jakarta.

One issue that tested ASEAN Centrality although in an oblique way was when the funds of the APT Cooperation Fund reached a critical level and there was danger that the planned activities and projects were going to be sidelined for this reason. There have been some gaps on the part of the ASEAN Secretariat in the administration of the funds resulting in this situation. As a result some of the Plus Three members hesitated to send in their contributions. Under the agreement establishing the APT funds, the ratio on fund contribution was 3:3:3:1, i.e., that the Plus Three will contribute three quarters each to the fund and ASEAN will collectively cover the last quarter. ASEAN quickly acted to remedy the situation by instructing the ASEAN Secretariat to develop a system whereby financial reporting could be speeded up to allow for more transparency and a trigger system to alert us if funds are in critical stages. As a result, there was a withdrawal of several long-pending projects that have been clogging the system, some project proposals that were not deemed beneficial were rejected, a tighter project appraisal and approval system was installed. This satisfied all concerned and replenishments to the fund were deposited by APT members. Thus, even in practical ways, ASEAN-led mechanisms should also be strengthened to serve the purpose for which they were created, as a response to ASEAN's critics for ASEAN to strengthen its institutions and mechanisms.

Failure to Practise ASEAN Centrality in ASEAN's Dealings with its External Partners in Jakarta

For balance, I am recounting here few instances when ASEAN Centrality, defined in this current framework, did not serve the interests of ASEAN. Previous to the establishment of procedures and mechanisms for negotiating the Leaders' Statements, one ASEAN DP proposed the negotiation and adoption of a Leaders' Declaration on nuclear non-proliferation. However, this proponent DP insisted on negotiating this document from its capital, a move that proved to be counterproductive for AMS, as it resulted in delays in responding to the concept note provided by the proponent since their resident embassies in that capital were not familiar with the technical issues being negotiated, plus the practical difficulty of negotiating a sensitive document via long distance.

Moreover, the DP insisted that the negotiating text should be drafted by it, thereby imposing its views and interests already in the initial draft, and allowing participating countries to merely provide their comments and suggestions in written form and for these to be submitted to the Mission of that DP for onward transmittal and processing by its Headquarters, and then returned again to the participating countries for their approval. This long distance negotiation was not ideal for ASEAN. Two EAS countries immediately rejected the issuance of such a document citing the fact that this topic was not among the priority areas identified by the Leaders of the EAS. (The six priority areas during this time were energy, education, finance, global health including pandemics, environment and disaster management, and ASEAN Connectivity). The document was almost discarded as one EAS country refused to participate but in the spirit of cooperation, two late night emergency negotiating sessions were conducted and the EAS adopted the East Asia Summit Statement on Non-Proliferation.

Another failure of ASEAN Centrality that persists to this day, is the refusal by external partners to include ASEAN in the determination of which cooperation projects to fund and the kind and level of participation from AMS. This arises from the fact that they have not established cooperation funds lodged in the ASEAN Secretariat the management of which should ideally be handled both by ASEAN and the DP. Normally, development cooperation funds used to implement the Plan of Action with external partners are lodged in the ASEAN Secretariat and are managed by a team composed of representatives of the DP and the ASEAN Secretariat and a member state, usually the Country Coordinator for those relations. This is true in the case of the ASEAN-Australia Development Cooperation Program now in its second phase (AADCP II), with at least AU$60 million at any given time; the Japan-ASEAN Integration Fund I and II (JAIF) (as of 31 May 2018, the total contribution amounted to more than US$660 million);[6] the ASEAN-Korea Fund with about US$124 million and the ASEAN-China Fund which had an initial allocation of US$10 million that could be replenished as soon as funds are exhausted. However, in the case of the other DPs, the funds dedicated for the implementation of the dialogue relations are managed by their respective capitals. Worse still, there are no dedicated funds to push cooperation with ASEAN, thus depriving ASEAN of the opportunity to determine what priority areas should be given focus for implementation and which beneficiaries of the activities and the modalities of implementing the activity should be identified. ASEAN also had to compete with the global pool of beneficiaries in the absence of dedicated funds.

The practice of unilaterally determining which projects should be given priority also resulted in bureaucratic red-tape because of the long-distance mode of negotiations that lacked transparency on the part of the approving body which was located in the capital of this DP. One particular case was a project involving the youth of ASEAN and those of one DP which was originally intended to be implemented during the chairmanship of the Philippines in 2017. The long-winded back-and-forth movement of the communications between the Philippines/ASEAN and the DP including the latter's long period of processing and complicated requirements delayed the conduct of this activity for three years! At one point, the Ambassador of this DP was even dictating to the Philippines/ASEAN what it was supposed to do! He had had written to me in April 2019:

> *At the same time, if the budget of the project proposal is amended as preliminary (sic) agreed with the Philippine National Youth Commission, it would require a re-approval process from the ASEAN Side before the JCC endorsement and money disbursement. I hope you will facilitate this phase of the process.*

I shot back a reply and emphasized that no, there was no need for ASEAN to re-approve the budget proposal as it had already previously done so. The project had already been long delayed. The Philippines had also agreed to remove from the budget proposal items that the DP deemed not required for the conduct of the event.

The same DP had tried to exploit the lack of coordination among the different mechanisms of ASEAN by going directly to the sectoral body concerned and requiring that body to establish a working group where this DP could push an agenda that it has long been trying to push in ASEAN. According to the ASEAN process, no new mechanism may be established unless approved by the CPR and the DP working in tandem under the JCC.

Notes

1. China has been pushing for its recognition as a Comprehensive Strategic Partner, a matter being debated since no such categorization has been identified and the lines dividing a Strategic Partner and a Comprehensive Strategic Partner are not clear.
2. In 2020, Japan would align its Indo-Pacific Strategy in a refined Strategy Paper adopted by ASEAN and Japan, entitled Concept Note to Realize Synergy Between Japan's Free and Open Indo-Pacific (FOIP) and the ASEAN Outlook on the Indo-Pacific (AOIP).
3. Datuk Nasharudin Mat Isa, GMMF President at the time, would later be charged with thirty-three counts of money laundering and criminal breach of trust, including using GMMF funds for his personal use. See https://www.thestar.com.my/news/nation/2019/10/21/nasharudin-mat-isa-to-be-charged-with-graft.
4. Permanent Mission of the Philippines to ASEAN, *PH Envoy to ASEAN Chairs Meeting of Committee of Permanent Representatives to ASEAN with U.S. Vice President Pence*, Press Release, 21 April 2017.
5. This was during the ASEAN-EU Ministerial Meeting held virtually on 1 December 2020.
6. https://www.aseansdgscities.org/about.

7

ASEAN CENTRALITY AS AN ASPIRATION TO RAISE THE LEVEL OF AWARENESS ABOUT ASEAN

Finally, the litmus test that should test the relevance and continuity of ASEAN as a regional organization is the disposition of its people to identify themselves as citizens of ASEAN. Therefore, the last dimension of my definition of ASEAN Centrality is my ardent aspiration for the peoples of ASEAN and those around the world, to increase their level of awareness about ASEAN, and concomitant to this is the need to raise their sense of identity or belongingness to ASEAN. ASEAN is an important regional organization; it should be known to those living within it and those outside. Unfortunately, this has not been the case. I have frequently lamented the lack of awareness and sense of identity by the people of ASEAN about their own regional organization despite its fifty years of existence. In a *Philippine Star* article I wrote for the 52nd anniversary of ASEAN (2019), I cited the following:

> For a long time, people from the Southeast Asian region have identified more with their colonial masters than with each other, prompting the former Thai Foreign Minister Thanat Khoman to complain that these countries were like *cloisons etanches* (airtight containers), looking more to their former colonizers,

than to each other, in searching their identity. Membership in ASEAN has changed all that. Today, the Filipino can boast of an identity that celebrates unity in diversity, the famous battle cry of ASEAN, signifying that people in the region can live in peace and harmony despite the differences among them. It has also enabled us to chart a common identity with the rest of ASEAN Member States (AMS). When Filipinos find a common identity with the rest of ASEAN, it does not mean that we should all have similar characteristics and ways of doing things. It means that we Filipinos have a shared dream with the rest of them, of living in peace and stability, enjoying economic prosperity and providing our people dignity, social protection and the means to face up to our common challenges.

My advocacy has been to make people become aware of ASEAN. ASEAN is not a perfect regional organization. Indeed, the many criticisms against it have factual foundations. Its member states are not the best exemplars of what the West would consider models of human rights promotion and protection. But ASEAN is more than the sum of its parts. When united in their vision and intent, they could work together to provide peace and security, economic prosperity and dignity to their people. The existence, indeed, the success of ASEAN could be a beacon to people to learn more about it, how to maximize its full potential and avoid the pitfalls that caused the demise of its early predecessors. Understanding this organization, what it can and cannot do can help a number of people including educators, farmers, job-seekers and business conglomerates. However, this is not yet the case.

I was also alarmed by two surveys on ASEAN Awareness conducted by the ASEAN Foundation and the Economic Research Institute for ASEAN and East Asia (ERIA) which both resulted in a very low level of awareness by ASEAN citizens about what ASEAN does for them. In the ERIA survey conducted in 2017 and subtitled "Feeling of ASEAN citizenship", the results were mixed. On the one hand, three-quarters of the respondents felt "moderately" to "very much" as ASEAN citizens but on the other hand, this result points only to awareness of the ASEAN Economic Community (AEC) and not of the other pillars. An earlier survey (2014) conducted by the ASEAN Foundation revealed an even more dismal picture of ASEAN awareness among the respondents, with the Philippines registering one of the lowest scores together with Myanmar. The results of both surveys indicate a lack of awareness, in general, among ordinary people of what ASEAN is and what it is doing for their benefit.

This has prompted me to urge the ASEAN Secretariat to conduct another survey of ASEAN Awareness in 2018,[1] with the hope that results would improve as a result of the Philippines' high profile initiatives to commemorate the 50th Anniversary of ASEAN the year before. The Philippine Presidential Communications Operations Office (PCOO) was also proactive in according adequate publicity to these commemorative events and the various meetings and forums held during the Philippine chairmanship. The Committee of Permanent Representatives (CPR) under my chairmanship has also urged the ASEAN Ministers Responsible for Information (AMRI) through the ASEAN Secretariat officer assisting them—Mr Romeo Arca, a Filipino Assistant Director at the time—to utilize their platforms to raise this level of awareness. The results of the 2018 Survey were encouraging. Polling a spectrum of respondents from businesses, civil society organizations (CSOs), and the general public, the ASEAN Secretariat came up with remarkable results indicating an increase in the sense of belonging to ASEAN among respondents. Across the region, 94 per cent of the general public identify themselves as ASEAN citizens at some level. This is an increase of 13 percentage points from the result of a previous study conducted by the ERIA in 2017. According to this ASEAN Secretariat survey, two-fifths of citizens strongly affiliate themselves with ASEAN. Filipinos, Indonesians, and Thais exhibited the strongest sense of belonging to ASEAN (50 per cent of the respondents indicated "very much"). In addition, the sense of belonging is also tied with a feeling of "Shared Identity", with economy being identified as the key factor creating a sense of belonging. Awareness of the three pillars varies from country to country where scores are still poor in some but the heightened identification as a citizen of ASEAN is a big boost to the ASEAN Community.[2]

Indeed, ASEAN can only exist as ASEAN if it remains relevant, responsive and caring to the people it serves.

I also embarked on a personal crusade to make ASEAN known to people as I was truly apprehensive that people were not aware of what

ASEAN is and are, therefore, quick to condemn it seeing it from the perspectives of outsiders instead of understanding it from the lenses of peoples who are directly affected by it. This is, from my view, one of the reasons for Brexit. People in the UK were not aware or were not satisfied with what their regional institutions are doing to promote their welfare. Despite my hectic schedule, I travelled to various parts of the world, from Victoria, Canada to Hiroshima in Japan, Seoul, Korea, various cities in China, in Canberra and Sydney, Australia, and the cities of Indonesia and Thailand, and the Philippines, to talk about ASEAN.

One of my first activities upon assumption of the chairmanship of ASEAN was to speak on 29 January 2017 at the Habibie Center's Talking ASEAN series, together with Indonesia Director General for ASEAN Jose Tavares and Jakarta Post columnist Jamil Flores (see Figure 7.1). In this talk, I spoke of the ASEAN processes and mechanisms and the principles followed by ASEAN. I also spoke about the priorities of the Philippine chairmanship of ASEAN. I explained the Philippine chairmanship's theme and priorities, emphasizing the Philippines' core goals of bringing about positive change in the lives of the peoples of ASEAN and maintaining ASEAN's role as the driving force in

**FIGURE 7.1
Speaking at the Habibie Center**

our regional architecture. I noted that said priorities are based on the ASEAN Community Vision 2025 and its Blueprints as well as rigorous consultations with the Philippine's sectoral body focal points and civil society. I underscored that corresponding deliverables for each priority have already been identified, including a legal instrument on the rights of migrant workers and the long-awaited Code of Conduct (COC) in the South China Sea. I also noted that ASEAN will celebrate its 50th anniversary this year and that activities to commemorate the milestone were also being planned.

In commemoration of the 50th anniversary of the establishment of ASEAN, Channel News Asia invited me to join a panel on their programme, "Perspectives", to talk about the relevance of ASEAN in today's world (see Figure 7.2). Joining me in the panel were Mr Ho Kwon Ping, Chairman of the Singapore Management University and Executive Chairman of Banyan Tree Holdings Limited, Mr Edmund Koh, Head of Wealth Management Asia Pacific, UBS and Ms Noni S. A. Purnomo, President Director of the Blue Bird Group Holding of Indonesia. CNA's Mr Teymoor Nabili was the anchor. The programme was aired in May

FIGURE 7.2
Co-panelist in the Perspective Show of Channel News Asia

2017. Among the questions Mr Nabili posed included: "What does the future hold for ASEAN in 2025? Is ASEAN still relevant for businesses today?" The other panelists, while guardedly optimistic about the future of ASEAN, were quite vocal in their condemnation of ASEAN as an ineffective body, as they deemed it more regulatory than helpful in their lines of business. They decried the many rules and regulations in Member States, preventing them from doing their businesses more freely and called out the many statements and declarations that Leaders issue but which are not legally binding and would not help their businessmen directly. One panelist said that yes, ASEAN helps politically and socio-culturally, but does not really help in the economic and technological spheres. Most damning of all was the statement by one panelist that Southeast Asia prospered and developed in spite of ASEAN! Panelists also shared the view that businessmen are not aware of or do not care much about ASEAN because they are not affected by it. One panelist even pointed out that there was no value calling ourselves citizens of ASEAN. This was a lot for me to counter, but I had to make a stand for ASEAN and this I did.

I said then that the single most important achievement of ASEAN for the last fifty years has been its ability to prosecute peace despite the fact that the region hosts two of the most flammable conflict flashpoints in the world, the South China Sea and the Korean Peninsula, and the fact that Member States have a hundred and one reasons to wage war against one another considering the many bilateral issues that could conflagrate into major conflicts. Instead, I emphasized, the Member States of ASEAN choose to live in harmony with one another and manage the instability posed by these challenges. The reason why you are able to conduct your business in peace and with remarkable profit, I concluded, was that there is peace and harmony in ASEAN, instead of its citizens scrambling for cover because countries have decided to hurl missiles and chemical weapons at one another, like many regions of the world do. I think this assertion has somewhat assuaged them and admitted that indeed, the peace and stability that ASEAN as provided has enabled them to do their business in peace. I also spoke about the many initiatives of ASEAN on Micro, Small and Medium Enterprises (MSMEs), connectivity and digital innovation, and free trade and investment regimes. I think that this assertion has somehow calmed the criticisms of my co-panelists and put their complaints in perspective. They also started to speak positively about ASEAN.

As a Speaker in the Maritime Security Conference held in Victoria, Canada in May 2017 and sponsored by the Hawaii-based Asia-Pacific Center for Security Studies[3] (APCSS), I spoke of ASEAN's desire to avoid becoming once again the theatre for major power projections, and that ASEAN is trying to develop a new security architecture that has ASEAN Centrality at its core (see Figure 7.3). I pointed to ASEAN-led mechanisms such as the East Asia Summit (EAS) and the ASEAN Regional Forum (ARF) where several workshops and conferences have been held to map out the evolving security architecture in the region. ASEAN has played a central and proactive role in driving regional processes and continues to have focused deliberations on strategic matters or issues of concern such as the South China Sea, through ASEAN-led mechanisms such as the EAS, APT, ARF and the ADMM-Plus. Ideally,

FIGURE 7.3
Speaking at the Maritime Security Conference in Victoria, Canada

the evolving regional security architecture should have the following characteristics:

a. A strengthened regional security architecture shall accommodate the security interests of all parties based on mutual benefit, mutual trust, transparency, good neighbourliness and partnership;
b. Enhanced concrete and practical cooperation to overcome security challenges within the region;
c. A rules-based approach is needed as well as coordination and communication;
d. Continued promotion of common responsibility in the endeavour to maintain the region's peace and security;
e. Commitment for common security, common stability, and common prosperity;
f. The exercise of mutual restraint in preventing escalation of dispute/conflict;
g. The use of peaceful settlement of disputes; and
h. To have a legally-binding instrument based on the Treaty of Amity and Cooperation in Southeast Asia (TAC) and EAS Bali Principles for the wider region built upon the vision of an EAS Treaty of Friendship and Cooperation.

In the University of the Philippines Asian Center where I was a Keynote Speaker at the ASEANnale held on 28 February 2018 (see Figure 7.4), my key message was for us citizens of ASEAN to tell the remarkable success story of ASEAN to each other and to the world. I told the story of how ASEAN which was born out of the poverty and political instability of the 1960s, has become regarded as one of the most successful regional organizations in the world. I said that the South China Sea and human rights issues are not the sum total of ASEAN and that there are many initiatives out there to discover about ASEAN, including the use of digital platforms to tell the story of ordinary peoples achieving extraordinary success in ASEAN.

I gave a number of other talks on ASEAN in various places which I always prefaced with: *"My name is Buensuceso. In Spanish, Buen means good and suceso indicates an event or news. Good news! Today, I am*

**FIGURE 7.4
Speaking at the ASEANNALE 2018**

bringing you good news about ASEAN". I then proceed to tell them the good news (as well as the bad) about ASEAN and end up exhorting all ASEAN citizens in the audience to tell their own ASEAN story.

This aspiration has also prodded me to enroll in the Master of ASEAN Studies (MAS) programme of the University of the Philippines Open University. When I told my colleagues this decision over lunch at the office kitchen in January 2018, a few days after we ended our chairmanship, their quizzed looks and pregnant silence screamed their unvoiced question—but why? Why would a sixty-three-year-old Ambassador with thirty-eight years of foreign service experience, nine of which were spent practising ASEAN diplomacy, want to go through the humiliating experience of becoming a student again, submitting assignments and taking examinations, on a subject that she is supposed to have mastered and about which she has given various lectures and speeches around the world? In my application to be accepted as a student, I had said in my essay that I had wanted to combine my practical experience with the discipline of scholarship and be able to raise the level of correct understanding about ASEAN. In other words, I wanted to teach ASEAN Studies in the easiest and most practical way that I could without going through the formalities of being employed as a teacher—by being technically a student. In all the essays I submitted and student forums of the MAS courses I took, I conveyed these views to my fellow students and the faculty. I was heartened by the responses of classmates that it was the first time they viewed ASEAN in the way I described it to them, following the framework that I used in this book. They said that they understand ASEAN better now.

A Final Word from the Author

I hope that this autoethnography could be another vehicle to give us a deeper insight into the ASEAN story, what it has been through over the more than fifty years of its existence, what it can and cannot do, what it is and what it does not purport to be and how it will sustain its relevance and usefulness not just to the governments, but to the peoples of ASEAN.

Finally, I wish to reconnect to the previous writers I cited who have made their own ideas about ASEAN Centrality known: ASEAN does not purport to be the same entity as other regional organizations in the world. It has its unique characteristics and will pursue its objectives in a manner befitting these unique elements. For writers who have expressed their expectation for ASEAN to exercise leadership, this autoethnographic account demonstrated how this concept of leadership could be operationalized.

Future researchers can also expound on the interesting topic of ASEAN chairmanships and their potential in shaping the regional architecture as well as the future of ASEAN. Whether it is Brunei or Singapore, each Chair endeavours to rally its ASEAN counterparts and external partners around causes that they find important.

Diplomats and other officials, especially those involved in negotiations, peace and security, peace processes and reconciliation, should use autoethnography in recording their experiences to equally enrich this field and to help others hone their own negotiating skills. For example, during the aforementioned Cebu Symposium on the Role of Women in Peace Processes, Professor Ferrer recounted a time when she distributed chocolates and roses on Valentine's Day to the male Moro Islamic Liberation Front (MILF) negotiators who had threatened to walk out of the negotiating table. As a Christian and a woman negotiating with male Muslim counterparts, this was an unconventional move, but it worked. This is the stuff that autoethnographies should be founded on.

Briefing papers used in meetings and negotiations should be enhanced to include personal circumstances and impressions so that they can aid in recollecting memories later.

I would advise students, practitioners, teachers of ASEAN studies and ASEAN observers to consider looking at ASEAN in the manner I had described in order for them to gain a better understanding of ASEAN. They might wish to study its mechanisms, formats, principles and processes, how it operates and how it promotes the welfare of its governments and its peoples, and not compare ASEAN with other regional organizations and avoid basing their assessment on what ASEAN does not purport to be. It is important to analyse ASEAN behaviour and meta-nation interaction among ASEAN Member States themselves and between them and their external partners, taking into account the elements found in this autoethnographic study. Those who work in regional and international non-governmental organizations (NGOs), and governmental organizations (GOs) such as the International Committee of the Red Cross (ICRC), the United Nations Economic and Social Commission for Asia and the Pacific (UNESCAP), corporate strategists of companies who have a regional and global coverage would benefit from such an approach as they would be provided with the skills and knowledge of navigating their way through the labyrinthian system and processes of ASEAN.

Practitioners of ASEAN should endeavour to advance ASEAN Centrality, using the examples illustrated in this book, when discussing and negotiating important pillars of the regional political, economic and socio-cultural architecture to sustain the relevance of ASEAN in this rapidly changing world. As demonstrated in this book, external partners of ASEAN will always endeavour to influence ASEAN to bend to their own mode of cooperation and their own agenda, procedures and venue. In the unfolding of the Indo-Pacific Concept or Strategy, for example, ASEAN diplomats should always bear in mind the ASEAN-centric dimension and direction of any undertaking in this regard, as I explained in the introduction section of this book. ASEAN Centrality is earned, it just does not happen, as Natalegawa admonished.

ASEAN has many faults and weaknesses, but it is the only regional organization that we have. It has fulfilled its promise to keep the peace and stability in the region that has enabled its people to pursue socio-economic development and promote the dignity and identity of its people. The point of view of one of its "natives" must be a correct way of looking at it. Such correct understanding might inspire students and teachers of ASEAN to contribute to making it a more effective and more efficient organization.

Notes

1. ASEAN Secretariat, *Poll on ASEAN Awareness 2018* (Jakarta: ASEAN Secretariat, 2019), https://asean.org/storage/2019/12/Poll-on-ASEAN-Awareness-2018-Report.pdf.
2. Building on the results of this survey, the ASEAN Secretariat has embarked on another new initiative on the ASEAN identity which is expected to be issued by the Brunei chairmanship in 2021. The project has the following parameters: 1. ASEAN Awareness: the percentage of ASEAN peoples that can associate themselves being part of ASEAN; 2. ASEAN Relevance: The understanding of how people should benefit from ASEAN; and 3. ASEAN Appreciation: the degree of appreciation of the people to be part of ASEAN and the acknowledgments of external parties of the unity and centrality of ASEAN Community.
3. I graduated from a three-month peace and security course from this school which is funded by the US Department of Defense.

BIBLIOGRAPHY

Acharya, Amitav. 1998. "Culture, Security, Multilateralism: The 'ASEAN Way' and Regional Order". *Contemporary Security Policy* 19, no. 1: 55–84.
———. 2017. "The Myth of ASEAN Centrality?" *Contemporary Southeast Asia: A Journal of International and Strategic Affairs* 39, no. 2: 273–79.
Acharya, Amitav and Alastair I. Johnston. 2007. "Comparing Regional Institutions: An Introduction". In *Crafting Cooperation: Regional International Institutions in Comparative Perspective*, edited by Amitav Acharya and Alastair I. Johnston. Cambridge: Cambridge University Press, pp. 1–31.
Anderson, Leon. 2006. "Analytic Autoethnography". *Journal of Contemporary Ethnography* 35, no. 4: 373–95.
Anderson, Leon and Bonnie Glass-Coffin. 2013. "I Learn by Going". In *Handbook of Autoethnography*, edited by Stacy H. Jones, Tony E. Adams, and Carolyn Ellis. Abingdon: Routledge, pp. 57–83.
ASEAN Foundation. 2014. "ASEAN Awareness Survey". http://www.aseanfoundation.org/project/asean-awareness-survey.
ASEAN Secretariat. 2017a. Chairman's Statement of the 30th ASEAN Summit. Manila.
———. 2017b. Chairman's Statement of the 31st ASEAN Summit. Manila.
Barnett, Michael N. 1997. "The UN Security Council, Indifference, and Genocide in Rwanda". *Cultural Anthropology* 12, no. 4: 551–78.
Bleiker, Roland. 2001. "The Aesthetic Turn in International Political Theory". *Millennium* 30, no. 3: 509–33.
Brigg, Morgan and Roland Bleiker. 2010. "Autoethnographic International Relations: Exploring the Self as a Source of Knowledge". *Review of International Studies*: 779–98.

Buensuceso, Elizabeth P. 2019. "The Modern Filipino: One with ASEAN, Better with ASEAN". *The Philippine Star*, 28 July 2019. https://www.philstar.com/lifestyle/business-life/2019/07/28/1938820/modern-filipino-one-asean-better-asean.

Caballero-Anthony, Mely. 2014. "Understanding ASEAN's Centrality: Bases and Prospects in an Evolving Regional Architecture". *The Pacific Review* 27, no. 4: 563–84.

Canagarajah, A. Suresh. 2012. "Teacher Development in a Global Profession: An Autoethnography". *Tesol Quarterly* 46, no. 2: 258–79.

Chang, Heewon. 2016. *Autoethnography as Method*. Vol. 1. New York: Routledge.

Dethloff, Carl. 2005. "A Principal in Transition: An Autoethnography". Unpublished PhD dissertation, Texas A&M University.

Drysdale, Peter. 2017. "ASEAN: The Experiment in Open Regionalism that Succeeded". In *ASEAN@50 Volume 5: The ASEAN Economic Community Into 2025 and Beyond*, edited by Rebecca Sta. Maria, Shujiro Urata, and Ponciano S. Intal, Jr. Indonesia: Economic Research Institute for ASEAN and East Asia (ERIA), pp. 64–86.

Ellis, Carolyn, Tony E. Adams, and Arthur P. Bochner. 2011. "Autoethnography: An Overview". *Forum: Qualitative Social Research* 12, no. 1, Art. 10. https://www.qualitative-research.net/index.php/fqs/article/view/1589/3095 (accessed 20 April 2019).

Emmerson, Donald K. 2007. "Challenging ASEAN: A 'Topological' View". *Contemporary Southeast Asia* 29, no. 3: 424–26.

———. 2008. "ASEAN's 'Black Swans'". *Journal of Democracy* 19, no. 3: 70–84.

Franklin, John K. 2006. *The Hollow Pact: Pacific Security and the Southeast Asia Treaty Organization*. Texas Christian University.

HarperCollins. 2019. "Principle". In *Collins English dictionary*. https://www.collinsdictionary.com/dictionary/english/principle.

He, Kai. 2006. "Does ASEAN Matter? International Relations Theories, Institutional Realism, and ASEAN". *Asian Security* 2, no. 3: 189–214.

Jones, Lee. 2010. "Still in the Driver's Seat, but for how long? ASEAN's Capacity for Leadership". *Journal of Current Southeast Asian Affairs* 20, no. 3: 95–113.

Jones, Stacy H., Tony E. Adams, and Carolyn Ellis, eds. 2016. *Handbook of Autoethnography*. Abingdon: Routledge.

Kamasa, Frassminggi. 2014. "ASEAN Centrality in Asian Regional Architecture". *Global South Review* 1, no. 1: 63–78.

Katsumata, Hiro. 2004. "Why is ASEAN Diplomacy Changing? From 'Non-Interference' to 'Open and Frank Discussions'". *Asian Survey* 44, no. 2: 237–54.

Koga, Kei. 2010. "The Normative Power of the 'ASEAN Way': Potentials, Limitations and Implications for East Asian Regionalism". *SJEAA* 80.

Koh, T. 2014. "Reviewing the ASEAN Charter: An Opportunity to Reform ASEAN Processes". Singapore: The Singapore Institute of International Affairs (SIIA). http://www.siiaonline.org/wp-content/uploads/2016/10/2014-10-Policy-Brief-Reviewing-the-ASEAN-Charter-An-Opportunity-to-Reform-ASEAN-Processes.

pdf?fbclid=IwAR14s5Hc9RxuNB6UUGbHoaAO4_33jPZRZOwoNC6lwbVEqN_yzoEui4LYGjw (accessed 1 November 2018).
Lee Hsien Loong. 2018. 51st ASEAN Foreign Ministers' Meeting and Related Meetings. Singapore.
Mahiwo, Sylvano. 2014. "ASEAN in the Meta-Nation State Interface". Globalization Seminar. https://www.youtube.com/watch?v=iEdeDJ8C1So.
Martin, Lisa L. 1992. "Interests, Power, and Multilateralism". *International Organization* 46, no. 4: 765–92.
McIlveen, Peter. 2008. "Autoethnography as a Method for Reflexive Research and Practice in Vocational Psychology". *Australian Journal of Career Development* 17, no. 2: 13–20.
Myrdal, Gunnar. 1968. *Asian Drama: An Inquiry into the Poverty of Nations*. Harmondsworth: Penguin.
Nair, Deepak. 2019. "Saving Face in Diplomacy: A Political Sociology of Face-to-Face Interactions in the Association of Southeast Asian Nations". *European Journal of International Relations* 25, no. 3: 672–97.
Natalegawa, Marty. 2018. *Does ASEAN Matter?: A View from Within*. Singapore: ISEAS – Yusof Ishak Institute.
Ness, Gayl D. 1962. ASA: The First Asian International [Letter to Mr. Nolte, Director of the Institute of Current World Affairs]. Selangor, Malaysia, 1 May 1962.
Neumann, Iver B. 2007. "'A Speech That the Entire Ministry May Stand for,' or: Why Diplomats Never Produce Anything New". *International Political Sociology* 1, no. 2: 183–200.
Permanent Mission of the Philippines to ASEAN. 2017. "Philippine Envoy to Chair CPR During ASEAN'S Golden Anniversary", 27 January 2017. https://jakartapm.dfa.gov.ph/sample-sites/pr/206-philippine-envoy-to-chair-cpr-during-asean-s-golden-anniversary.
———. 2018. "ASEAN Secretary-General Leads Launch of ASEAN Women For Peace Registry", 13 December 2018. https://jakartapm.dfa.gov.ph/index.php/sample-sites/pr/384-asean-secretary-general-leads-launch-of-asean-women-for-peace-registry.
Pitard, Jayne. 2017. "A Journey to the Centre of Self: Positioning the Researcher in Autoethnography". *Forum: Qualitative Social Research* 18, no. 3. http://dx.doi.org/10.17169/fqs-18.3.2764.
Pollard, Vincent K. 1970. "ASA and ASEAN, 1961–1967: Southeast Asian Regionalism". *Asian Survey* 10, no. 3: 244–55.
Rolls, Mark. 2012. "Centrality and Continuity: ASEAN and Regional Security since 1967". *East Asia* 29, no. 2: 127–39.
Santamaria, R. 2019. "RCEP: Challenging ASEAN Centrality". Lecture presented at ERIA Inaugural Seminar in Indonesia, Jakarta, 21 April 2019.
Scott, Joy D. 2014. "Memoir as a Form of Auto-ethnographic Research for Exploring the Practice of Transnational Higher Education in China". *Higher Education Research & Development* 33, no. 4: 757–68.

Severino, Rodolfo C. 2001. "ASEAN: Building the Peace in Southeast Asia". Jakarta: The ASEAN Secretariat, 6–7 February 2001. https://asean.org/?static_post=asean-building-the-peace-in-southeast-asia-2.

Sparkes, Andrew C. 2000. "Autoethnography and Narratives of Self: Reflections on Criteria in Action". *Sociology of Sport Journal* 17, no. 1: 21–43. DOI:10.1123/ssj.17.1.21.

Storey, Ian. 2017. "Anatomy of the Code of Conduct Framework for the South China Sea". The National Bureau of Asian Research (NBR), 24 August 2017. https://www.nbr.org/publication/anatomy-of-the-code-of-conduct-framework-for-the-south-china-sea/.

Strategic Comments. 1995. "Vietnam Joins ASEAN". *Strategic Comments* 1, no. 5: 1–2. DOI: 10.1080/1356788950154.

Stubbs, Richard. 2008. "The ASEAN Alternative? Ideas, Institutions and the Challenge to 'Global' Governance". *The Pacific Review* 21, no. 4: 451–68.

———. 2014. "ASEAN's Leadership in East Asian Region-building: Strength in Weakness". *The Pacific Review* 27, no. 4: 523–41.

Tan, See Seng. 2017. "Rethinking 'ASEAN Centrality' in the Regional Governance of East Asia". *The Singapore Economic Review* 62, no. 3: 721–40.

Tay, Simon and Cheryl Tan. 2015. "ASEAN Centrality in the Regional Architecture". Policy Brief. Singapore: Singapore Institute of International Affairs. http://www.siiaonline.org/wp-content/uploads/2016/10/2015-05-Policy-Brief-ASEAN-Centrality-in-the-Regional-Architecture.pdf (accessed 11 May 2018).

Taylor, Alastair M. 1964. "Malaysia, Indonesia — and Maphilindo". *International Journal* 19, no. 2: 155–71.

Tullis, Jillian A. 2016. "Self and Others". In *The Handbook of Autoethnography*, edited by Stacy H. Jones, Tony E. Adams, and Carolyn Ellis. Abingdon: Routledge, pp. 244–59.

Wall, Sarah. 2012. "Ethics and the Socio-political Context of International Adoption: Speaking from the Eye of the Storm". *Ethics and Social Welfare* 6, no. 4: 318–32.

Woon, Walter. 2012. "Dispute Settlement: The ASEAN Way", 11 December 2012. https://cil.nus.edu.sg/wp-content/uploads/2010/01/WalterWoon-Dispute-Settlement-the-ASEAN-Way-2012.pdf.

Xinhua. 2018. "Chinese State Councilor Meets CPR to ASEAN Delegation", 10 September 2018. http://www.xinhuanet.com/english/2018-09/10/c_137458644.htm.

Annexes

Annex A

LIST OF DOCUMENTS ISSUED BY ASEAN IN 2017

a. ASEAN Declaration to Prevent and Combat Cybercrime
b. ASEAN Declaration on Innovation
c. Action Agenda on Mainstreaming Women's Economic Empowerment in ASEAN
d. ASEAN Leaders' Declaration on Anti-Microbial Resistance (AMR): Combating AMR through One Health Approach
e. ASEAN Leaders' Declaration on Disaster Health Management
f. ASEAN Leaders' Declaration on Ending All Forms of Malnutrition
g. ASEAN Declaration on the Adoption of the ASEAN Youth Development Index
h. ASEAN Declaration on 'Culture of Prevention' for a Peaceful, Inclusive, Resilient, Healthy and Harmonious Society
i. ASEAN Declaration on the Gender-Responsive Implementation of the ASEAN Community Vision 2025 and Sustainable Development Goals
j. ASEAN Joint Statement on Climate Change to the 23rd Session of the Conference of the Parties to the United Nations Framework Convention on Climate Change (UNFCCC COP-23)
k. Joint Statement on Promoting Women, Peace and Security in ASEAN
l. ASEAN Framework Agreement on the Facilitation of Cross Border Transport of Passengers by Road Vehicles

In addition, the following documents were also either issued, signed or adopted:

APT documents

- Manila Declaration on the 20th Anniversary of the ASEAN Plus Three
- ASEAN Plus Three Leaders' Statement on Food Security Cooperation
- ASEAN Plus Three Plan of Action 2018–2022

ASEAN+1 documents

- Chairman's Statement of the 5th ASEAN-U.S. Summit to Commemorate the 40th Anniversary of ASEAN-U.S. Dialogue Relations
- Co-Chairs' Press Statement of the ASEAN-Canada Commemorative Summit on the Occasion of the 40th Anniversary of the Establishment of ASEAN-Canada Dialogue Relations
- Press Statement of the ASEAN-EU Commemorative Summit on the Occasion of the 40th Anniversary of the Establishment of ASEAN-EU Dialogue Relations
- Chairman's Statement of the ASEAN-China 20th Summit

EAS documents

- Manila Plan of Action to advance the Phnom Penh Declaration on the East Asia Summit Development Initiative (2018–2022)
- Chairman's Statement of the 12th East Asia Summit, Manila, 14 November 2017
- East Asia Summit Leaders' Statement on Chemical Weapons, Manila, 14 November 2017
- East Asia Summit Leaders' Statement on Cooperation in Poverty Alleviation, Manila, 14 November 2017

- East Asia Summit Leaders' Statement on Countering Ideological Challenges of Terrorism and Terrorist Narratives and Propaganda, Manila, 14 November 2017
- East Asia Summit Leaders' Statement on Anti-Money Laundering and Countering the Financing of Terrorism, Manila, 14 November 2017
- Chairman's Statement of the 7th East Asia Summit Foreign Ministers' Meeting, Manila, 7 August 2017

In 2017, ASEAN also commemorated the following milestones in its relations with Dialogue Partners: (i) 40th anniversary of ASEAN's dialogue relations with the United States of America, Canada, and the European Union; (ii) the 25th anniversary with India; and (iii) the 20th Anniversary of the ASEAN Plus Three. The ASEAN Inter-Parliamentary Assembly (AIPA) also marked its 40th year.

Annex B

TERMS OF REFERENCE FOR THE JOINT CONSULTATIVE MEETING (JCM)

I. Role and Functions

The JCM shall:
1. Assist the ASEAN Coordinating Council (ACC) in addressing cross-sectoral and cross-pillar issues at the Senior Official's level in the following aspects:
   a. Providing recommendations to the ASEAN Community Councils, ACC and ASEAN Summit in addressing strategic cross-cutting and ASEAN community-building issues, as well as challenges/obstacles to the community-building process;
   b. Promoting policy coherence and effective coordination among the ASEAN Community pillars, including through identifying a lead implementing sectoral body to coordinate the implementation of cross-pillar matters where appropriate, and work closely with ASEAN Member States who serve as coordinators on specific issues where applicable; and
   c. Following up on the implementation of decisions by the ASEAN Community Councils, ACC and ASEAN Summit on cross-sectoral and cross-pillar issues.
2. Support the ACC to prepare for the meetings of the ASEAN Summit in the following aspects:
   a. Identifying and prioritizing strategic cross-cutting and ASEAN community-building issues, and preparing the necessary

documentation, for the discussion and decision by the ACC and the ASEAN Summit, in consultation with the relevant ASEAN Organs. Only in specific cases where coordination and a common decision among the three pillars of the ASEAN Community is required, the JCM may submit its recommendations to the ACC for consideration.
   b. Assisting in the coordination of outcome documents for submission to ACC and ASEAN Summit, including documents to be noted, issued, adopted, or signed by the ASEAN Summit.
   c. Promoting cross-sectoral and cross-pillar coordination through the placement/assignment/secondment of AEC and ASCC officials from ASEAN Member States to their respective Permanent Missions to ASEAN in Jakarta.
   d. In line with the foregoing, the Committee of Permanent Representatives to ASEAN (CPR) and the ASEAN Secretariat will assist the JCM in the implementation and monitoring of the implementation of Leaders' decisions on cross-sectoral and cross-pillar issues.

II. Composition and Chairmanship

3. The JCM shall comprise all Members of the ASEAN Senior Officials' Meeting (ASEAN SOM), Senior Economic Officials' Meeting (SEOM), Senior Officials' Committee for the ASEAN Socio-Cultural Community Council (SOCA) and Committee of Permanent Representatives to ASEAN (CPR).
4. The JCM shall be chaired by the Chair of the ASEAN SOM.
5. In the absence of the JCM Chair, the Member State holding the ASEAN Chairmanship shall designate an alternate of Senior Official rank to serve as the Chairperson.

III. Agenda

6. The Chair of the JCM shall prepare the agenda for the JCM, in consultation with the Chairs of SEOM, SOCA, CPR and where applicable, ASEAN coordinators on specific issues. The agenda

shall focus on issues related to cross-sectoral and cross-pillar coordination and other issues related to the preparation of Summits for discussion and decision by the ACC and the ASEAN Summit.
7. The Agenda should be circulated at least thirty days prior to the JCM.

IV. Frequency of Meeting

8. The JCM shall meet in advance of the ASEAN Summit, at a time to be determined by the Chair in consultation with Member States. Such meetings shall be hosted by the Member State holding the ASEAN Chairmanship.
9. Special meetings may be convened at the initiative of the Chair or at the request of any Member State with the concurrence of all other Member States. Such meetings may be convened in any Member State.
10. The JCM shall also coordinate intersessionally as required, including through electronic means, to ensure substantive discussions.

V. Participation

11. All Member States shall ensure appropriate representation for the SOM, SEOM, SOCA and CPR during meetings of the JCM.
12. The JCM may invite the Chairs of relevant sectoral bodies to attend its meetings as appropriate.

VI. Reporting Mechanism

13. The JCM shall submit its reports and recommendations to the ACC.

VII. Rules of Procedure

14. The JCM shall prescribe its own Rules of Procedure.

VIII. Amendment

15. Any amendments to these Terms of Reference shall be done by consultation and consensus and shall be adopted by the JCM.
16. ASEAN SOM, SEOM, SOCA and the CPR and individual ASEAN Member States may propose amendments to these Terms of Reference.

Annex C

TERMS OF REFERENCE FOR THE ASEAN CONNECTIVITY COORDINATING COMMITTEE (ACCC)

I. Background

1. The ASEAN Connectivity Coordinating Committee is established under the ASEAN Coordinating Council pursuant to the decision of the 17th ASEAN Summit on 28 October 2010 and as espoused in the Ha Noi Declaration on the Adoption of the Master Plan on ASEAN Connectivity.

II. Purposes

2. The ASEAN Connectivity Coordinating Committee shall work to ensure the effective implementation of the Master Plan on ASEAN Connectivity to:
   - promote economic growth;
   - narrow development gaps;
   - enhance ASEAN integration and community-building process;
   - enhance competitiveness of ASEAN;
   - promote deeper social and cultural understanding and mobility of people; and
   - connect ASEAN Member States within the region and with the rest of the world.

III. Roles and Functions

3. The ASEAN Connectivity Coordinating Committee shall:
   a) Monitor, evaluate and review on a regular basis, or as appropriate, the implementation of the strategies, actions and projects of the Master Plan on ASEAN Connectivity;
   b) Coordinate with the National Coordinators, the Committee of Permanent Representatives to ASEAN, relevant ASEAN sectoral bodies and subregional arrangements to ensure that the implementation of the strategies, actions and projects are in line with the Master Plan on ASEAN Connectivity;
   c) Identify issues and challenges, which arise from the implementation of the Master Plan on ASEAN Connectivity, and make appropriate recommendations to the ASEAN Summit through the ASEAN Coordinating Council;
   d) Coordinate with ASEAN Dialogue Partners, multilateral development banks including various international and regional financial institutions. Adopted by the ASEAN Coordinating Council 17 January 2011 two international organizations, private sector and other relevant stakeholders to promote the implementation of Master Plan on ASEAN Connectivity and mobilize all possible sources of funding;
   e) Evaluate and recommend additional strategies, actions and prioritized projects to the ASEAN Summit through the ASEAN Coordinating Council;
   f) Liaise with the National Coordinators to carry out outreach activities and consultations with stakeholders to raise awareness of ASEAN Connectivity;
   g) Explore strategies to strengthen connectivity between ASEAN and other regions including East Asia and beyond; and
   h) Undertake other activities as instructed by the ASEAN Coordinating Council.

IV. Composition of the Committee

4. The ASEAN Connectivity Coordinating Committee shall comprise the Permanent Representatives to ASEAN or any other special representatives appointed by ASEAN Member States.

V. Chairmanship

5. The ASEAN Connectivity Coordinating Committee shall be chaired by the Member State assuming the ASEAN Chair.

VI. Reporting Mechanism

6. The ASEAN Connectivity Coordinating Committee shall report, on a regular basis and well in advance of the ASEAN Coordinating Council meetings, the progress of implementation of the Master Plan on ASEAN Connectivity to the ASEAN Coordinating Council. The ASEAN Coordinating Council shall make appropriate recommendations, in consultation with the ASEAN Political-Security Community Council, ASEAN Economic Community Council and ASEAN Socio-Cultural Community Council, to the ASEAN Summit.

VII. Decision Making

7. All decisions of the ASEAN Connectivity Coordinating Committee shall be taken by consensus. Adopted by the ASEAN Coordinating Council 17 January 2011.

VIII. Participation

8. The ASEAN Connectivity Coordinating Committee may invite National Coordinators, relevant sectoral bodies, Asian Development Bank (ADB), the World Bank, Economic Research Institute for ASEAN and East Asia (ERIA), the United Nations

Economic and Social Commission for Asia and the Pacific (UNESCAP), the private sector, or representatives of Dialogue Partners and other external parties, to participate in their meetings and other relevant activities, as and when necessary.

IX. Establishment of Sub-committees and Coordinating Mechanisms

9. The ASEAN Connectivity Coordinating Committee, if necessary, may establish a sub-committee to facilitate its work as well as in coordinating with interested Dialogue Partners and external parties.

X. Frequency and Venue Of Meetings

10. The ASEAN Connectivity Coordinating Committee shall convene at least two meetings a year.
11. All meetings of the ASEAN Connectivity Coordinating Committee shall be held at the ASEAN Secretariat or other venue as agreed by the Committee.

XI. Role of the Asean Secretariat

12. The ASEAN Secretariat shall provide the necessary resources and support for the effective functioning of the ASEAN Connectivity Coordinating Committee.

XII. Review

13. The Terms of Reference of the ASEAN Connectivity Coordinating Committee shall be subject to review by the ASEAN Coordinating Council as and when necessary and by consensus.

Annex D

TERMS OF REFERENCE FOR THE ASEAN INSTITUTE FOR PEACE AND RECONCILIATION (AIPR)

The ASEAN Institute for Peace and Reconciliation (hereinafter referred to as "the Institute") shall be established under Provision B.2.2.i of the ASEAN Political-Security Community Blueprint. As a follow-up to the ASEAN Leaders' Joint Statement on the Establishment of an ASEAN Institute for Peace and Reconciliation adopted on 8 May 2011, the Institute shall be an entity associated with ASEAN under Article 16 of the ASEAN Charter.

The Institute shall operate in accordance with the following Terms of Reference (TOR):

1. Headquarters

The headquarters of the Institute shall be in the Republic of Indonesia, hereinafter referred to as "the Host Country", and shall be based in Jakarta.

2. Legal Personality

The legal personality of the Institute shall be established under a Memorandum of Understanding (MoU) between the Host Country and the Institute.

3. Principles

The Institute would operate in accordance with the ASEAN Charter and be guided by the principles of the Treaty of Amity and Cooperation in Southeast Asia, inter alia:
   a. respect for the independence, sovereignty, equality, territorial integrity and national identity of all ASEAN Member States;
   b. shared commitment and collective responsibility in enhancing regional peace, security and prosperity; and
   c. non-interference in the internal affairs of ASEAN Member States.

4. Mandate and Functions

4.1. *Mandate*

The Institute shall be the ASEAN institution for research activities on peace, conflict management and conflict resolution, as requested by ASEAN Member States. The Institute's work will include, inter alia, promotion of those activities agreed in the ASEAN Political-Security Community Blueprint and additional activities as agreed by ASEAN Member States.

4.2. *Functions*

The Institute may undertake, among others, the following activities:

Research

- Undertake research and compile ASEAN's experiences and best practices on peace, conflict management and conflict resolution as well as post-conflict peace-building, with the view to providing appropriate recommendations, upon request by ASEAN Member States, to ASEAN bodies;
- Undertake studies to promote gender mainstreaming in peace building, peace process and conflict resolution; and
- Study and analyse existing dispute settlement mechanisms in ASEAN with a view to enhancing regional mechanisms for the pacific settlement of disputes.

Capacity Building

- Hold workshops on peace, conflict management, and conflict resolution;
- Hold seminars/workshops/training in promoting the voice of moderation to contribute to the Global Movement of the Moderates, as well as to advance work in the area of interfaith dialogue; and
- Knowledge building among relevant government officials, scholars or think-tanks on conflict management and resolution.

Pool of Expertise and Support for ASEAN Bodies

- Develop a pool of experts from ASEAN Member States as resource persons to assist in conflict management and conflict resolution activities;
- Where appropriate and at the request of ASEAN governments, provide policy recommendations to ASEAN governments on promotion of peace and reconciliation based on their own studies, as well as facilitation for peace negotiation; and
- Assist ASEAN bodies, upon request of ASEAN Member States, on activities and initiatives related to peace, reconciliation, conflict management and conflict resolution.

Networking

- Function as a knowledge hub by establishing linkages/network with relevant institutions and organizations in ASEAN Member States, as well as other regions and at the international level, which have similar objectives aimed at promoting a culture of peace; and
- Collaborate with relevant UN agencies, regional organizations and international think tanks to exchange expertise and experiences on peace, conflict management, and conflict resolution.

Dissemination of Information

- Disseminate best practices, lessons learned and relevant information to ASEAN Member States;

- Outreach and engagement with the civil society and other relevant stakeholders to promote peace, reconciliation, conflict management, conflict resolution and peace-building; and
- Promote awareness of the work of the Institute among the general public.

5. Budget and Funding

- ASEAN Member States shall make a contribution to support the operations of the Institute for each budget year. ASEAN Member States may consider making additional contributions to support the operations of the Institute within the same budget year.
- The Institute may seek additional project-based voluntary funding from ASEAN Member States on an ad hoc basis, which should be requested in a timely manner.
- The Institute shall mobilize additional resources from ASEAN Dialogue Partners, interested countries, international and regional organizations, financial and any other institutions, corporations, foundations or individuals to fund project-based activities.
- The resources mobilized to fund the project-based activities will also be allocated as deemed appropriate to support the operations of the Institute.

6. Structure

The Institute shall be composed of the Governing Council, the Executive Director and an Advisory Board Governing Council.

6.1. The Governing Council, hereinafter referred to as "the Council", shall consist of:
   a. a Representative of each ASEAN Member State to be appointed by and accountable to the respective appointing Governments;
   b. the Secretary-General of ASEAN as ex-officio member; and
   c. the Executive Director as ex-officio member.

6.2. Each Member of the Council, except for the ex-officio members, shall work for a term of three (3) years and shall be eligible for one re-appointment.

6.3. The Chair of the Council shall be the Representative of the ASEAN Member State holding the Chairmanship of ASEAN.

6.4. The Members of the Council, except for the ex-officio members, shall elect two (2) Vice-Chairmen from among themselves each for a term of one year.

6.5. The Council shall:
   a. formulate the guidelines and procedures for the activities of the Institute;
   b. have the overall responsibility for the funds of the Institute and shall be responsible for the formulation of policy for the procurement and the utilization of the funds;
   c. approve the annual operating budget for the Institute;
   d. perform such other functions as may be necessary to carry out the objectives of the Institute; and
   e. meet at least twice a year.

Executive Director

6.6. The Executive Director of the Institute shall be a national of an ASEAN Member State and shall be appointed by the Governing Council through open recruitment for a non-renewable term of three years.

6.7. The Executive Director in discharging his/her functions to serve ASEAN Member States, shall represent the Institute, not his/her country or any other institution.

6.8. The Executive Director shall:
   a. represent the Institute in all administrative and operational matters, manage the activities of the Institute and perform such other functions as may be assigned by the Council from time to time;
   b. have authority to appoint such professional, secretarial and administrative staff as are necessary to achieve the Institute's objectives; and
   c. undertake activities to raise funds for the Institute's activities, in accordance with guidelines and procedures as established by the Council.

6.9. The Executive Director shall be responsible to the Council.

Advisory Board

6.10. An Advisory Board, hereinafter referred to as "the Board", shall consist of:
   a. representative appointed by the government of each ASEAN Member State, hereinafter collectively referred to as "Representative"; and
   b. the Executive Director as ex-officio member.

6.11. Representatives shall work for a term of three years and shall be eligible for one re-appointment.

6.12. Representatives shall be eminent persons in the field of peace and reconciliation, including, but not limited to, academics, parliamentarians, senior or retired civil servants and civil society representatives.

6.13. Representatives on the Board, with the exception of the Executive Director, shall not serve concurrently on the Council.

6.14. The Board shall advise the Council on the research priorities for the Institute.

7. Decision-making

Decision-making in the Institute shall be based on consultation and consensus in accordance with Article 20 of the ASEAN Charter.

8. Reporting Mechanism

The Executive Director shall make regular reports on the work of the Institute through the relevant senior officials to the ASEAN Political-Security Community Council (APSC Council).

9. Review Mechanism

This TOR shall be initially reviewed five years after the official launching of the Institute. This review and subsequent reviews shall be undertaken by the APSC Council supported by the relevant senior officials.

INDEX

Note: Page number followed by n refers to end notes.

A

Abhisit Vejjajiva, 57
Adams, Tony, 18, 19, 23
Aesthetic Turn in International Political Theory, The (Bleiker), 20
Agreement on Maritime Cooperation, 112
AIPR Symposium on International Humanitarian Law, 103
Alcala, Angel, 54
Anderson, Leon, 23, 65
APT Cooperation Fund, 150, 152
APT Cooperation Work Plan (2018–2022), 151
ASEAN
    agenda-setting role by, 37
    brief history of, 8–11
    Chair of, 22
    and China, 114
    community pillars, 72
    Coordination Meetings, 140
    corporate identity, 31, 69
    critics of, 27
    Dialogue Partners, 42, 78
    documents, 79, 80
    economic development of, 109, 115
    external partners, 40, 66, 78, 89, 166. *See also* external partners, ASEAN
    Founding Fathers of, 8, 55
    infrastructure projects, 119
    lack of unity, 16
    level of awareness about, 5
    membership, 15
    Permanent Representatives to, 96
    Philippine and, 23, 40, 159
    policymakers, 36
    power or ability of, 34
    precursors of, 5–8
        Association of Southeast Asia (ASA), 7
        Malaysia-Philippines-Indonesia organization (MAPHILINDO), 7–8
        Southeast Asian Treaty Organization (SEATO), 5–7
    as regional institution, 31

regional organizations, 5–6
resolution on EAS Plan of
  Action, 132–34
role in Asia's Regional
  Architecture, 27
strategy, 145
Timor-Leste as 11th member of,
  15–16
unity and centrality, 84
weaknesses, 5
ASEAN-Australia Development
  Cooperation Program II (AADCP
  II), 98, 153
ASEAN-Australia Plan of Action, 88
ASEAN-Australia Relations (2012–
  2015), 142
ASEAN-Australia Special Summit
  (2018), 115
ASEAN-Australia Summit, 115
ASEAN-Canada Joint Cooperation
  Committee, 42
ASEAN-Canada Relations
  (2015–2018), 142
ASEAN Centrality, 1, 77
  in the ASEAN Connectivity
    Coordinating Committee,
    96–101
  in ASEAN Institute for Peace
    and Reconciliation, 101–6
  in ASEAN+1 mechanism,
    140–43
  in ASEAN Plus Three Meeting,
    149–52
  awareness of, 26
  concept of, 4, 36
  conflicting bilateral disputes, in
    spite of, 81–82
  in CPR. *See* Committee of
    Permanent Representatives (CPR)

  criticism of, 82
  definition of, 4, 5, 32, 33, 156
  despite inability to amend/update
    ASEAN Charter, 89–93
  as diplomacy principle. *See*
    diplomacy, ASEAN
  dynamics of, 66
  in EAS Ambassadors' Meeting in
    Jakarta, 119
  in emerging regional security
    architecture, 1
  external partners. *See* external
    partners, ASEAN
  failure of, 36, 122
  insistence on, 26–29
  through Joint Consultative
    Meeting, 73–76
  and leadership, 29
  principle of, 123, 151
  processes and procedures, 64
  in regional political security
    architecture, 29, 115
  security perspective of, 35
  support for, 2
  through ASEAN consensus or
    without, 82
ASEAN Charter, 2, 16, 25, 64, 68, 79,
  89–93
  proposed amendments to, 91
  and Treaty of Amity and
    Cooperation, 28
ASEAN-China Centre, 112
ASEAN-China Centre Joint Council,
  42, 66
ASEAN-China Cooperation Fund,
  55, 146
ASEAN-China Cooperation on
  Infrastructure Connectivity, 118
ASEAN-China Fund, 153

Index

ASEAN-China Ministerial Meeting, 109
ASEAN-China Project Management Team, 146
ASEAN-China Relations (2018–2021), 142
   Country Coordinator of, 146
ASEAN-China Statement, 119
ASEAN-China Summit (2017), 146
ASEAN Community, 16–17
   documents related to realizing, 11–14
   in Jakarta, 50
   in Kuala Lumpur, 43
   pillars of, 43, 73, 78
   post-2025 Vision, 14
ASEAN Community Vision 2025, 14, 43, 49, 79, 126, 160
ASEAN Connectivity, 97–99, 116
ASEAN Connectivity Coordinating Committee (ACCC), 4–5, 66, 76, 96–101
   with external partners, 116–19
ASEAN consensus, 92
   ASEAN Centrality through, 82
   on Illegal Unreported and Unregulated Fishing, 87–89
   on South China Sea issue, 82–87
   "VX sarin", 89
ASEAN Convention on the Trafficking in Persons (ACTIP), 49
ASEAN Coordinating Council (ACC), 14, 15
ASEAN Coordinating Council Working Group (ACCWG), 15
ASEAN Council of Chief Justices, 70
ASEAN Declaration on the Protection and Promotion of the Rights of Migrant Workers (2007), 47

ASEAN diplomacy, 3–5, 24, 27, 29–32, 67, 164
   academics of, 5
   and ASEAN Centrality, 37–38
   consensual brand of, 32
   culture of, 31
   "face-saving" practices in, 29–30
   in Jakarta, 30
   practitioners of, 5, 68
   two dimensions/stages of, 31
ASEAN Disability Forum (ADF), 60, 70, 71, 78
ASEAN Economic Community (AEC), 45, 157
ASEAN Economic Ministers' Meeting (AEMM), 99
ASEAN-EU relations, 148, 149
ASEAN Foreign Ministers' Meeting (AMM), 90, 94
ASEAN Foundation, 66, 76, 157
ASEAN Free Trade Area, 10
ASEAN-HK Free Trade Agreement, 45
ASEAN-India Centre, 112, 113
ASEAN Institute for Peace and Reconciliation (AIPR), 5, 60, 66, 76, 101–6
ASEAN Integration (IAI) Task Force, 42
ASEAN Intergovernmental Commission on Human Rights (AICHR), 71
ASEAN-Japan Centre, 112
ASEAN-Korea Centre, 112
ASEAN-Korea Fund, 153
ASEAN leadership, in negotiations, 122–23
ASEAN-led forum, 122
ASEAN Mayors Association, 72

ASEAN Mayors' Forum (AMF), 70
  accreditation of, 72
ASEAN+1 mechanism, 140–43
ASEAN Member States (AMS), 11,
  14, 26–27, 30–31, 40, 42, 109, 157
  and non-AMS PCs, 121, 124,
  128
  relations of, 31
ASEAN Outlook on the Indo-Pacific
  (AOIP), 17n1
ASEAN Plus One, 5
ASEAN Plus Three (APT) meeting,
  5, 34, 70, 110, 149–52
  cooperation projects, 150
ASEAN Political and Security
  Community (APSC), 45
ASEAN Protocol Handbook, 76
ASEAN Regional Forum (ARF), 34,
  35, 162
ASEAN Rohingya Association, 71
ASEAN-Russia Centre, 112
ASEAN Secretariat, 5, 142–43
  ASEAN Connectivity
    Coordinating Committee and,
    100, 119
  and Committee of Permanent
    Representatives, 41, 73
  concept paper, 54
  headquarters in South Jakarta, 8
  Member States and, 14
ASEAN Secretariat Annual Budget,
94
ASEAN Secretariat Financial Rules
  and Procedures (AFRP), 58
ASEAN Socio-Cultural Community
  (ASCC), 45, 75
  mechanisms and priorities, 75
ASEAN Socio-Cultural Community
  Council (SOCA), 15

ASEAN Staff Rules and Regulations
  (ASRR), 58
ASEAN Summit, 28
ASEAN-US Senior Officials' Meeting
  (SOM), 109
ASEAN Vision 2020, 12
ASEAN Way, 93–94, 96
ASEAN Women Experts on Peace
  and Reconciliation, 103
ASEAN Women for Peace Registry
  (AWPR), 103–5
ASEAN Women Mediators Network,
  101, 102
ASEAN Youth Social
  Entrepreneurship Awards, 56–57
Asia-Europe Meeting (ASEM), 86,
  87
Asian Infrastructure Investment Bank
  (AIIB), 118
Asia-Pacific architecture, 33
Asia-Pacific Center for Security
  Studies (APCSS), 162
Asia-Pacific regional institutions, 34
Asia's Regional Architecture, 27
Association of Southeast Asia (ASA),
  7
Australia, Indo-Pacific Foreign Policy
  of, 2
autoethnography, 3, 4, 40, 61, 165
  aesthetic approach of, 21
  analytical framework of, 18–21
  ASEAN diplomacy and, 24
  brand of, 65
  ethical considerations of, 23–24
  "feminine traits" of, 22
  memoirs and, 18
  method, 32
  nature and sources of data, 24–25
  purposes or goals of, 19–20

reflexivity in, 21–23
as research method, 18, 24

B
Bali Concord I, 11, 12
Bali Concord II, 29
Bangkok Declaration (1961), 7
Bangkok Declaration (1967), 8, 9, 26, 54
Belt and Road Initiative (BRI), 2, 118
bilateral diplomacy, 69
bilateral disputes, 81–82, 86
Bochner, Arthur, 18, 23
Brunei chairmanship (2021), 167n2
Brunei's leadership, 62n1

C
Cambodia, Laos, Myanmar, and Viet Nam (CLMV), 10, 42, 80
Cambodia-Thailand dispute, 29
Cayetano, Alan Peter, 44, 54, 58, 62
Cebu Declaration on Migrant Workers (2007), 47
chairmanship of ASEAN
  Committee of Permanent Representatives, 41
  expectation of, 39
  Foundation, 42
  logo of, 44
  Mission, 41, 59
  Philippine diplomatic, 43
  Philippine Mission to ASEAN and, 50–62
Chemical Weapons statement, 124–27
China
  ASEAN's relations with, 145–46
  Belt and Road Initiative of, 2
  "China-centric" attitude of, 33
  Ministry of Commerce of, 119
  in the regional political and security architecture, 1
  and United States, 33
civil society organizations (CSOs), 78, 158
Code of Conduct (COC), 45–46
Cold War, 6, 10
  colonialism and, 27
  stigma, 26–29
colonialism, 7
  and Cold War, 27
Committee of Permanent Representatives (CPR), 4, 41, 66, 71, 73, 109, 110, 158
  agenda of, 78–81
  ASEAN Centrality in, 69–72
  ASEAN Protocol Handbook, 76
  chairmanship of, 79
  format of, 76–77
  interface with high level officials, 111–15
  and Joint Consultative Meeting, 73–76
  and Michael Pence, 144–45
  Plus Three Ambassadors Meeting, 150
  refusal to meet with unfriendly partners, 115–16
  tone and language of, 93–96
  Work Plan, 79
Common Effective Preferential Tariff (CEPT) Scheme, 10
communism
  "domino effect" paranoia of, 10
  spread of, 6
constructivism, 30, 33
Country Coordinator, 110
  for ASEAN-Canada relations, 143
  of ASEAN-China relations, 146

ASEAN's relations with DP, 143
Dialogue Partners and, 140
relations with SDPs, 142
COVID-19 pandemic, 62n3

D
Democratic People's Republic of Korea (DPRK), 150
Department of Foreign Affairs and Trade (DFAT), Australia, 115
Dialogue Partners (DPs), 53, 55, 108–10, 116, 152, 153
    ASEAN's relations with, 143
    and Country Coordinator, 140
Does ASEAN Matter?: A View from Within (Natelagawa), 29

E
EAS Ambassadors' Meeting in Jakarta (EAMJ), 70, 119, 133, 136
    membership of, 137
    physical format of, 120
EAS Development Initiative, 131, 132
East Asia Summit (EAS), 1, 34, 37, 59, 110, 119
    Ambassadors of, 121
    creation of, 29
    as Leaders-led strategic forum, 37
    Leaders' Statements. *See* Leaders' Statements
    Manila Plan of Action on, 131
    membership, 149
    non-ASEAN partners in, 121, 140
    Participating Countries, 127, 130
    Plan of Action, ASEAN resolution on, 132–34
    platform in Jakarta, 120
    priority area of cooperation, 131–32
    statements, ASEAN leadership in negotiating, 122–23
    Terms of Reference, 135–38
    Workshop on Regional Security Architecture (RSA), 133
East Asia Summit Statement on Non-Proliferation, 153
Economic Cooperation Organization (ECO), 110
Economic Research Institute for ASEAN and East Asia (ERIA), 57, 98, 157
Ellis, Carolyn, 23
European Union (EU), 31, 68
extended Plan of Action (POA), 131–32
external partners, ASEAN, 40, 66, 72, 78
    ASEAN Connectivity Coordinating Committee with, 116–19
    formal partnerships with the world's major powers, 107
    high level officials, CPR interface with, 111–15
    in Jakarta, dealings with, 152–54
    lecturing by, 146–49
    meeting with, 109
    Treaty of Amity and Cooperation by, signing the accession to, 107

F
female diplomacy, 22
Foreign Service Institute of the Philippines, 58

Framework Agreement on the Code of Conduct, 45–46
Free Aceh Movement (GAM), 102
Free and Open Indo-Pacific (FOIP), 155n2
Free and Open Indo-Pacific Strategy (FOIPS), 1, 116, 145

G

GAM. *See* Free Aceh Movement (GAM)
Global Movement for Moderates Foundation (GMMF), 130
Global Movement of Moderates (GMM), 80, 130
Gulf Cooperation Council (GCC), 48, 110

H

Handbook of Autoethnography, 19
Hanoi Plan of Action, 12
High-Level Task Force (HLTF), 14

I

Illegal Unreported and Unregulated Fishing (IUUF), 80
    ASEAN consensus on, 87–89
Indonesia
    Indo-Pacific Strategy and, 1
    Kalimantan in, 8
    and Malaysia, *Konfrontasi* between, 8
    Miangas issue, 81
    non-traditional security, 88
    Philippine Embassy in, 50
    Philippines and, 72, 80
    Sukarno, 8
Indo-Pacific Concept, 167
Indo-Pacific Foreign Policy of Australia, 2

Indo-Pacific Strategy (IPS), 1
Intellectual Property Rights Organization, 71
International Court of Justice (ICJ), 86
international law, 85, 87
international relations (IR), 20–23, 65
    constructivist theory of, 94
    theories, 30
International Rice Research Institute (IRRI), 55
International Women's Day, 49

J

Jack Ma, 114, 115
Jakarta
    ASEAN diplomats based in, 30
    ASEAN-led mechanisms in, 67
    Chair of ASEAN mechanisms in, 22
    Committee of Permanent Representatives, 110
    CPR Plus Three Ambassadors Meeting in, 150
    cultural community of, 40
    DP Ambassadors in, 110
    East Asia Summit platform in, 120
    external partners in, 152–54
    hub of regional multilateralism, 67–69
    modus vivendi in, 67
    platform, conceptual framework of, 65–68
    socio-cultural milieu in, 31
Jakarta Channel, 41, 42
Jakarta Philippine Mission (JPM), 51
Jakarta platform
    conceptual framework of, 65–67

Japan
　delegation, 116
　Free and Open Indo-Pacific, 155n2
　infrastructure financing by, 117
　initiatives, 117
　Quality Infrastructure Program of, 2
Japan-ASEAN Integration Fund (JAIF), 57, 153
Japan-ASEAN meetings, 109
Japan Bank for International Cooperation (JBIC), 118
Japan International Cooperation Agency (JICA), 117
Japan Overseas Infrastructure Investment Corporation (JOIN), 117
Joint Communique (2012), 29, 33, 84, 89, 94
Joint Consultative Meeting (JCM), 14, 73–76
Joint Cooperation Committees (JCCs), 70, 110, 143
Joint Sectoral Cooperation Committees (JSCCs), 110, 141, 142

K
Koh, Tommy, 92
Konfrontasi, 8, 9
Kuala Lumpur Declaration, 136

L
Lahad Datu incident, 82
Leaders' Statements, 49, 74, 121, 122, 152
　on anti-money laundering, 127–28
　on Chemical Weapons, 124–27
　on cooperation in poverty alleviation, 128–29
　on countering ideological challenge of terrorism and terrorist narratives and propaganda, 129–31
Lead Implementing Body (LIB), 99, 100
Lee Hsien Loong, 28
Le Luong Minh, 41, 49, 54
Li Keqiang, 146
Lim Jock Hoi, Dato, 105

M
Malaysia, 80
　Batu Puteh issue, 81
　federation in 1963, 7
　Indonesia and, 8
　Tun Abdul Razak, 53
　Tunku Abdul Rahman, 8, 9
Malaysia-Philippines-Indonesia organization (MAPHILINDO), 7–8
Malik, Adam, 53–54
Manila Plan of Action (POA), 131–33
　Preambular Paragraph of, 134
marine protected areas (MPAs), 54
maritime cooperation, 131–32
Master Plan on ASEAN Connectivity (MPAC) 2025, 72, 79, 97, 116, 118
Mekong-Japan Connectivity Initiative, 117
Member States, 32, 57, 141. *See also* ASEAN Member States (AMS)
　and ASEAN Secretariat, 14, 71
　ASEAN's relations among, 64
　bilateral disputes among, 81–82
　Biodiversity Heroes of, 54
　and CPR. *See* Committee of Permanent Representatives (CPR)
　degrees of economic development of, 36

and Dialogue Partners, 46
and external partners, 37, 59
Joint Consultative Meeting of, 73–76
meta-nation interaction among, 31
rice scientists and technologists of, 55
Memorandum of Understanding (MOU), 112
Micro, Small and Medium Enterprises (MSMEs), 115, 161
migrant workers, rights of, 46–50
Moro Islamic Liberation Front (MILF), 102, 166
MPAC 2025 Forum on Initiatives and Project Concepts, 118
multilateral diplomacy, 50, 67, 69, 78
Myanmar
of human rights violations, 96
Thailand and, 81

N

national sovereignty, 27
negotiation process
ASEAN leadership in, 122–23
EAS Terms of Reference in the, 135–38
effective technique in, 122
on Manila Plan of Action, 131
of new Plan of Action, 131–32
procedures employed in, 138–40
neorealism, 30
New Delhi Declaration, 112
Nippon Export and Investment Insurance (NEXI), 117
Non-Aligned Movement (NAM) Summit, 116

non-ASEAN Participating Countries (PCs), 119, 121, 123–26, 128, 130, 134, 138–40
non-confrontational approach, 95
non-traditional security, 30, 35, 88, 146
North American Free Trade Agreement, 35

O

official development assistance (ODA) loans, 117
Organization for the Prohibition of Chemical Weapons (OPCW), 124

P

Pacific Alliance (PA), 110
Pence, Michael, 111, 144–45
Permanent Court of Arbitration (PCA), 83
Permanent Representatives (PRs), 42, 43, 75, 77, 90
to ASEAN, 96
to Jakarta, 43
of Myanmar, 77
of the Philippines to ASEAN, 43
persons with disabilities (PWDs), 70, 71
Philippine Department of Agriculture, 55
Philippine Mission, 21, 43, 48, 52, 75
to ASEAN, 50–62
EAMJ mangrove planting event organized by, 59
Philippine Presidential Communications Operations Office (PCOO), 158
Philippines, 80
agencies and NGOs, 21

Ambassador/Permanent
 Representative of, 66
ASEAN and, 23, 40
chairmanship of ASEAN. *See*
 chairmanship of ASEAN
 against China in 2013, 84
claim to Sabah (1962), 7–8
cuisine and cultural traditions, 53
diplomacy, 50, 87
foreign service, 3
and Indonesia, 72, 80
Miangas issue, 81
Permanent Representative, 42, 43
Ramos, Narciso, 9
sovereignty claims of, 81
and Thailand, 6
31st ASEAN Summit hosted by,
 28
and Viet Nam, 80
Phnom Penh Declaration on the EAS
 Development Initiative, 131–33
post-Cold War experiences, 9, 26
post-colonial nationalism, 6, 26–29
Poverty Alleviation Statement, 126

Q
Quad (United States, India, Japan and
 Australia), 1

R
Rajaratnam, S., 9, 54
Ramos, Fidel, 57
Ramos, Narciso, 9, 54
realpolitik, 69
Regional Comprehensive Economic
 Partnership (RCEP), 16, 36, 38n1,
 45
regional multilateralism, 67–69

regional security architecture (RSA),
 131, 134, 163

S
Sectoral Dialogue Partners (SDPs),
 42, 78
Senior Economic Officials' Meeting
 (SEOM), 71, 73, 76, 97, 99, 118
Senior Officials Meeting on Social
 Welfare and Development
 (SOMSWD), 71
Senior Officials Meeting on
 Transnational Crime (SOMTC),
 112
Silk Road Fund, 118
Singapore, Batu Puteh issue, 81
social constructivist theory, 94
social network method of analysis
 (SNA), 34
Socio-Cultural Community Council
 (SOCA), 15
socio-cultural cooperation, 7, 150
South China Sea, 33, 80
 Code of Conduct in, 85, 160
 dispute, 16
 Framework Agreement on the
  Code of Conduct in, 45–46
 and human rights issues, 163
 issues, ASEAN consensus on, 82
 and Korean Peninsula issues, 120
peace and stability in, 114
Southeast Asian Treaty Organization
 (SEATO), 6–7
Sparkes, Andrew, 21–22, 23
Strategic Dialogue Partners (SDPs),
 108
 of ASEAN, 115
 Country Coordinator for, 110

Substainable Development Goals (SDGs), 62n1

T
Technical and Vocational Education and Training (TVET), 80
Terms of Reference (TOR), 73, 75, 97, 101
   of ASEAN Institute for Peace and Reconciliation, 101–6
   EAS, delay in negotiating, 135–38
   negotiations for, 138
Thailand, 80
   Cambodia and, 81
   and Myanmar, 81
   Philippines and, 6
   Singapore chairmanship and, 62n2
Thanat Khoman, 9, 54, 156
Timor-Leste
   ASEAN Coordinating Council Working Group on, 15
   membership of ASEAN, 15
   as 11th member of ASEAN, 15–16
Treaty of Amity and Cooperation (TAC), 9, 16, 25, 28, 80, 107, 109
Trump, Donald, 1, 122, 145
Tun Abdul Razak, 53
Tunku Abdul Rahman, 8, 9

U
United Cities and Local Governments Asia Pacific (UCLG ASPAC), 72
United Nations Convention on the Law of the Sea (UNCLOS), 83–85, 87, 114
United Nations Security Council, 109
United Nations Substainable Development Goals (UNSDG), 10
United States
   ASEAN Summit with, 1
   China and, 33
   diplomats, 19
   Free and Open Indo-Pacific Strategy of, 2
   instrument by, 7
   Southeast Asian Treaty Organization in 1954, 6
UN Security Council Resolution 1325 on WPS, 49
U Thein Sein, 57

V
Vientiane Action Programme (VAP), 13
Viet Nam
   Ambassador of, 17n2
   communism, 10
   Philippines and, 33, 80, 85
Viet Nam War, 9
"VX sarin", 89

W
Women, Peace and Security (WPS), 49
World Trade Organization, 114

X
Xi Jinping, 118

ABOUT THE AUTHOR

Ambassador Elizabeth Buensuceso is currently the Acting Undersecretary (Vice Minister) in the Philippine Department of Foreign Affairs and Philippine ASEAN SOM Leader. She was the Ambassador/Permanent Representative of the Philippines to ASEAN for over six years. She has been with the Philippine Foreign Service for more than forty-one years. She was formerly Ambassador to Norway, with concurrent accreditation to Denmark and Iceland. She was also Ambassador to Laos. In the Home Office, she oversaw Philippine- European relations as Assistant Secretary for European Affairs and had stints at the ASEAN, economic diplomacy and policy (political) offices. She was also the Philippine Representatives to the ASEAN Intergovernmental Commission on Human Rights (AICHR) from July 2019 to April 2021.

She has a Master of ASEAN Studies degree from the University of the Philippines and a Bachelor of Arts, major in English, *magna cum laude*. She was awarded the Presidential Grand Cross, Gawad Kamanong, rank of Commander in 2017. Ambassador Buensuceso has an adopted daughter, Carina, and two granddaughters, Claire Elise and Angelique Isabelle.

www.ingramcontent.com/pod-product-compliance
Lightning Source LLC
Chambersburg PA
CBHW071355290426
44108CB00014B/1551